STILL
TRENDING

STILL
TRENDING

*A Divided America
From Newspaper to Newsfeed*

Kenneth N. Weiss

SENTIENT PUBLICATIONS

First Sentient Publications edition 2024

A paperback original
Book design by Timm Bryson, em em design, LLC

Library of Congress Control Number: 2024939986
Publisher's Cataloging-in-Publication Data
Names: Weiss, Kenneth N., author.
Title: Still trending : a divided America , from newspaper to newsfeed / Kenneth N. Weiss.
Description: Includes bibliographical references. | Boulder, CO: Sentient Publications, LLC, 2024.
Identifiers: LCCN: 2024939986 | ISBN: 978-1-59181-312-5 (paperback) | 978-1-59181-313-2 (ebook)
Subjects: LCSH Mass media—Social aspects—United States. | Mass media—Social aspects—United States—History. | Mass media—Political aspects—United States. | Mass media—Political aspects—United States—History. | Politics and culture—United States. | Politics and culture—United States—History. | Social media—Political aspects—United States. | Communication in politics—United States. | Communication in politics—United States—History. | BISAC SOCIAL SCIENCE / Media Studies | HISTORY / Social History | SOCIAL SCIENCE / Technology Studies
Classification: LCC HM258 .W45 2024 | DDC 302.2/34—dc23
Printed in the United States of America
10 9 8 7 6 5 4 3 2 1

SENTIENT PUBLICATIONS
A Limited Liability Company
PO Box 1851
Boulder, CO 80306
www.sentientpublications.com

Contents

This book is for all Americans who
value the benefits of democracy and the
foundational constitutional principles upon which
our nation was built—even as they continue to evolve.

Introduction

From Soapbox to Social Media

I n late October 2022, Elon Musk declared to the world: "The bird is freed." For Musk, "the bird," which referenced his $44 billion purchase of the social media platform Twitter, quickly morphed into an albatross. Musk's deal created immediate turmoil (most of it self-inflicted), as he laid off half the staff, or about 3,700 employees, and demanded that those who remained with the company commit to working "long hours at high intensity," or resign. Eventually, Musk turned to a Twitter poll to determine his own fate as the platform's CEO. And Musk's continued ownership has only continued to generate controversy.

Back in March 2006, when Twitter began as Twttr—with a name derived partly from bird sounds—few could have envisioned how the platform designed as a short messaging service (SMS) for groups of people would blossom to one day tout roughly 440 million users.

Twitter's concise tweets became synonymous with virtually instantaneous commentary on all matters political, cultural, and social. One commonly heard, "Did you see what so-and-so tweeted?"

And Twitter wasn't the first or largest social media platform. Mark Zuckerberg and some college friends and roommates started Facebook as FaceMash on October 28, 2003, and today it has roughly 3 billion users worldwide.

As Twitter and Facebook—and other social media companies—expanded, the spotlight focused on what the platforms were doing to monitor misinformation, disinformation, and outright propaganda spread by some of its users. The issue grew exponentially to today.

On March 23, 2023, TikTok CEO Shou Zi Chew was grilled for five hours by a bipartisan U.S. House panel that raised national security concerns given what it claims are the popular Chinese-based platform's ties to that country's Communist Party. On April 24, 2024, President Joe Biden signed into law a bill giving TikTok until early 2025 to identify a non-Chinese buyer. A failure to do so would effectively lead to a U.S. ban of the platform. Two weeks later, TikTok sued the federal government saying the measure violates the First Amendment rights of its more than 100 million U.S. users. The issue is likely to end up before the Supreme Court.

In March 2023, Utah became the first state to prohibit social media services from allowing access to minors without parental consent. Citing concerns over the mental health of teens, Governor Spencer Cox signed two bills requiring social media companies to confirm the age of a user and imposing a 10:30 p.m. to 6:30 a.m. curfew that locks out minors unless a parent overrides the block. The legislation is likely to face legal action brought by civil liberties groups.

In any event, as social media companies come and go, which could be attested to by those who once worked at or used MySpace, one thing remains clear: "Our language and our ecosystems are becoming more caustic online," Nora Benavidez, senior counsel for Free Press, an advocacy group for digital accountability, summed up in a *New York Times* story by Steven Lee Myers and Sheera Frenkel on October 20, 2022.

In early May 2022, Musk reportedly had almost 90 million followers on Twitter, although almost half of those were identified as fake, according to Twitter auditing tool SparkToro. Still, the number of people Musk—or, in theory, anyone else—could reach in a split second was staggering. And the fact that Twitter reportedly was in financial trouble after Musk's purchase mattered little in the scheme of things.

Inexpensive personal computers and software enabled almost everyone to share information and opinions with a global audience, wrote author Scott Gant back in 2007. That reality, along with technological developments such as smartphones and tablets, has made for a far more complicated world than existed even before the relatively recent year 1993, when Mosaic, the first web browser, was introduced for the general public's use.

By 1995, some 18 million American homes were online, but just 3 percent of online users had ever signed onto the World Wide Web, according to the Pew Research Center. But by 1999, 41 percent of adults were using the internet, although the most popular information search was for the weather.

Prior to the late 1990s, the average American turned to television, radio to a lesser extent, local newspapers, and maybe a few national magazines for their news coverage.

"In so limited a universe of information, achieving information literacy was less daunting than in the digital world where information overload is the one constant," wrote Donald A. Barclay in his book *Fake News, Propaganda, and Plain Old Lies: How to Find Trustworthy Information in the Digital Age.*

With the rise of digital information sourcing, however, objectivity and factuality were discarded, Barclay noted, adding that critics say we are now living in a "post-truth" world.

The consequences have been profound for society. While some online disputes have been big-picture insignificant—social media debates abounded after the *Game of Thrones* finale aired—others have had a dire impact on the citizenry. The "big lie" regarding the 2020 presidential election probably has been the largest.

Danielle Allen, a Harvard University political theorist and a contributing columnist for *The Washington Post*, wrote on January 31, 2023, that social media "has blasted one of the original pillars of our Constitution out from under us." She explained that the dispersal of citizens around the country had been a buttress for democracy; it basically kept extremists from congregating.

"But the internet—and social media especially—has shrunk the nation down to one crowded neighborhood," Allen wrote.

Six months following the uprising in Washington, D.C., on January 6, 2021, the Southern Poverty Law Center issued a report that Twitter failed to address the use of the platform by far-right extremists to spread disinformation. "Perhaps above any other platform, Twitter enabled the January 6 insurrectionists to organize their attack on the U.S. Capitol," said Michael Edison Hayden, a senior investigative reporter for the SPLC's Intelligence Project.

A compelling *Washington Post* story on January 17, 2023, detailed how the fastidious committee in the House of Representatives that investigated January 6 undersold the impact of social media messaging leading up to the fateful day, according to staff members.

Congressional investigators found evidence that platforms, especially Twitter, feared retribution if they went after ex-President Donald J. Trump or right-wing activists at the time.

The spread of disinformation in the wake of Trump's insistence that the election was stolen, despite a lack of evidence, is more widespread these days than before, said Nina Jankowicz, an expert on disinformation, in the *New York Times* story. Making matters worse, the fact-free online environment comes even though the media, academics, and social media companies themselves have pressed for ameliorative measures for years, the story said.

The outsized impact of social media influencers also has played a major role in spreading points of view that can be disruptive to society. The influencers exploit Twitter users' "addiction to the pacy, adrenaline-fueled, call-and-response dynamics between them and those who follow them," wrote author Sara McCorquodale.

McCorquodale quotes BBC journalist Michael Wendling, who opined: "Social media has, in effect, flattened authority. If someone has 100k followers and a local newspaper has 100k followers, these two things are now seen as being the same."

Wendling's observation seems to align with what famous newspaper columnist Walter Lippmann said decades before, that "true opinions can prevail only if the facts to which they refer are known; if they are not known, false ideas are just as effective as true ones, if not a little more effective."

The Washington Post published a story by reporters Elizabeth Dwoskin and Jeremy B. Merrill on September 20, 2022, with the headline, "Trump's 'big lie' fueled a new generation of social media influencers," that said the ex-president's claim produced "sky high" follower counts for a number of conservative pundits. The *Post* analysis found that right-wing commentators who already had large audiences still increased their followings by more than 50 percent by posting about supposed election fraud.

Of the seventy-seven "big lie" influencers identified by the *Post*, Twitter banned only twelve in the period around the 2020 election and the January 6 attack on the Capitol. Eight others already had been banned or were later banned. Meanwhile, Facebook banned just two of the seventy-seven influencers.

Even though the midterm election results in 2022 were seen as a rebuke of election denialism, the belief that the use of misinformation and disinformation will disappear from the social media landscape would be naïve. The promotion of misinformation is easy; it has the advantage of speed and can be posted before fact checkers can attempt to discredit it.

During election periods, such as the midterms, media companies like Facebook and TikTok developed partnerships with fact-checking groups, employed warning labels, removed posts, and banned users.

A typical broadsheet newspaper of the day from 1831. (Courtesy of Library of Congress)

But fact checkers can only address "a fraction" of the online lies in any event, Stephan Lewandowsky, a professor at the University of Bristol in England, told *New York Times* reporters Nico Grant and Tiffany Hsu in a story on August 24, 2022.

"We need to teach people to recognize the misinformation playbook, so they understand when they are being misled," he said.

For better or worse, today's social media platforms offer the means to react instantaneously—whether factually or falsely—to issues in local communities and on the national and international scenes.

And commentary can be served up on a platform that is used widely or one that is more targeted to a particular political viewpoint. The array of sites, which rises and falls, is impressive and includes Instagram, Reddit, YouTube, Mastodon, Snapchat, Tumblr, Tribel, Discord, Truth Social, Bluesky Social, Gab, Parler, Telegram, etc., etc. (A study found that almost 33 percent of British teens used Instagram as their primary news source, while 28 percent turned to TikTok, and another 28 percent used YouTube.)

And, of course, the newest elephant in the room—and perhaps the biggest threat to Twitter—was Zuckerberg's rollout of Instagram companion Threads, which garnered 100 million users in its first week in July 2023. Musk responded by threatening to sue rival Zuckerberg over theft claims involving "trade secrets and other intellectual property." As Twitter lost users, Musk in July 2023 re-branded his platform as "X."

Nevertheless, if people today can reach thousands or even millions of others immediately via a relatively low-cost personal computer, tablet or smartphone, what did people in the old days do to try to get their viewpoint across to a "mass" audience?

Before addressing that, it might make sense to take a look at who is likely to post a comment for others to see, regardless of the sophistication of the platform.

In a 2018 study, four Swedish researchers found that those most inclined to participate in political discussions online simply didn't care what others think. They conclude that this particular personality trait might contribute to the harshness of much of the online rhetoric and accompanying societal divisiveness.

Supposing for a moment that people in colonial days and subsequent decades had similar psychological needs, how did they reach more than an individual or a relatively few people at a time?

Their options clearly were limited in the days before broadcast and social media. They could maybe plaster a flyer to a building, speak at a public meeting, or mount a soapbox, a platform to address crowds of people that was especially popular in the decades preceding World War I.

But in reality, their voices couldn't reach many people by applying those methods, and they would have had little ability to gauge the impact of their message. A more effective means was to turn to a newspaper letter to the editor.

The 85 essays that came to be known as the Federalist Papers, which made the case for the U.S. Constitution and a strong federal government, were originally published as letters in New York newspapers in 1787 and 1788. Some newspapers subsequently printed the arguments of the so-called anti-federalists.

The fact that many posters nowadays are anonymous through the use of online pseudonyms undoubtedly makes it easier to spew vitriolic comments. Newspapers today generally require letters in print to be signed and verified, but in past centuries, letter writers used either their real name, their initials or a pseudonym such as "A Constant Rider," "A Patrol Boy," "Old Harmony," and "A Booster."

The right of newspapers to basically print what they wanted was guaranteed with passage of the First Amendment to the U.S. Constitution on December 15, 1791, as one of the ten amendments of the Bill of Rights. Thomas Jefferson, among the strongest advocates of a free press, famously said: "The freedom of the press is one of the great bulwarks of liberty and can never be restrained but by a despotic government."

In a statement that certainly resonates today regarding social media, John Adams said: "Facts are stubborn things; and whatever may be our wishes, our inclinations, or the dictates of our passion, they cannot alter the state of facts and evidence."

In the early days of the nation, newspapers often were published by printers as a sidelight. From the 1790s into the nineteenth century, political parties sponsored newspapers to reach their supporters.

In 1833, the *New York Sun* spawned a new business model. The publisher cut the price of his newspaper on the street to increase readership among immigrants and workers and then turned to eager advertisers to make the publication profitable, according to the *Oxford Dictionary of Journalism* by Tony Harcup.

Around that time, the United States had more than 1,200 newspapers, just ninety of which were daily.

Soon, a couple of societal developments spurred the growth of newspapers. A manufacturing economy was producing millions of new consumers, wrote author Anthony Smith, who added that by 1850, 3 million American children in primary schools were becoming readers. In fact, by mid-century, the country had 400 dailies along with 3,000 weeklies.

Early in the nineteenth century, a newspaper, at best, had a circulation in the low thousands. But by mid-century, the circulation could reach hundreds of thousands. By 1850, the total annual circulation of U.S. newspapers hit 500 million copies serving a population of just under 23.2 million people, according to the American Antiquarian Society.

During the nineteenth and early twentieth centuries, while a number of newspapers ran letters to the editor from the public, many did not, except maybe for an occasional letter on the front page or editorial page.

The earliest letters tended to be long and often rambling. Sometimes newspapers were given permission to run letters from the recipient of a personal letter. There's little indication that the letters were edited for content or fact

An editorial page, including letters to the editor, from the *Detroit Times* on January 16, 1908. (Courtesy of Library of Congress)

checked. Often the letters were serious in tone, taking on weighty issues. The letters could convey outrage or feign indignation.

For example, George L. Beatty had a letter in the *Lubbock Avalanche* of Texas, on June 24, 1921, on what constituted a "big man" in politics. It said, in part:

> . . . It is not the brain power of a Calhoun or Webster that makes a big man. If Washington had depended alone on his brain power he would not have lived in history as a big man. As a statesman his brain power was not that of a Calhoun or Webster cast, but the fact that he always stood firm for what he thought was right and best for government and people regardless of self, made him a big man.
>
> . . . Today all kinds of issues are afloat, and seem to be popular. Some of these issues strike — hard — at the fundamental issues upon which our government was founded. The man in office or one who seeks office

that feels his way, will never live in history as a big man, no matter how brainy.

But sometimes, the letter topics were rather mundane, and the writing was sarcastic or downright comical.

It was not unheard of for a letter to the editor to weigh in on ordinary, everyday topics. (Courtesy of Library of Library of Congress)

For example, an early letter from "R." that appeared in the *Berkeley and Jefferson Intelligencer* of Martinsburg, Virginia (now West Virginia), on July 8, 1803, addressed, of all things, women's hairdos. It said, in part:

> Mr. Editor,
>
> I believe it will be difficult to ascertain the cause, and account for the corruption of taste, which could give rise to the present fashion amongst our *Belles*, of wearing the hair over the eyes.
>
> Some have been of opinion that this custom was adopted upon economical principles, to serve as a substitute for veils. However *this* may be, it is certainly a fashion imported from France, whose corrupt manners we are too fond of aping; and it is probable the practice was imitated from the most sluttish and worthless class of females, among

whom *only* it formerly prevailed, and which among decent persons is truly ridiculous.

. . . Unless all correct ideas of elegance and propriety are absolutely eradicated, I have no doubt the female face will be but a short time in eclipse; the person will again assume its once elegant drapery; — and instead of a rough mop, we shall soon have the flowing tresses and the graceful ringlets.

And, a rather amusing letter from "Marianne" on local flooding appeared in the *Daily Crescent* of New Orleans, on May 17, 1849. Headlined "The Overflow," it took aim at a Mr. Dunbar, who apparently was in charge of emergency services in Louisiana's largest city. The letter said, in part:

Eds. Crescent — Today my neighbors are becoming more and more alarmed. If you were here about ten o clock this morning you would surely have laughed to see the bustle and confusion of removing furniture, etc. I am still undaunted, although the water has increased considerably since I last wrote.

In fact, if I did not feel anxious about the serious losses that many of our citizens are likely to sustain, I should make your column the medium of conveying my thanks to Mr. Dunbar for being instrumental in affording an amusement that I cherish above all others. Boating, gentlemen, is my hobby.

I am delighted when I anticipate the pleasure I will experience in hopping from my balcony into one of the *municipal skiffs.* . . .

As the nineteenth century progressed, events such as the Civil War were fodder for personal accounts or broad declarations. For example, early in the war, on June 21, 1861, the *Abbeville Press* of South Carolina published a succinct letter from H.W. Lawson: "I propose to be one of Seventy-Five Men to arm ourselves and pay our own expenses for six months, to go to Virginia to help clear the Old Dominion of Lincoln's Pirates."

And, the *Daily Green Mountain Freeman* of Montpelier, Vermont, on February 28, 1863, reran a letter from "W.," a soldier with the Sixteenth Vermont Regiment in camp near Fairfax Station, Virginia. The letter, which initially was published in the *Christian Messenger* of Middlebury, said, in part:

. . . As nearly as we can judge, our Vermont Regiments in this section are not losing their interest in the great national cause they have at heart.

. . . They will be glad to see their homes again, when their time of service expires, but it is thought that a large portion of them, will be willing to enter the service again, if the country still needs their help to put down this nefarious rebellion.

Letters to the editor served as an outlet for distraught Americans in the wake of the shooting of President Abraham Lincoln just five days after Confederate General Robert E. Lee surrendered to Union General Ulysses S. Grant at the Appomattox Courthouse in April 1865. Lincoln died the next morning.

On April 17, 1865, the *Evening Argus* of Rock Island, Illinois, printed one such letter from "M" that said, in part:

The doleful telegraph dispatches received from Washington should admonish every man and woman of intelligence in the country, north and south, east and west, to encourage cool, calm deliberation and to discourage precipitate action on the part of any and every person who can command power or influence in any government department or who may be able to wield influence in civil or military society.

. . . There are certainly no men of intellect, in either the north or the south, opposed to the administration who would not very much rather have the administration of Mr. Lincoln and his cabinet continued than to take the chances of the administration which may follow.

Many letters to the editor over the years focused on quality-of-life issues. Some of those letters were aimed at national crises or political or social developments, including the purchase of Liberty Bonds to help finance World War I and the contentious issue of Prohibition and temperance.

An example of the latter was a letter warning of the dangers of drink that ran in the *Breckenridge News* of Cloverport, Kentucky on August 30, 1893. The letter from "Voter" said, in part:

Why civilized society or a community half-civilized submit to the barbarous and demonizing rum traffic is beyond comprehension. Who is he that denies or does not positively know that the open saloon is an expression of all the evils of which hell itself is heir to? These sinks of iniquity are opened wide in the name of liberty. Liberty for what?

... Why should our nation bear even the name of a Christian civilization? There is no half-civilized or barbarous country on the face of the earth which is dominated and ruled by a greater curse than these United States, by the rum power.

Still, most quality-of-life letters addressed local issues. For example, "A Lover of Quiet" had a letter on September 25, 1844, in the *Brooklyn Eagle and Kings County Democrat* of New York, railing against a local fire department practice. It said:

To the Editor of the Eagle:

I reside near one of our principal thoroughfares, Myrtle Avenue, and the rest of an invalid in my family is almost nightly broken by the racing of fire engines, cries of fire, yells, &c., the whole of which, I verily believe, originates among the half grown boys who manage to have the engines out, and who do their full share to bring the Fire Department of our city into disgrace. They never stop to think, it seems, whether there is a fire or not.

The moment any one — a boy for instance — *out of fun* screams 'fire,' it is considered by them to be an alarm, the engines are dragged out, and a scene of riot ensues which baffles description. Must the sick be made the victims of these thoughtless individuals? Is there no remedy?

While the letter to the editor has been a fixture of American life for more than two centuries, print newspapers have been in noted decline in recent decades, suffering from reduced readership and crucial advertising revenue. In the 1980s and 1990s, newspaper circulation slid 10 percent overall. "In the past few years the drop has accelerated, fueled in part by the growing audience for Internet-based news," wrote Harvard professor Thomas E. Patterson in an article on the Nieman Foundation website.

With revenue shrinking, the size of newspapers also has decreased. The reduced space for editorial content often has affected the number of letters that can be printed. While most newspapers that publish letters appear to continue to vet and/or edit letters in their print editions, the landscape online—where a number of newspapers and online news sites still run letters/comments—sometimes resembles the Wild West.

It's not unusual for large newspapers with a national readership that have made a successful transition to online publication to garner a large number of responses to their articles and columns. *The New York Times* is one of those publications and clearly is more restrictive in what it allows readers to post than, say, the more laissez-faire *Washington Post*, which often has thousands of online comments on a story.

Of course, for newspapers generally, the major competition for public discourse is from social media outlets, where many potential readers have turned. In part for that reason, and to show how certain topics have remained salient over the decades, this book is focusing on republishing letters from the distant past that connect with today's readers.

The chapters in this book address issues that often were controversial back in the day, with many remaining so. Many arguments for or against a topic are shockingly alike in the different eras. For example, the reasons given in support of or opposition to vaccines sound quite familiar. And in 1872, immigration, as noted in one newspaper account, included a policy that almost a century and a half later outraged much of the public.

What becomes apparent in researching this book is that xenophobia, racism, the questioning of science, a mistrust of politicians, sexism, and metathesiophobia, or fear of change, among other conditions and reactions to events, were as prominent then as now.

Even so, a good editorial page editor of a newspaper can fact-check letters to the editor and clean up misinformation, or even discard missives that promote disinformation. But the almost instantaneous nature of social media posts makes them much harder to vet, if an attempt is even made. Plus, the case can be made that the very sitting down to write a letter to the editor of a newspaper serves to moderate one's thoughts, while the quick reaction time often associated with a social media post leads to vitriol.

Still, the impact of social media disinformation is still a relatively new phenomenon. Interestingly, a Pew Research Center survey of nineteen advanced countries in 2022 indicated that a median of 57 percent of those polled said social media has been a positive for democracy. Meanwhile, the United States was described as a "clear outlier," with only 34 percent of adults citing social media as good for democracy, while 64 percent said it was having a negative impact.

The role social media ultimately plays regarding the fabric of society is a source of great concern for many, but is still largely uncertain. The implications call to mind the late Canadian media theorist Marshall McLuhan's phrase that the "medium is the message." In this case, the medium is affecting the very way people communicate.

Regardless, the reality that many of the contentious issues nowadays were also divisive in the old days (before broadcast media) should also offer a measure of hope for those who fear that the foundation of democracy is teetering. The fact is, the country has managed to subsume verbal—and occasionally violent—discord over the years and, hopefully, will survive it today as well.

As it happens, the content similarities over the many years call to mind that sententious quote from French writer Jean-Baptiste Alphonse Karr, who in 1849 penned the words: "*Plus ça change, plus c'est la même chose*," or "The more things change, the more they stay the same."

Chapter 1

Capitol Attacked!—1814

Well before the January 6, 2021 attack on the U.S. Capitol by supporters of defeated incumbent President Donald J. Trump, the first invasion of the home of Congress took place on August 24 and 25, 1814. But unlike the more recent assault from "within," the early-nineteenth century attack was from without, by the British.

That earlier offensive occurred during the War of 1812, which historian J.C.A. Stagg said is viewed as the "most unsatisfying and least well understood" of wars fought by the United States.

The United States had declared war against Britain for several reasons, including the continued seizure of American shipping. The U.S. wanted to end British influence in America and make inroads into territories held by the British, Spanish, and Indians. Some war hawks even wanted to conquer British-ruled Canada. In any event, a defeat of the British, with their Native-American allies, would assert American sovereignty.

The British had been at war with France, and with the defeat and exile of Napoleon Bonaparte, they were able to consolidate their forces for the war in the United States.

In the 1814 attack on Washington, D.C., British troops set fire to the Capitol building as well as to the White House and other public properties.

The British invasion of Washington was made possible by that nation's defeat of an American army at Bladensburg, Maryland. In that battle of August 24, American forces, numbering 6,500 and under the command of General

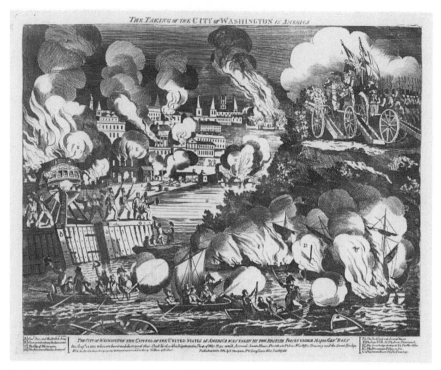

Early illustration of the invasion and burning of Washington, D.C., by the British in 1814. (Courtesy of Library of Congress)

William Winder, suffered embarrassing losses against a British force of 4,500 under General Robert Ross.

American forces were essentially a militia of poorly trained soldiers. After the battle, Winder was roundly criticized for not preparing his men for an organized retreat that might have led to an assembled defense of Washington. Instead, the British eyed a clear path to the heart of the U.S. government.

Ross was ordered by General George Prevost to destroy property on his march to Washington. Despite Ross' protestations, Prevost prevailed, and Ross reluctantly agreed to burn down the President's House and the Capitol Building, according to journalist author A.J. Langguth.

The impact and shock of the British incursion into the nation's capital was captured in an extract of an unsigned letter with a dateline of Alexandria, Virginia, that ran in the *Augusta Herald* of Georgia on August 26, 1814. Initially published in the Richmond *Daily Compiler* of Virginia, the extract said, in part:

. . . Every public building in Washington is in ashes, and that city and George Town in quiet possession of British troops. This morning the barracks and the old ships at the navy yard were fired. For two nights our streets have been lighted by the flames at Washington, which is still smoking. Part of the bridge is destroyed. We are momently expecting a visit from them at this place.

You can scarcely conceive the distress, alarm and consternation that prevails in that place, women and children crying and screaming, in every direction hurrying out of Town, all bustle and confusion.

On September 8, 1814, the *Columbian Museum and Savannah Advertiser* of Georgia ran a rather remarkable extract of an unsigned letter to the editor dated August 20 and datelined St. Mary's County, Maryland, that presaged the attack on Washington and British intentions to move down the coastline. The extract said:

I saw an account in the papers that Mr. Kilgour of this county was on board the Admiral's ship, and that he was informed there would be a Peace or Armistice in less than 30 days. I have since been on board the Admiral's ship and conversed with several officers, who expressed a great desire for peace, but were in hopes they should burn Baltimore first, and seize the President.

The conversation I heard in the officer's apartment, where I went to see a relation who is on board. As soon as I was recognized, they were silent, but asked me many questions about Richmond.

On September 3, 1814, the *Carolina Federal Republican* of Newbern (now New Bern), North Carolina printed an extract of a letter that Captain Bernard Peyton had sent to his brother, an aide to Brigadier General Robert Porterfield. Dated August 24, 1814, at 9 p.m.—the first day of the attack on Washington—it gave further details of the offensive, saying, in part:

The British entered Washington this evening at 6 o'clock, and are now in peaceable possession of it. The President's house, Navy Yard, and all the offices, are now in flames and no doubt the whole town will share the same fate tho' it is said Lord Hill has issued a proclamation; making it death for infringing on private property. The Navy Yard, ships and all naval stores burnt by our own people.

An extract of an unsigned letter from Alexandria, Virginia, dated August 26, 1814, appeared in the *Virginia Argus* of Richmond, five days later. It said:

> The British Army are still in Washington. On Wednesday it attacked our army at Bladensburg, defeated it, and took the artillery. On the evening of that day it took possession of the city. About eight P. M. the Navy Yard was set on fire by order of our Government. About nine the British fired the Capitol, and at midnight the President's House.
>
> . . . Private property has hitherto been respected, and the most rigid discipline observed. The enemy cannot now cross the Potomac — so far we are pretty safe, but there are six frigates coming up and we have every thing to fear from the plundering system they have pursued else where.
>
> The militia at Bladensburg behaved shamefully, with the exception of the Baltimore Cavalry, and some fine regiments and the Artillery under Barney, who was wounded and taken.

Langguth's book, *Union 1812: The Americans Who Fought the Second War of Independence*, recounts more specific details of the British seizure and burning of the Capitol Building.

Initially, British soldiers fired their rifles into the eastern windows in case snipers were positioned there. Then the doors were broken down and a search party looted the building for souvenirs.

Woodwork was cut up and fires were started. Then rockets were aimed at the Hall of Representatives and "shattered the hundred squares of imported English glass-plate at the roof," Langguth wrote.

The British then moved on to the President's House. Upon entering, they drank President James Madison's wine and stole a miniature painting of first lady Dolley Madison as a war prize. The troops then doused rags in oil and set the mansion on fire.

The *Carlisle Weekly Herald* of Pennsylvania, on September 2, 1814, ran an extract of an unsigned letter dated August 27, with a Baltimore dateline, that advanced the narrative. It said:

The British have retired from Washington the way they came, except about five hundred men, who, it is said, have taken the road to Queen Ann, where there is a great quantity of tobacco. They have destroyed all the public buildings in Washington, except the one where the post office was kept.

The *United States Gazette* of Philadelphia, Pennsylvania, printed the extract of a personal, unsigned Washington, D.C., letter to the editor of the *Baltimore (Democratick) American*, dated August 27, that addressed the toll the invasion was taking on the public—both physically and mentally. It said, in part:

I am almost fatigued to death since Sunday last. I slept little, eat little, and marched till my feet are all blistered, and after the whole we are completely disgraced. The enemy took possession of the City, burned the Capitol, the President's House, Treasury and War offices and some private houses; but to give the Devil his due, his conduct here was as good as could have been expected.

. . . I do not say that thousands who were present, who never fired a shot during the action, would not have behaved as well as they did, but for some reason a retreat was ordered, and although three fourths of our forces were eager to fight they were never permitted to make a stand, but marched to the high grounds about three miles from Georgetown, where they encamped for the night.

. . . If the British visit Baltimore I have no doubt you will receive them in American style — we are disgraced.

The *Lancaster Intelligencer* of Pennsylvania, on September 9, 1814, published an extract of a letter dated August 29 that was sent by Secretary of the Navy William Jones to Commodore John Rodgers regarding the British "terms of capitulation" for the town of Alexandria, Virginia. The letter described the conditions as "so degrading and humiliating as to excite the indignation of all classes of people." It said, in part:

The arrogant foe has required the surrender of all articles of produce and merchandize (sic), even retrospectively to the 19th inst. including all that has been sent from the town subsequent to that date, together with all the shipping, whether afloat or sunk, to be delivered to him in perfect order, to carry off his immense booty, which he is now busily engaged in loading and preparing for departure.

On September 10, 1814, the *Enquirer* of Richmond, Virginia, had an item with a Washington dateline that listed property destroyed or damaged in the British attack. The introductory line of the listing said: "Sufferers by the pillage and burning of the British in Washington City." The list included residents' homes and businesses that were set afire or looted (for example, "Mr. Crampton's shoe store, plundered").

Under "PUBLIC PROPERTY DESTROYED," the list showed:

Capitol.
President's House.
War Office.
Treasury Office.
Fort and magazine at Greenleaf's Point.
Public Stores, &c. at the Marine Barracks.

On August 26, the *Baltimore Patriot* ran a detailed, unsigned letter from a seemingly prominent eyewitness to the capture of Washington. It said, in part:

To the Editors of the Baltimore Patriot.
    Friday Evening, Aug. 26
    Gentlemen —
    Having witnessed the late unhappy occurrences at Washington, I will, agreeably to your request, put them on paper; that, if necessary, they may be used to correct some of the many erroneous reports which are circulating.
    I arrived at Washington on Sunday, the 21st instant. At that time the officers of government, and the citizens were very apprehensive of an attack from the British, who had landed a force on the Patuxent— Their numbers had not been ascertained, but reports were various, stating them from 4 thousand to 16 thousand.
    Gen. Winder was stationed near the Wood Yard, with about 2 thousand men, hourly expecting large reinforcements from every quarter,

particularly from Baltimore, 3 thousand men having been ordered to march immediately from that place. On Sunday, the public officers were all engaged in packing, and sending off their banks, & the citizens their furniture.

. . . Reports were current, that Winder had received reinforcements; so that it was believed by many well informed persons, that he would have 10,000 men embodied in the course of the week.

. . . On Wednesday morning I walked through the army, and remained at the bridge until 10 o'clock, when advice was received that the enemy had taken the Bladensburg road. The troops were immediately put in motion, and by 12 o'clock the whole were on their march, in the hope of forming a junction with the Baltimore troops, before the enemy reached Bladensburg. This was only partially accomplished, when the battle commenced, & was contested by the Baltimore troops and the men from the flotilla, with great spirit and gallantry, until it appeared useless for so small a force, very badly supported, to stand against six thousand regulars, all picked men and well supplied — a retreat was ordered, when the President, who had been on horseback with the army the whole day, returned from the mortifying scene, and left the city on horseback.

On Thursday morning, I proceeded on with the army, to Montgomery Court House, where Gen. Winder's head quarters were established. I had some conversation with him. He appeared to regret very much that he had not been enabled to have made a greater resistance . . .

Letters to newspapers during this period questioned Winder's competence. Secretary of War John Armstrong, who had opposed President Madison's appointment of Winder to head the military district to protect Washington and Baltimore, wrote an accusatory letter that the *Baltimore Patriot* published on September 3, 1814. It concluded with:

That from what is now known of the enemy's force, of the loss he sustained in the enterprise, of the marks of panic under which he retreated, &c. &c. it is obvious, that if all the troops assembled at Bladensburg, had been faithful to themselves and to their country, the enemy would have been beaten, and the Capital saved.

Along the same lines, an unsigned letter, apparently from a high official, ran in the *Kentucky Gazette* of Lexington on September 12, 1814. Datelined Washington, the letter of September 4 said, in part:

> To the Editors,
>
> The capture of the city must be ascribed to our commanding General's want of military knowledge and experience. The unprincipled enemy promised to spare private property — but a number of houses were consumed with every thing they contained.
>
> . . . It is rumored that the seat of government will be removed, but the president is opposed to it — and from the melancholy fate that has befallen the city I trust it will not be attempted.

Most damning, perhaps, was an extract in the *Maryland Republican* of Annapolis, on December 10, 1814, that was reprinted from the *Baltimore American*. Headlined "Governor and General Winder Blamed for the Destruction of the American Capitol," it said, in part:

> . . . From these facts, it appears evident *that the proper exertions were not made, or the proper disposition was not felt by the* EXECUTIVE OF MARYLAND *to comply, in good time, with the requisitions of Gen. Winder, and the administration*; that a partial failure took place in that respect; that enough troops were put by the government at the disposal of General Winder; that the Gen. did not in time make a specific call upon Pennsylvania for her 5000 troops; that for some days previous to the battle, he acted and changed his resolutions as if he knew not what to do; that he harassed and exposed the troops he had actually under his command to such an extent, as to incapacitate them from being as efficient as they otherwise would have been; that he scattered and divided them too much; that he never at any time, until too late, procured correct intelligence of the force and movements of the enemy; that he suffered the enemy to march fifty miles through a hilly and woody country, almost without attempting to retard their progress, or to cut up their troops, which he might have done even with half the British force . . .
>
> . . . and that thus, and by these means, was the American capitol invaded, the public property destroyed, the American arms and name

disgraced. It is clear to me although some of the men did not act with bravery, but disorderly, there was a sufficient force on the ground, if it had been well arranged to have beaten the enemy; that the general is unfit for any important command, and that to him, principally, the enemy is indebted for his success of that day's.

However, Secretary of War Armstrong himself wasn't free from blame. Madison had instructed him to develop a defensive plan to protect the entire American coastline. His bare-bones strategy called on the governors of the potentially affected states to establish militias and volunteers of 93,500 men.

The *Lancaster Intelligencer* of Pennsylvania published an item on September 16 that demonstrated the frustration and public anger fomented by the attack on the Capitol, leading volunteers to act:

> On hearing of the destruction of our Capitol, a number of the most respectable young gentlemen of Lancaster armed themselves with swords & pistols, mounted their horses and marched off in a few hours. They were joined by several others from Marietta and Columbia, and were the first Pennsylvania troops who entered Baltimore. They volunteered their services, we understand, for ten days, and then 10 days more, and so on as long as Baltimore was considered in danger.

Following the attack, the editorial pages of newspapers reflected the nation's shame, which quickly morphed into defiance and calls for revenge.

For example, on August 27, 1814, the *Enquirer* of Richmond, Virginia, ran an editorial commentary with the headline "TO ARMS! TO ARMS!" that began:

> At length a blow is struck, which must rouse the most listless and incredulous — a blow, which would near 'create a soul under the ribs of death.' Prepare, prepare; the Philistines be upon you.
>
> In what words shall we break the tidings to the ear? The blush of shame, and of rage, tinges the cheek, while we say that Washington has been in the hands of the enemy! — The Capitol and the President's house are in ruins! — The particulars of this melancholy news have reached us

A wood engraving of the capture and burning of Washington, D.C., by British troops. (Courtesy of Library of Congress)

in so confused a way, that we are unable to state them with system or precision. Such as they are, we give them precisely as we get them.

On September 3, 1814, the *Virginia Argus* ran an unsigned letter from a party outraged by the "execrable" actions of the British. It said, in part:

> . . . Infatuated Britons! your atrocities recoil on your own heads. Yes! they break the talisman, dispel the charm, which fascinated even *your friends*. You thus create a centrifugal force which counteracts the gravitation of some parts of our country towards you — and, perhaps, to the indignant spirit which your outrages now rouse every where, the preservation of our liberties for ages to come, will be due. What signifies the capture or even the destruction of our towns by such a foe! This is not Europe — Vitality does not here center in one spot — It is diffused through the whole body of the nation — we may emphatically say *our* country!
>
> The whole surface of the United States teems with a republican population. — Burn, ravage, destroy a few ripuary settlements; if, however, your barbarous career is not checked even there, it is nothing in a

political point of view — you can not conquer us. Oh! Royalty, once, at least, republicanism may thank thee for shewing thyself in thy true colours — Savage, ruthless, execrable! and for thereby producing an abhorrence which nothing can ever overcome!!

While Washington understandably was the focus of much attention, some newspapers emphasized the need to fortify local defenses. The nearby city of Baltimore, for example, created a thirty-member Committee of Vigilance and Safety, chaired by Mayor Edward Johnson and consisting of professionals and businessmen, to oversee the city's civilian defense. Similar actions took place in other cities as well.

On September 14, 1814, the *Georgia Journal* published a letter-resolution from Savannah by the chairman and secretary of the Joint Committee of Council and Officers—Matthew McAllister and John H. Ash, respectively—on its recommendations for defending the city. It said, in part:

> . . . Your committee, knowing the patriotic character of their fellow citizens generally will not use the language of excitement to this necessary duty — Should there, however, be any who can still doubt, let them behold the smoking ruins of the Capitol of our great and beloved Republic, and then say what reason we have to expect safety, without preparation.
>
> On motion Resolved, That the chairman of the joint committee address the Major General of the first division of the Georgia Militia, requesting that he will immediately throw a sufficient force into Savannah or its vicinity, which, with the regular and militia force within and in the vicinity of the city, may be able to face and to beat off the enemy.

A few months after the attack on the Capitol, a letter to Congress, from "An Old Soldier," castigating the governing body was published in the *Kentucky Gazette* of January 9, 1815. It said, in part:

> The person who now addresses you is one of those who, with millions of his fellow-citizens, has become disgusted and sickened at the long and windy speeches, which have been pronounced in your council chambers.
>
> . . . You have been debating near three months since you convened, meantime the dangers of the country have been encreasing (sic) daily, and but for a few tax bills that you have passed, better, far better would it

have been, that you never had met. Your indecisive conduct, and permit me to add in the sincerity of my soul, your dubious patriotism have invited the enemy external as well as internal, to oppress us with increased vigor, in strong hopes of effecting our ruin.

. . . Now as we have a powerful army in the North as well as the South to contend with — and as the internal enemy is becoming bolder and more respectable, because of your imbecility, &c. and as you have not thought proper to provide any defence (sic) for the country it is fair to ask you, whether it be your wish or not, for it to fall into the hands of the public enemy? For, if the former be your intention, your countrymen will thank you to capitulate immediately.

In the aftermath of the attack, the *Maryland Herald, and Hagers-town Weekly Advertiser* of Hagers-town (now Hagerstown) published the findings of a report on the projected cost of repairing the Capitol and other buildings:

From that report it appears, that $458,000 will be sufficient to repair the Public Buildings, and that it will require $250,000 of that sum to repair the Capitol. The whole first cost of these buildings appears to have been $1,215,110, so that the damage sustained by the entry of the enemy into our Capital amounts only to $757,110.

(The more recent January 6 attack on the Capitol caused about $1.5 million worth of damage to the building, according to a May 2021 estimate by the Architect of the Capitol.)

As noted in the *Augusta Chronicle, and Georgia Gazette* of May 3, 1819, Congress, on March 3, 1819, authorized the president to build "two good and sufficient" fire houses, with "one to be located on the Capitol Hill, near the Capitol, and one near the President's house and public offices."

The final major combat in the War of 1812 was the Battle of New Orleans on January 8, 1815. It actually occurred two weeks after the Treaty of Ghent, ending the war, had been signed by British and American delegates in Belgium, although the news was slow to spread, and the document wouldn't be ratified unanimously by Congress until February 16.

In the Battle of New Orleans, the British saw more than two thousand casualties, while the Americans, under the command of General Andrew Jackson

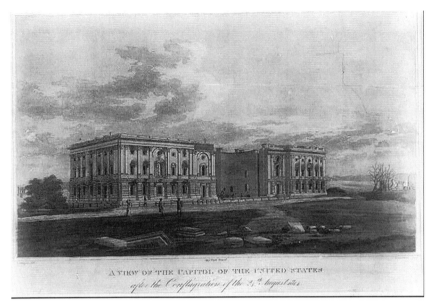

A view of the Capitol building after it was set ablaze in 1814. (Courtesy of Library of Congress)

of the Seventh Military District, suffered just seventy-one. For quite a few days leading up to the decisive battle, the British tried to make inroads into the city.

A letter from New Orleans, dated December 30, 1814, that appeared in the *Franklin Repository* of Chambersburg, Pennsylvania on February 1, 1815, gave a firsthand account of a "gentleman" to a friend in Pittsburgh about the situation in Louisiana. It said:

> The British (about 5000 men) are within four and an (sic) half miles of the city. I have been in the field for eight days. —
>
> Yesterday we had a brisk cannonade, and by report of deserters killed 120 of the enemy — our loss four killed. All kind of business at a stand. Every able bodied man in the field of battle. Should the enemy receive no reinforcements, we shall repulse him in a short time.

PHOTO: First Attack on the Capitol, either Screenshot 5 or 6 (whichever shows up better in print)

CAPTION/CUTLINE (the same for either photo):

After the Battle of New Orleans, Richard Terrell, apparently a wealthy cotton broker in Natchez, Mississippi, had a letter to the editor dated January 17,

Illustration of the Battle of New Orleans, the last major military confrontation of the War of 1812. (Courtesy of Library of Congress)

1815, in the *Richmond Enquirer* of Virginia about a demand of Andrew Jackson to the British. The letter, which also ran on February 10 in the *Charleston Courier* of South Carolina, said:

> SIR, —
>
> ... There are several letters in town, that state the loss of the British more, and say they lost *three* of their Generals killed, and *one* mortally wounded.
>
> In the first attack, they took an Irishman by the name of Laverty, and since the last battle, Jackson had demanded his exchange, and he has sent the Commander word if they do not give him up, he will keep ten of his officers; if they dared to kill him, he would kill ten of their best officers. This is stated in several letters in town.

The War of 1812 exposed weaknesses in the U.S. military that John C. Calhoun began addressing. Calhoun had been a war hawk while serving as a congressman from South Carolina and was secretary of the War Department from December 1817 to 1825. Among the changes, according to historian Stagg, was a nearly fourfold increase in the size of the Army and the formalization of professional training for officers. Calhoun also beefed up that service's Corps of Engineers. Meanwhile, he expanded the Navy's fleet and standardized shipbuilding.

Almost seven months after the end of the war, the *Virginia Argus* on September 9, 1815, ran a letter from "C." that first appeared in the *Boston Patriot* and savaged the behavior of a British officer who had been taken prisoner. It said, in part:

> This doughty hero having also been vanquished and made prisoner, was in want of money. The American commander, relying on what uniform experience has shewn (sic) can in but very few instances be trusted, generously advanced him one thousand dollars to relieve his embarrassments, and received a bill of exchange payable in England.
>
> This gallant Briton had received every attention which a generous and humane conqueror could bestow, but after his return to his country, retreating behind the bulwark of the LAW, *which does not permit an alien enemy to maintain an action, he refused to pay his Bill!*
>
> To such SWINDLING the 'honor' of a British officer could stoop for one thousand dollars! A common pick-pocket would have blushed at an action so base. Nevertheless, Britain is the bulwark of our religion, the last retreat of honor, truth, good government and *mercantile* morality!

Under the terms of the Treaty of Ghent, the British agreed to give up claims to the Northwest Territory; the United States, meanwhile, established credibility as a foreign power while pledging to work with Britain to stop the slave trade, according to the National Archives.

As for the far more recent attack on the Capitol, as of early January 2024, more than 1,230 people had been charged with federal crimes and about 750 had been sentenced, with nearly two-thirds receiving some prison time, according to the *Associated Press*.

Stewart Rhodes, founder of the far-right Oath Keepers militia, and Ethan Nordean, one of the leaders of the Proud Boys, were convicted of seditious conspiracy and handed eighteen-year sentences. On September 5, 2023, Enrique Tarrio, former chairman of the Proud Boys, was given the longest sentence—twenty-two years in prison for seditious conspiracy and leading a failed plot to prevent the presidential transfer of power.

Chapter 2

Controversy over Vaccines, "Spanish" Flu Response

After December 1, 2019, when the first case of COVID-19 was reported, the world grappled with a pandemic that took more than 1.1 million lives in the United States and almost 7 million lives worldwide. A then-new coronavirus, later named SARS-CoV-2, was the cause.

On May 5, 2023, the World Health Organization declared an end to COVID-19 as an international public health emergency, although as of late August 2023, *Worldometer* reported the number of cases worldwide still at a staggering 694 million-plus; nearly 108 million in the U.S. Medical personnel continued to worry about the emergence of new variants of the coronavirus.

Operation Warp Speed, a federal effort in the United States undertaken during the Trump administration that supported COVID-19 vaccine development, helped with the early arrival of the vaccine. Despite its groundbreaking emergence, the vaccine and vaccinations quickly became politicized. A number of so-called anti-vaxxers even espoused the opinion that the COVID vaccine caused deaths from the disease.

Eventually, the rates of those inoculated in the U.S. were highest in the blue, or Democratic, states and lowest in the red, or heavily Republican, states, according to the *New York Times*. Robert F. Kennedy Jr., a third-party candidate in the 2024 presidential election, was even running in large measure as a vaccine skeptic.

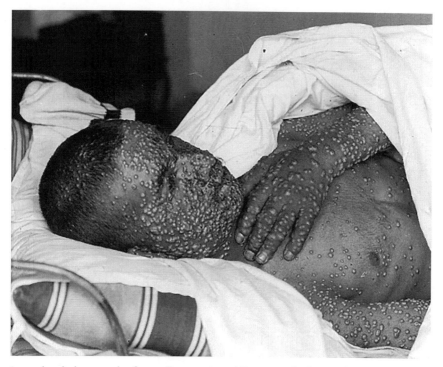

An undated photograph of a smallpox patient. (Courtesy of Library of Congress)

Still, controversy over vaccines, which have been around for centuries, is not new. The earlier contentiousness centered around the smallpox vaccine.

Smallpox was believed to have killed more than 300 million people in the twentieth century alone, according to Laura Spinney on the website of the journal *Nature* in 2020. The dreadful symptoms included lesions in the mouth and throat, making it painful to swallow food and drink. While many didn't survive past the second week, those who did were marked by pitted scars for the rest of their lives.

Smallpox arrived in the Americas with Spanish forces in 1507. At the time the Pilgrims landed at Plymouth Rock in 1620, the region's native population was said to have been reduced by as much as 90 percent, wrote Dr. D.A. Henderson in his book *Smallpox: The Death of a Disease*. Smallpox had spread two years earlier from a French settlement in Nova Scotia.

On January 6, 1777, General George Washington wrote to Dr. William Shippen Jr., ordering him to inoculate all of the troops that passed through Philadelphia against variola, a less-deadly form of the smallpox virus.

Although its origins remain somewhat murky, variolation, or the smearing of cowpox on a skin tear to convey smallpox immunity, was believed to have been applied in China as early as the year 1500, Mariel Tishma noted in a summer 2020 article in *Hektoen International, A Journal of Medical Humanities.*

At the time of the American Revolution, the practice of inoculation was widespread in Europe; during the war, most British troops were immune to variola, giving them a decided battlefield advantage.

In 1796, Edward Jenner, a British physician and scientist, inoculated his gardener's thirteen-year-old son with cowpox to promote smallpox immunity. Jenner had noticed that milkmaids exposed to the cowpox virus rarely came down with the more virulent smallpox, according to *The Vaccine: Inside the Race to Conquer the COVID-19 Pandemic*, a book by Joe Miller with Dr. Özlem Türeci and Dr. Uğur Sahin. The first actual smallpox vaccine was developed in 1798.

Concerns over smallpox were evident throughout the nineteenth and a good chunk of the twentieth centuries. One example was this news item that appeared in the *Augusta Herald* of Georgia on March 14, 1816, regarding an outbreak in Savannah. It said, in part:

> We regret to state that cases of the smallpox have appeared in Savannah, notwithstanding the vigilance of the constituted authorities. The Council have removed them — but citizens! be on your guard! To "make assurrance (sic) doubly sure," adopt proper measures to oppose the spreading and the ravages of this destructive disease! Vaccination furnishes an infallible means of prevention. There is plenty of the vaccine virus in town.

A letter of support from physician Thompson Bird that appeared in the *Georgia Journal* of Milledgeville on March 20, 1816, said, in part:

> Seeing in the Savannah papers a recommendation by the worthy Mayor of that City recommending the inhabitants to be vaccinated in order to prevent the spreading of that great scourge of the human race, the small-pox — and having had an opportunity equal, or perhaps superior to most of my Medical brethren in the state, of proving the efficacy of the kine-pox, as a preventive of the small-pox, I herewith communicate my experience to induce those who have entertained doubts of its being a preventive, to submit to vaccination.

. . . It was I believe in the year 1804 or 5, that A. Miles, esq. (whom you know) took a trip to the lower part of the state, & was accidentally exposed to the small-pox contagion. In a day or two after he got home he was taken unwell & during the eruptive state of the disease, I was called to visit him.

. . . I inoculated Mrs. Miles and the servants that waited on Mr. Miles, with the small-pox. I then selected 24 persons, chiefly children, and inoculated eleven with the kine-pox and 12 with the small-pox.

. . . The result was, 10 had the kine & 14 the small-pox. Some that had the kine-pox eat and slept with those who had the small-pox, and yet no symptoms of the small-pox ever appeared on those where the vaccine disease prevailed.

. . . I can confidently recommend vaccination to my fellow citizens, as securing them from a troublesome and dangerous disease.

Dr. S.L. Jepson, the health officer of Wheeling, West Virginia, had a letter in the *Wheeling Register* on November 1, 1895, that sought to dispel a misconception about the vaccine. It said, in part:

To the Editor of the Register.

Sir:—Small pox is a germ disease, and people contract it by the germs entering their mouth and nostrils and finally getting into the blood.

. . . Physicians protect themselves solely by vaccination. They know of no other method of protection. The prevalent idea that when a person is vaccinated and takes small pox soon after, the disease is rendered more severe, is entirely erroneous.

. . . Not a single dose case of small pox has occurred of a person who was ever successfully vaccinated. Not a single death has occurred of a person who was ever successfully vaccinated. Death from small pox need never occur if vaccination and revaccination be persistently tried.

A letter on varioloid, the mild form of smallpox occurring in people previously vaccinated or who had had the disease, was published in the *Northern Star, and Farmers' and Mechanics' Advocate* of Warren, Rhode Island, on March 6, 1830. The letter, which sounds familiar today regarding the COVID-19 vaccines, addressed the hesitancy of some. It wasn't signed but ended with "To be continued" and said, in part:

> . . . The inconveniences attendant on small pox inoculation and its fatality in some instances, and the dread it occasioned in the minds of the timid, constituted serious objections to its universal adoption.
>
> Hence the number was infinitely small, compared with those which have been vaccinated and the chances for small pox to occur a second time in the same subject, proportionably few.

A long, prescient letter headlined "Prevention of Small-pox—Inoculation and Vaccination," that was simply signed "+," ran in the *Brunswicker* of Brunswick, Missouri, on February 28, 1857. It said, in part:

> That the public mind does not believe in the protective power of vaccination, is frequently evinced in the unnecessary degree of alarm, exhibited by a community — no matter how thoroughly they may have been vaccinated, upon the apperance (sic) of Small-pox.
>
> Perhaps nothing tends more to increase this want of public confidence in vaccination, than those members of the medical profession, who manifest their own want of reliance in its virtues, by an unworthy exhibition of personal dread of the Small-pox contagion.
>
> The universal practice of vaccination would doubtless result in the disappearance of Small-pox.
>
> . . . Let there be made a law, that every child born in the State shall be carefully vaccinated before a certain age, and again after a certain age and we would soon find that Small-pox would die out for the want of victims to feed upon.

Still, not everyone was convinced vaccination was a viable strategy. For example, a letter from Rufus K. Noyes in the *Boston Evening Transcript* on June 23, 1881, said, in part:

> To the Editor of the Transcript:
> . . . Whenever vaccination is held to be a substitute for smallpox, as it now very generally is by scientists, it is directly admitted that it does

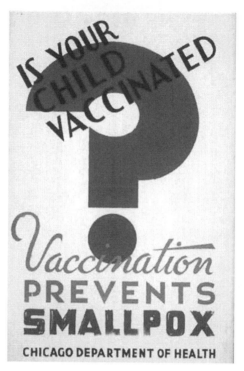

A poster in Chicago on getting youngsters vaccinated against smallpox. (Courtesy of Library of Congress)

not prevent or modify smallpox. That one disease cannot be substituted for another is a fact which all honest doctors will admit. Vaccination is a superstitious rite — a mental substitute for smallpox.

Virus manufacturers do not inform their patrons that many chemical substances, as well as decomposing animal and vegetable substances, will produce virus when applied to denuded flesh of cattle, which can be transferred to the human system, producing local sore and constitutional disturbance analogous to that of vaccination. Bearing in mind this fact, it is easy to see how 150,000 *vaccinated* Europeans fell victims to smallpox in 1871-2.

Even some in the medical profession questioned vaccinations, as demonstrated in a letter from Dr. Henry L. Houghton, of Winchester, Massachusetts, that also ran in the *Boston Evening Transcript* on January 15, 1902. His long letter said, in part:

To the Editor of the Transcript:

Ordinarily, health is supposed to be the best safeguard against disease; to be careful about one's diet, regular in a normal amount of sleep, and to avoid excesses of all kinds, has been the advice given in the past during epidemics of disease other than smallpox.

. . . If one takes the time to read the early history of vaccination, as practised (sic) by Jenner and his followers, it will be found that a certain percentage of those vaccinated were subject to smallpox in the same way as a certain percentage of the unvaccinated.

. . . Smallpox was on the wane before the introduction of vaccination and has been since, but its decline has not kept pace with that of typhus. Why is there this discrepancy between the rate of disappearance of these two kindred filth diseases? The one difference in the fighting of the two diseases has been the use of vaccination in the case of smallpox; in the case of typhus dependence has been placed wholly on sanitary and hygenic (sic) measures.

The argument touting hygiene to combat smallpox also was proffered by "A Baltimore Physician" in the *Sun* of Baltimore, Maryland, on January 9, 1873. The letter said, in part:

[For the Baltimore Sun.]

There is now no doubt that, in spite of the immense number of vaccinations performed by the physicians connected with the board of health and those in private practice, the small-pox is still amongst us in a virulent form and rapidly increasing — located, it is true, mostly in the smaller streets and alleys, but passing daily from them to the dwellings of the more fortunate in this word's (sic) goods. It is plain now that vaccination is not the only remedy.

We would, therefore, call upon the board of health to use all hygienic measures that can be advantageously resorted to. We would suggest the employment of physicians to attend at stated hours at the different station-houses, to examine all persons that are to be committed to any institution, jail, Bayview Asylum, &c.

We would further suggest that the same physicians should visit all cases reported by the police and order the premises to be thoroughly ventilated and disinfected, the bedding, &c., to be promptly removed, and authorize the removal of cases which have no proper attendance to the hospital.

The Baltimore doctor's letter, however, got blowback from Dr. J.S. Conrad, a resident physician at that city's Marine Hospital, on January 13, 1873. Conrad's letter said, in part:

> *Messrs. Editors:* — An article which appeared in your paper of the 9th, from 'A Baltimore Physician,' is calculated to do a great deal of harm to the public welfare. I refer especially to his remarks on vaccination, in which he says that 'it is not the only remedy,' &c., thus giving the impression to the public that vaccination is not to be relied upon as a means of protection from small-pox, &c.
>
> From my standpoint of observation, in which institution over 1,000 cases have been treated since the epidemic began, in November, 1871, I feel it my duty to the public to correct this impression, and in evidence of the *inestimable value of vaccination* add the weight of my testimony to this great and *only* means of protection.
>
> During the fiscal year ending October 31, 1872, there were 787 small-pox cases treated in this hospital. Of this number only .38 of 1 per cent (thirty-eight hundredths of one per cent.) died having one or more *good* marks, whilst 62.5 per cent died having no marks or imperfect ones. What greater exhibit of the value of the great discovery of Jenner could be offered in proof of its value?

More recently, the Centers for Disease Control and Prevention reported in early 2022 that unvaccinated adults were ninety-seven times more likely to die from COVID-19 than boosted adults.

Over the years, some letter writers proposed home remedies to prevent smallpox. For example, the following letter, from Mrs. Florence E. Hawes, could have been detailing an early twentieth-century equivalent of horse paste or bleach. Appearing in the April 18, 1912, edition of the *Independent-Reporter* of Showhegan, Maine, the letter said, in part:

> Some years ago through the kindness of a lady living in Massachusetts, whose character I personally know to have been unimpeachable, I received the following formula as a preventative for smallpox.

. . . Acid Muriate, 3 drachms;

Acid Sulphuric, 4 drachms;

Acid Phosphoric, 1 ounce.

Mix in one gallon of water and take 1 teaspoonful in 1-3 of a tumbler of water three times a day before meals.

It tastes much like lemon juice in water, with also a puckery taste like alum.

In mixing one must be cautious not to get the acids on the hands or clothing, but with care there will be no danger.

Similarly, the *Daily Alta California* of San Francisco ran this brief item on its front page of December 30, 1872:

The Atlantic Medical and Surgical Journal publishes the following: Dr. G.D. Norris, at a recent meeting of the Alabama State Medical Association, stated that during the prevalence of small-pox in Huntsville certain families at the instance of some one unknown, had resorted to the free use of the tea of the Cimicifuga Racemosa, or black snake root of the United States Pharmacopia (black cohosh) as a preventive of small-pox.

In the families using the cimicifuga there occurred no case of smallpox; though some were exposed to the disease.

(An aside: Native Americans used black cohosh, or black snakeroot, as a natural medicine. Some women use it nowadays for symptoms of menopause, including to offset profuse sweating and hot flashes.)

A brief letter from "Small-Pox" in the *Cincinnati Commercial* of Ohio, on May 6, 1882, accused the Board of Health of dereliction of duty. It said:

To the Editor of the Commercial:

On Saturday, April 29, there was a small-pox poster put up on the entrance to a house on Hunt street, between Spring and Pendleton streets. On Monday, May 1, in spite of the fine against doing so, the poster had been torn off.

The Board of Health was notified that same day, and promised to replace the poster immediately, but up to Friday morning it has not been done.

That same day, the *Commercial* ran a letter from "C" about a smallpox "pest-house," a building that isolated victims of communicable disease. It said, in part:

> To the Editor of the Commercial:
> This morning, referring to the care of small-pox patients, you say, among other suggestions, that 'What is needed is a pest-house of simple and comfortable dimensions, supplied with every article needed for the comfort of the patient, with a corps of experienced nurses, and the whole establishment equipped like a first-class hospital,' &c., and further on you say 'such a hospital or pest-house should be constructed and furnished as would insure the patient the same comfort and attention as he would have in his own house.'
> I beg to assure you that the hospital authorities have erected such a house and supplied it with the most complete accommodations for the treatment of that class of patients.
> ... With all the hue and cry about small-pox for the past six months, there have never at any time been over seventy-five patients in this Branch Hospital, or Pest-house, if you choose so to call it.
> ... Not a half-dozen people of note have died of small-pox in this city during this visitation. It is almost exclusively confined to a certain class who refuse to be vaccinated. There is no danger whatever to persons who are successfully vaccinated.

A letter from "Taurus" in the *Chicago Daily Tribune* of January 12, 1880, had questions concerning quarantining smallpox cases. It said:

> To The Editor of The Chicago Tribune.
> Will you kindly inform one of many interested citizens of the Eighteenth Ward as to the discretionary or other powers in connection with quarantine vested in the City Health Department? And further, whether a case in mild form can be so thoroughly isolated as to admit of the full occupation by healthy persons of the same house? A case in point is a building in this ward which bears a well-nigh illegible query, 'Small-pox here, — are you vaccinated?' yet is filled with Scandinavians, and is situated in a central position with relation to recent North Side cases of this disease.

A vaccination is administered at a New York City lodging house in 1908 or 1909. (Courtesy of Library of Congress)

This unsettling item appeared in the *Reno Evening Gazette* of Nevada on December 27, 1887, under the headline "Well Vaccinated":

> Vaccine virus is in great demand in San Francisco just now, and a gross of points was sent to one of the orphan asylums. The parcel was entrusted to a chubby youngster to take to the Matron. He, however, investigated the contents and shared the points with his playmates. They mistook the points for toothpicks, and soon sucked all the virus off, which will, however, produce no evil effects.

The *Seattle Post-Intelligencer* of Washington, on July 3, 1892, published a brief account by Dr. E. Buchanan regarding his vaccination campaign on the Tulalip Indian reservation. The letter made reference to Native Americans' well-founded fear of smallpox. In some documented cases, the colonists tried to pass on smallpox to Indians through infected blankets. While the success of this insidious practice is subject to debate, there's no disagreement over the fact that smallpox devastated Native-American communities.

SCIENTISTS ASSERT THAT ALL DISEASES CAN BE PREVENTED BY INOCULATION.

An illustration from an 1885 edition of *Puck*, America's first humor magazine, with the caption "SCIENTISTS ASSERT THAT ALL DISEASES CAN BE PREVENTED BY INOCULATION."

Buchanan's letter said, in part:

> . . . I have vaccinated about 200 at Tulalip, and there are at Sumner, Muckleshoot, Madison and Duwamish about 600 more who need the operation. Some three years ago I vaccinated 760, and this time I am taking those we missed then, or those upon whom the virus did not take. The Indians, as a whole, are very willing to be vaccinated, for they know what ravages the smallpox makes among them, and they are in great dread of the disease.

In the early twentieth century, smallpox vaccination still had its detractors. An item in the May 15, 1908, edition of the *Waterbury Evening Democrat* of Connecticut, described a local meeting of about one hundred members of the Excelsior Pomona Grange in which a resolution aimed at the state legislature was referred to committee for the group's next meeting. The resolution said:

> Whereas: We realize that vaccination constitutes an operation of innoculation, (sic) or introducing, into the body of a healthy human being, the products of decayed animal tissue, (the matter from a sore or diseased

beast), that this matter is otherwise undefinable, its power for evil unknown, and that it cannot be guaranteed that no evil effects or untoward results will follow, nor that a vaccinated person will be rendered immune to attacks of smallpox, therefore — Resolved: That the compulsory enforcement of vaccination by law or otherwise is unjustifiable, in direct violation of the inherent and constitution rights of the citizens of a free country, and, therefore, Excelsior Pomona grange, No. 7, P. of H., protests against, and urges the repeal of, all law compelling vaccination by the incoming legislature.

James T. Irwin, of Pomona, California, wrote a letter to the *Los Angeles Herald* that also referenced a state law. It appeared on December 24, 1909, and said, in part:

[Editor Herald]: What is the opinion of Letter Box contributors on the subject of compulsory vaccination?

. . . In this state a child is refused admittance to school if vaccination has not been successful. The law requiring it is so unpopular that many parents keep their children out of school rather than have them submit to it.

I believe the last state legislature passed a bill making it optional, but the governor neglected to sign it, so it remains as before.

An editorial that sounds as though it could have been written nowadays, especially given that medical practitioners worried about the low rate of citizens who sought booster shots and fears that more coronavirus variants could emerge, was published in the *St. Joseph News-Press* of Missouri, on March 25, 1925. The commentary said, in part:

That smallpox is more prevalent in the United States than in any country save the most backward is revealed in the report of the surgeon of the public health service. Only China, Russia, Greece and India exceed us in number of patients.

. . . Vaccination has meant such a tremendous change in the status of the disease that the feeling has grown that it is no longer a menace. Yet it flourishes to the extent that vaccination is neglected. In view of the increase of this disease in the United States, there should be renewed emphasis by health and educational authorities upon the indispensable precaution.

Dr. M. Hagan, the Los Angeles health officer, in his annual report that the local *Daily Herald* published on December 28, 1887, made a plea and, by extension, a prediction when he wrote: ". . . Were universal vaccination adapted (sic) by every nation and people on earth, no abiding place would be left for this loathesome (sic) disease. Smallpox would become totally extinct."

Almost a century later, on May 8, 1980, the World Health Assembly, which governs the World Health Organization, declared the variola virus, which causes smallpox, eradicated. (An aside: WHO announced in 2022 that the smallpox vaccine was also effective in protecting against mpox, formerly known as monkeypox.)

The "Spanish" flu

As the number of COVID-19 cases climbed, many looked back more than one hundred years to a pandemic that took at least 50 million lives worldwide and 675,000 in the United States, according to the Centers for Disease Control and Prevention. The reign of the so-called "Spanish" flu extended roughly from February 1918 until April 1920. The commonly used name derived from a misunderstanding, according to the *History* website. Spain was neutral during World War I and Spanish journalists were reporting on the outbreak of the illness generally. With war-participating countries in a media blackout, the Spanish accounts received wide readership, with the erroneous assumption being that the flu must have been identified initially in Spain.

Caused by an H1N1 virus, the widespread flu first surfaced in the U.S. military in spring 1918. The main wave of the pandemic ran from September to November 1918, according to the National Center for Biotechnology Information.

Early in the COVID-19 pandemic, some people opposing vaccines claimed that the 1918 pandemic was caused by a vaccine, but there was no flu vaccine at the time, as noted by *Reuters*.

Many healthy people, including children under five, died in the earlier pandemic. Without a vaccine, officials resorted to strategies including isolation, quarantine, hygiene, disinfectants, and limits on public gatherings, which, according to the CDC, "were applied unevenly." Needless to say, as the pandemic spread throughout the U.S., newspaper coverage was extensive.

The *Omaha Daily Bee* of Nebraska, in its lead story on Page 1 on October 5, 1918, gave insight into what specific locales faced in trying to control outbreaks of the deadly illness. The story, headlined "City Takes Step to Prevent Any Epidemic Here," said, in part:

> Health Commissioner Manning's formal order in connection with the Spanish 'flu' situation, specifically closes churches, schools, theaters, movies, dances, lodges and similar gatherings and in general refers to all indoor public gatherings.
>
> . . . The order has a far-reaching effect upon the everyday life of the city. No dances will be allowed tonight and all churches will be closed on Sunday. A bazaar, which was to have been held in the Auditorium, has been postponed. The dance halls are closed.
>
> The health commissioner hopes that the situation will warrant lifting the order about the middle of next week. If there is no serious spread of the disease within the next few days, the city will return to its normal activities.

No part of the country, whether big city or rural enclave, escaped the scourge of the pandemic. Newspaper obituaries were commonplace. For example, the *Headlight* of Stromsburg, Nebraska, published a small item on February 6, 1919, that began:

> Two very sad deaths occurred the past week, that of Mrs. Aug. Anderson and her little eight year old son, Archie, the result of the Spanish flu. Mrs. Anderson died on Thursday and the boy on Friday and a double funeral was held on Sunday at the Benedict cemetery. Mrs. Anderson was the mother of eight children, the youngest but a year old.

The *Pascagoula Chronicle* of Mississippi ran a front-page warning in its December 14, 1918, edition that included some advice. Headlined "WATCH OUT FOR INFLUENZA," it said, in part:

> A new outbreak of Spanish influenza at Mobile and Hattiesburg has necessitated a general closing order for places of public assembly. There has also been a considerable increase of the disease at Gulfport and Biloxi.

American Red Cross canteen workers on October 16, 1918, in Charlotte, North Carolina, attend to a Black settlement stricken with the flu, providing several hundred meals daily.

. . . Following are suggestions by the leading health authorities as best calculated to prevent spread of influenza, and should be religiously followed by every person in the city.

> Keep your feet warm and dry.
> Do not go visiting oftener than is absolutely necessary.
> Keep out of crowds.
> Keep your sleeping room windows open at night.
> If you contract the disease,
> go to bed and stay there until you are well.
> 'Cover up each cough and sneeze,
> If you don't you'll spread disease.'

James Hale, of Omaha, Nebraska, in a letter to the *Daily Bee* on October 14, 1918, described his personal experience with the flu and offered some advice. The letter said, in part:

To the Editor of The Bee:

. . . I commenced vomiting in the evening, until I thought I must be empty, but still kept this up until late, when I was taken with a severe chill and a burning fever. I did nothing but take a hot foot bath, so hot that I fairly scalded my limbs. I took a heavy physic and went to bed, and drank all the cold water I could, and dampened a cloth in cold water and placed upon my head. Of course, I had inward fever throughout the night, but kept drinking more cold water.

My 'modus operandi' is simple. The result is today I never felt better in 10 years. And my unfortunate friend, taken at about the same time, is to be buried this afternoon. He was under care of a physician, and I tried to use common sense.

The *Wheeling Intelligencer* of West Virginia ran a letter on October 15, 1918, from a former reporter, Private F. Reed Frasher, who was with a Canadian military unit in the midst of World War I but at the time was hospitalized with the flu. His letter, addressed to a newspaper colleague, said, in part:

Dear Hop:

. . . Well, old boy, how is every little thing in old Wheeling.

. . . There are about three hundred cases of Spanish 'Flu' up here, although for most the cases are not serious. Several of the fellows have however 'bit the dust,' and one of my close friends here, a fellow by the name of McNabb, died last night.

I was certainly sorry for the poor chap, as he was a returned man, and had seen three and one half years service on the battlefields of France. He had been wounded twice and gassed once.

As reported in a brief in the *Evening Journal* of Wilmington, Delaware, on October 17, 1918, even a baseball icon wasn't spared illness:

George (Babe) Ruth, batting ace of the World's Champion Boston Red Sox, is a sufferer with Spanish Influenza at his home in Baltimore.

. . . Called to Baltimore on a business mission, he fell a victim of the scourge. His condition is reported as not serious.

A letter from Mary E. Bettinger in the *Seattle Star* of Washington on October 31, 1918, advocated quarantining, saying, in part:

> . . . Why not take the same precautions against contagion that are used in such simple diseases as mumps, measles and chicken pox?
>
> When Seattle people are dying at the rate of 15 to 30 per day, and 25,000 Seattle citizens are afflicted with the pest, why muzzle the well and still continue to leave the way open for the disease to be propagated by permitting the diseased people to come and go freely and to be visited by their friends and the public without restriction?

As with smallpox, some had home remedies for the flu. The *Omaha Daily Bee* ran one such "cure" from Mrs. F.B. Hough on October 7, 1918, that called for employing a foul-smelling, bitter-tasting plant that often was referred to as the "devil's dung." Her letter said, in part:

> To the Editor of The Bee: Will you kindly publish the enclosed remedy for the Spanish 'flu.' It may seem much like grandmother's receipt, but it is not. It was prescribed by one of the greatest physicians the world has ever known, long since dead — I forgot his name.
>
> . . . Make a small white bag two inches square, put into bag piece of asafoetida, sew up the bag, pin to under garment next to the chest as close to the throat as possible.

The *Sunday State Journal* of Lincoln, Nebraska, ran letters from young readers on how they spent their vacation, including one from Ruby Firey, who had to assume multiple roles due to the flu. It said:

> Dear Editor: If this letter is as interesting to your readers as my new line of work was to me, I know they will enjoy it. As I intended to work at Miller & Paine thru vacation.
>
> The lady where I stay took sick with Spanish flu and I had to be housekeeper and cook. I hung my first washing on the line which I thought was impossible for me to do, and at nine o'clock that same evening I found my whole washing ironed, mended and put away.
>
> As I had several good compliments on my cooking by the mister it made me feel as if there was nothing impossible for me to do.

I sure would not take anything for the experience I got in housekeeping thru vacation.

Private J.R. Harmon, stationed at Camp Pike, Arkansas, during World War I, sent a letter to his hometown newspaper, the *Sioux County Pioneer* of Fort Yates, North Dakota, that ran on October 17, 1918. The letter, addressed personally to the editor, noted measures being taken at the camp, saying, in part:

Dear Chris: —

. . . Well, Chris, I just got out of one of the field hospitals where I have been the past few days fighting it out with Spanish Influenza. If I could get the kaiser as quick as I got the Flu this war would be over soon. At that the Flu isn't anything to joke about and it makes a fellow sick enough to forget how to laugh.

The camp is under a strict quarantine and there has been over 13,000 cases so far and the hospitals are kept filled up, but the death rate is very low, except when it turns in pneumonia. One boy from Bismarck, N.D., died last Sunday. His name was Murray.

With a comical spin, the Langdon Sanatorium offered, in the *Courier Democrat* of Langdon, North Dakota, how to protect against contracting the flu. The advice, dated October 30, 1919, said, in part:

. . . Spanish Flu or Pneumonia is the final symptom of a weakened constitution. A person in vigorous health seldom contracts these or other diseases and when he does he usually throws them off quickly.

. . . Some day we will tell the truth in the death certificates and the reports will be out like this:

'Died after thirty years of overeating.'

'Smothered himself to death. Worked and slept in unventilated rooms.'

'Poisoned by his wife who cooked too well.'

'Burned out — Slept only six hours a night.'

'Killed by high living.'

Good health is a luxury which all of us can enjoy if we are willing to play the game on a long law of averages.

Eat lightly, drink lots of water, breathe fresh air night and day, get plenty of sleep, keep clean inside and outside and Father Time will pass you by.

On March 11, 1920, the *St. Johns Herald* of Arizona published a front-page editorial, headlined "About the Flu!'" that draws strong parallels to today. It said, in part:

> . . . It would seem that there are some people within our city who place their opinion of disease superior to the knowledge of any physician and when they find that they have been mistaken they make the cry, 'why I thought that we only had a bad cold and had no idea that it could be such a thing as the flu.' When at the same time there would be three or four of them sick at the same time.
>
> This alone ought to be enough for a reasonable person to known (sic) that whatever it was, it was very contagious, and if they had any love or respect for their fellow-neighbors and friends they would take steps to let the public know that they were suffering with some sort of a contagion and do everything possible to help the health board get rid of it. They may be the cause of the death of some dear one.
>
> To say the least it is very discouraging to the board of health after working hard to try and avert an epidemic, to have the people whom they are trying to protect, be the very ones who will not report an illness when it is in their family because they are afraid they might be quarantined a few weeks.
>
> Yet some of these same people would make a terrible howl if some one else did the same thing that they are guilty of.

Chapter 3

"Civilizing" Native Americans Through Education

O n June 22, 2021, Deb Haaland, the first Native American to serve as a
cabinet secretary as head of the U.S. Department of the Interior, directed
the department's agencies to investigate the federal Indian boarding school system, which the government operated or supported between 1819 and 1969.

The Federal Indian Boarding School Initiative Investigative Report was submit-
ted to Haaland, a tribal member of the Pueblo of Laguna in New Mexico, on
April 1, 2022, and released publicly the next month.

As Bryan Newland, the assistant secretary for Indian Affairs, noted in his
letter accompanying the report, the 408 boarding schools in thirty-seven states
(or then-territories), including twenty-one schools in Alaska and seven in Ha-
waii, "directly targeted American Indian, Alaska Native, and Native Hawaiian
children in the pursuit of a policy of cultural assimilation that coincided with
Indian territorial dispossession." (A *New York Times* story in August 2023 said
a "new accounting" showed there were at least 523 boarding schools and that
408 received federal funds.)

Going back in time, along with the institution of slavery, the most sor-
did chapter in the founding of the United States was the treatment of Native
Americans.

As pointed out by author David Wallace Adams, the thorniest issue facing
the nascent national government in the 1790s was the future of the Indians.

Thomas Jefferson spoke of a "coincidence of interests" in which Indians had land and were in need of "civilization," while white people had civilization but needed land, Adams wrote.

The intent of the government from early on was to turn Indians into sedentary farmers. That policy was quite clear years later on the Plains when white men killed buffalo for their hides, a practice that starved the Indians but was encouraged by the government in an effort to keep the Indians on their reservations, according to Michael L. Cooper in his book, *Indian School: Teaching the White Man's Way*. The reservation system was created when Congress approved the Indian Appropriations Act in 1851.

As for the government's relations with Native Americans in the early and mid-nineteenth century, many Indian treaties confirmed education as a priority. After treaty-making ended with another Indian Appropriations Act in 1871, existing treaty obligations purportedly remained intact. (For almost a century prior to 1871, some 368 treaties were signed with various tribes, many of which were routinely broken by the U.S. government in the wake of westward expansion, according to Sarah Pruitt, writing on the *History* website.)

Education was viewed by the government as the best means to acculturate Indians in white society's ways. Older Indians were considered too fixed in their beliefs and traditions to change; the youngsters were viewed as more pliable.

Several reasons were given to make the case for education. The belief was that the Native Americans could be driven directly from "savagism to civilization" through schooling, Adams wrote. Education also was viewed as advantageous economically for the country. By teaching the Indians and promoting their self-sufficiency, the government would no longer have to feed and clothe them.

Finally, a practical, but gruesome, argument was made by some that it was much cheaper to school Indians than to wipe them out.

The boarding school report presented the fact that after 1871 Congress passed laws to force often-reluctant Indian parents to send their children to school and instructed the Interior secretary to "secure the enrollment and regular attendance" of eligible children in Indian or public schools.

Under this policy, the secretary of the Interior in 1893 was authorized to "withhold rations, including those guaranteed by treaties, to Indian families whose children did not attend schools," according to the report.

Indigenous sovereignty was abrogated with passage of the Curtis Act in 1898, and Congress formally invalidated past Native-American treaties in 1903.

A math class at the Carlisle Indian Industrial School in Pennsylvania in 1901. (Courtesy of Library of Congress)

Education for Indian students was handled in three ways: through reservation day or boarding schools or off-reservation boarding schools. The latter were the most scrutinized and controversial, but also were favored by many officials as the best way to civilize and "Christianize" students. The government subsidized some religious institutions with money and tracts of reservation land to run a number of the schools.

By 1900, there were twenty-five off-reservation boarding schools, including the famous Carlisle Indian Industrial School in Pennsylvania, and of the 21,586 Indian students, nearly 18,000 were attending either reservation or off-reservation boarding schools.

Indian students sent to the off-reservation schools were stripped of their hair, clothes and even their names, Cooper wrote. For some, the haircutting was most traumatic; the Sioux, for example, cut their hair only as a sign of sadness or shame.

Speaking of that barbering practice, the *Wichita Daily Eagle* of Kansas, on February 21, 1902, had an irreverent editorial comment on the racist pronouncement by William Jones, the commissioner of Indian Affairs, that Native Americans should have their hair clipped. It said, in part:

> What Commissioner Jones is after is to break the Indians of the unprofitable habit of being Indians. Indians who retire from the stage, give up the picturesque, and assume the garb and implements of industrial acquisition, doubtless get on better in the world and make their Great Father less trouble than those who don't. The commissioner's intentions are doubtless good and possibly his orders are wisely conceived, but they sound shocking.

An annual report by A.R. Howbert, the U.S. Indian Agent of the Sac and Fox Indians of Iowa, that ran in that state's *Burlington Weekly Hawk-Eye* on December 10, 1874, typified the attitude of many whites toward Native Americans when it came to education. The report said, in part:

> . . . With few exceptions I am not able to report any great progress in the way of civilization during the past year. These Indians cling with great tenacity to their old ideas. They follow their natural instincts, and regard these instincts as the voice of the 'Great Spirit' to them.
> . . . Only a few have, or seem to have, a disposition to adopt the 'white man's way of living.' If they are to be civilized they must be educated, and this cannot be done as long as they roam about more than half of the year, engaged in hunting and trapping.
> . . . As long as they persist in roaming over the country at their pleasure it is utterly impossible to accomplish much in the way of their civilization and Christianization.

The *Indian Missionary*, a newspaper in the Choctaw Nation subdivision in Atoka, Indian Territory (Oklahoma), ran a letter on April 1, 1890, from J.R. Nigh of the Lone Wolf Mission on how a particular tribe had adapted its lifestyle to the new reality. It said, in part:

> Editor Indian Missionary.
> . . . I have had considerable acquaintance with the Kiowa Indians for three years and have seen the changes that have taken place among them.

A sewing class in the early 1900s at the Bismarck Indian School in North Dakota. (Courtesy of Library of Congress)

Then they wanted to hunt, now they want to work, to farm, to give their children an education, and to 'go the white man's road.'

In the past they looked with suspicion on all white men, and for this they had a good cause; now a few white men have their confidence and are getting along well with them, buying from them what they have to sell and trading fair and square. The Kiowas are now ripe for missionary work and a large majority are eager to receive the necessary instructions to make them self-supporting.

Frank D. Voorhies, a former resident of Rocky Ford, Colorado, and apparently a teacher or administrator at an Indian school in Porcupine, South Dakota, had a letter in the *Rocky Ford Enterprise* that ran on March 16, 1899, detailing what he saw as the important role of the day school. His letter, which ends appallingly, said, in part:

To the Editor of the Enterprise:

. . . In these Day Schools the child attends from 9 to 4 the same as at public schools, going home at night and carrying maybe ever so little, yet something of civilization home with him.

. . . Often when a young child who has older brothers or sisters in school, first starts to school he knows something of the English language having learned it from elders. This is a decided advantage. It seems very difficult for an Indian child to learn English.

. . . The very old Indians and many of the women are a decided drawback to the work and the sooner a good providence permits them to behold the happy hunting ground the better for younger ones.

Sioux Chief Swift Bear had a letter, in broken English, in the *Omaha Daily Bee* of Nebraska, on August 27, 1888, in support of Native-American students being force-fed the white man's language. It said:

To the Editor of The Omaha Bee:

I am again say to the people of the united states, that I am in favor of the order of the indian department issued in Sept. 87 Forbidding the use of the native language in all the Schools up on the reservations Whether those under Government patronage or under private or missionries (sic) control.

We are all of us indians now face to face with the White men, and we want to do away with the teaching of our language in all the schools in Dakota and I hope our great father (the president) Will enforce the order of the Indian department, and not mind those missionaries talks. Those missionaries teaching religion in our language are sowing ruin among our nation. We do not want these missionaries teaching us in our own language which do us no good.

We are indian enough without these missionaries teaching us more Indian. We want our children be teached in english and be educated in english like White people, so they can do business with the White people without interpreters. Those missionaries did not obey the order of the indian department, they still continued teaching our language among us.

W.H. Benefiel, of the Cibecue School in White River, Arizona, wrote a letter that appeared in the *National Tribune* of Washington, D.C., on December 3, 1908, in which he conveyed similar thoughts. It said, in part:

Editor National Tribune:

. . . Indian school children should not be allowed to talk Indian language; neither should employés in the Indian school service be allowed to talk Indian language. Our business should be to teach civilization all along this line, and our motto should be 'One country, one language and one flag.'

. . . We also find that the introduction of various National games, baseball, etc., wherein the employes take part with the Indian children has a tendency to encourage as well as to aid the children in speaking and acting English.

Mrs. Lillie M'Coy, of the Office of Superintendent, The Pawnee School, had an upbeat letter in the *Weekly Eagle,* of Wichita, Kansas, on June 3, 1898, in which she said the names of a few students mirrored that of the newspaper. It said, in part:

To the Editor of the Eagle, Wichita, Kan.

Dear Sir: — Every morning as I enter my school room my pupils greet me with, 'What news did the Eagle tell you last night?' I have seen the large boys draw straws to decide which should have the Eagle first at recess. I have five eagles in my room — eagle, bald eagle, high eagle, black eagle and sitting eagle — and these children feel sure that your paper was named for them.

The Moqui Indian School in 1905 in Keams Canyon, Arizona. (Courtesy of Library of Congress)

A letter from W.H. Rogers in the *Christian-Evangelist* of St. Louis, Missouri, on October 8, 1891, was blunt in calling for Christianizing Native Americans while in passing dismissed current educational efforts. It said, in part:

> . . . The U.S. government has sought the settlement of the Indian question by three methods: starvation, extermination, education. All these have failed.
>
> . . . Give the red man a new heart, and a new hope. He will never be civilized until he is first Christianized.
>
> . . . Five hundred million dollars have been spent in putting lead into the Indian's body. I know not whether one twentieth of that amount has been spent in putting truth into his heart.

The desire to Christianize the Indians—and Black people—as Catholics was directly stated in a letter from James Cardinal Gibbons, archbishop of Baltimore, Maryland; John Cardinal Farley, archbishop of New York, and Edmond F. Prendergast, archbishop of Philadelphia, Pennsylvania, that ran in the *Catholic Bulletin* of St. Paul, Minnesota, on February 8, 1913. It said, in part:

> . . . The Indian and Negro must be converted. This can only be accomplished by God's true Church. Hence we cry out to the entire Catholic body to come to our assistance with both men and means. We earnestly beg the clergy to plead for vocations for this home missionary work, and we appeal to the laity to contribute generously to the establishment of schools, to the building of churches, and to the support of the priests and sisters who are devoting their lives to the red and the black skin wards of the American nation, and of the Catholic Church.

At the time, many believed that the mission-run schools were doing an admirable job and had worthy goals. An example of such an assessment was a letter from O.B. Turrell in the *Redwood Gazette* of Redwood Falls, Minnesota, on November 9, 1904. The letter, regarding the Barthold Reservation, said, in part:

> TO THE EDITOR: — The Port Barthold Indian reservation on the Missouri river in central North Dakota has a history, and is carrying on a work in the development of the Indian problem and evolution of the Indian that calls for more than passing notice.

... There is a boarding school at Elbowoods of about 100 scholars, the board and tuition being free and three days of school at different places. There are ten teachers, all white, in the boarding school, the employees however are Indians.

... The spiritual welfare of the tribes is looked after by the American Missionary Association, under the auspices of the Congregational church and a Catholic mission, the following being pretty equally divided between the two.

... I saw some of the Barthold Indians every few days for two months and formed a favorable impression of the work of the government, Maj. Thomas and the missionaries, and feel that though slowly the Indian is attaining an advanced position in character and habits and that very soon by severing his tribal relations and placing himself under another environment, though still a son of the Aborigines he will be a full fledged American citizen.

However, the recent federal report commissioned by Interior Secretary Haaland cited an earlier governmental report from 1928 in which the mission-run schools were criticized for lacking central oversight and sometimes being administered by poorly educated and trained staff.

A short article headlined "About Indians" in the *Daily Independent* of Elko, Nevada, on September 2, 1899, included the following statistical information:

Here are in the United States 65 Indian agents. There are 317 distinct tribes that are to some extent under the control of the Government. There are 81 reservation boarding schools, and 145 day boarding schools. It requires 2,994 employes (sic) to teach the 18,000 Indian children now in these schools. Of these teachers, 1,118 are Indians.

The *Chippeway Herald* of White Earth, Minnesota, in its April 1903 edition, carried a letter from N. Benjamin Hurr about the crucial role of the Native-American teacher. It said, in part:

... The Indian teacher must not be forgotten. The Indian, knowing the queer disposition of his race can more easily devise methods of getting them to take up the white man's civilization, than those unfamiliar with

Indian characteristics. Some tribes of Indians need just such teachers to assist in wearing off the dread some have of pale face ways.

. . . We believe every Indian teacher realizes the great responsibility resting upon him, and that he will continue to use every effort in advancing his race; and, through his teaching make them feel and know the importance of self help, love of land, home and country; while the Indian is naturally inclined toward patriotism, still he need to be taught to love the Stars and Stripes.

Make him understand that every Star is beaming for man's right and every Stripe is waving for freedom.

W.A. Caldwell had a letter in the *Indian Chieftain* of Vinita, Indian Territory (Oklahoma), on November 24, 1898, on the need for curriculum standardization and a teachers' association in the Indian schools. The letter said, in part:

To the thoughtful observer, it is rather surprising that, with the great number of teachers now at work in the Indian Territory, there has been no attempt to bring the educational forces together. The common complaint has been, that there was but little system in the teaching, no uniformity in 'course of study' and no professional pride.

. . . At present there are many enthusiastic teachers in our midst. They consider teaching a profession and a worthy one. They are devoted to it, not for the value received, but for the grand opportunities to influence the young lives for good.

. . . The urgent demand for better teaching, and the interest taken in educational affairs, all these things point to a new era in school teaching in the Territory.

Organization is essential to effective work in any class or profession. The Indian Territory teacher's association should be an actual fact.

Frances C. Sparhawk, chair of the Department of Indian Libraries and Industries of the Women's National Indian Association, wrote a letter from Salisbury Point, Massachusetts, to the *New-York Tribune* of November 28, 1893, clearly dismissing a stereotype that Indian children didn't want to learn by emphasizing how Native Americans had taken to reading. While concluding questionably, the letter said, in part:

To the Editor of The Tribune.

Sir: One who last summer was visiting an Indian school on a Montana reservation writes: 'I was standing by the front door one morning when the superintendent came down from the postoffice. There was a general rush by both boys and girls to meet him, and he was greeted with cries of "Oh, Mr. B----, are there any new papers?" "Did the picture papers come?" "Shall we have papers for Sunday-school to-morrow?" And a general wail of disappointment went up when they found he had returned empty-handed.

The next day I went all about the grounds after Sabbath-school and found little Indians, and big ones, too, sitting around in corners on benches on the ground in the shade of the low buildings — for there are no trees — reading old Sunday-school papers that had been sent to them by some Eastern school, and that by these children had been read and reread until they were dropping to pieces.

. . . To fill the eyes of these Indian children with pictures of the triumphs of Christian civilization, and their minds with the knowledge of the outside world, and their hearts with stories of the sweetness of home life and the pursuits and pleasures of white children is to set between them and the old reservation life the barriers of intelligent thought and high aspiration.

In his book, *Education for Extinction: American Indians and the Boarding School Experience, 1875-1928*, Adams noted that while some students came to appreciate and thrive in their formal education, others resisted in various ways, including running away and setting buildings on fire.

An item in the *Sioux County Pioneer* of Fort Yates, North Dakota, on June 23, 1916, gave one such example of individual resistance. It said: "Dan Johnson, a run-away Indian boy from the Flandreau Indian school, who belongs at Poplar, was captured here last week by the Indian police, and will be returned to the school."

The *Progress*, of the White Earth Agency in Minnesota, had a brief commentary, headlined "Dastardly Attempt at Incendiarism," on January 28, 1888, on a close call involving fire. The arsonist was unknown at the time. It said:

Last Tuesday night, a dastardly attempt to bum the Government Boarding School was made by some unknown person or persons. Had this attempt been successful, there is no doubt that many of the children

The Indian Schoolhouse in Mount Vernon, Alabama. (Courtesy of Library of Congress)

who are boarding at the school would have lost their lives, oweing (sic) to the inadequacy of fire escapes with which the school is not properly supplied.

Those having children at the school should agitate this subject, and insist that the school should be provided with proper means of escape in case of fire.

While responsibility for a fire on January 12, 1918, at the Dwight Indian Training School was unclear, the conflagration resulted in tragedy. A brief account, datelined Muskogee, Oklahoma, that ran in the *Omaha Daily Bee* and was picked up by the *Oglala Light* of the Pine Ridge Reservation in South Dakota, said:

Thirteen Indian boys and girls were burned to death early this morning in a fire which destroyed the boys' dormitory of the Dwight Indian training school at Marble City, Okla., forty miles southeast of here. The origin of the fire is unknown. Over one hundred boys scantily clad escaped into the cold.

In fact, according to the federal report in 2022: "To date, across the Federal Indian boarding school system, the Department investigation has identified approximately 53 marked or unmarked burial sites." And, the report continues, an increase in the number of sites is expected.

The *Guthrie Daily Leader* of the Oklahoma Territory, had a curious, amusing item in its February 9, 1904, edition in its Leaderettes column that spoke to the collegiality that had developed between white and Indian students:

> The teacher at the Red Store has a complaint to make aglnst (sic) her pupils. The Red Store is an Indian trading post, as old as Fort Sill, and the children who live there have grown up attending the mission school with the Indian children and associating with them in their play.
>
> As a result the white children have learned the Indian language, wear gaudy sashes, paint their faces and put feathers in their hair. They shoot arrows as well as young bucks.
>
> They are now attending their first district school, and, though holding high regard for authority, refuse to be taught as civilized people. They read their lessons aloud in study and insist on wearing feathers, sashes, paint and brass earrings and finger rings in the school room. They jabber half the time in Comanche and continue to run away to the mission school, where the Indian children are.
>
> The teacher has resolved that educating an unbroken white child in the Indian language is quite as onerous as educating the real Indian.

The *Ottumwa Tri-Weekly Courier* of Iowa, on its Courier Junior page of May 29, 1906, ran an insightful letter from T.R. Porter, of St. Nicholas, Iowa, describing the educational experience for some Indian students—and ultimately why they lagged behind white students. It said, in part:

> Every year three or four of the brightest pupils at each school are taken down to the Agency, where the Indian agent lives, and are there placed in the boarding-school, which is equipped by the government. At this big school there are always several hundred Indian boys and girls, and the government pays all their expenses.
>
> . . . But after the little Indian is through school he is still far, far behind the average white boy or girl; for he has never had an opportunity of seeing railroad trains and street cars, and electric lights and gas stoves,

and sewing machines, and thousands of things with which white children are surrounded.

A physical education class at the Carlisle Indian Industrial School in Pennsylvania between 1901 and 1903.

The *Evening Times-Republican* of Marshalltown, Iowa, on October 24, 1916, published an article with a dateline of Sioux City that quoted Cato Sells, the commissioner of Indian Affairs, on education. Sells said:

> Five years ago we needed policemen to drive Indians to school. Today we need policemen to keep them out of school. There has been a wonderful change.
>
> The Indian of today is able to successfully compete with the white man. The saying that Indians, after having obtained an education, forsake the white man's ways and goes back to the blanket, no longer holds true.
>
> The school completely transforms the Indian. He is unlike the white child in that his ancestors never were given schooling, and he has no knowledge of anything that pertains to an education. The transformation is so rapid and gratifying that it is almost unbelievable.

Like many newspapers, the *Kansas Weekly Capital* of Topeka had a section devoted to kids ("Junior Capital"). Oleta Littleheart, of Sulphur, Oklahoma and the Chickasaw tribe, wrote a letter in the December 16, 1909, edition that promoted inclusion, saying in part:

> Dear Editor: Will you let an Indian girl, a Chickasaw, join your band of Junior Cousins? My fullblood cousin, Arrow Littleheart, recently subscribed for the Weekly Capital, and she and I and other Indian girls have become interested in our paleface cousins' letters and the instructive farm news matter published in the Capital.
>
> . . . All of my people are becoming deeply interested in scientific farming and stock raising, and we read eagerly speeches and letters from scientific men on these subjects, for there is not one of us, not even a child, but what has an allotment of valuable land.
>
> . . . Our chiefs had still another object in educating us children well in only the white people's language and ways. They wished to fit us for association and contact and comradeship with the scientifically educated young paleface men and women who would flock into our nation when our lands were opened to settlement by the white man — wanted to fit us for intermarriage with the best of the paleface race.
>
> . . . My people themselves are rapidly passing away through intermarriage with paleface. Now, cousins, don't you think our taking our lands in severalty and adopting the white people's language and ways, marks an interesting epoch in the history of the world's civilization? And the romance of the passing of my people themselves through intermarriage with the paleface is as fascinating to the Indian as it is to the white people.
>
> I will exchange postals with all who may write to me.

On June 20, 1902, the *Southern Herald* of Liberty, Mississippi, was among a number of newspapers that published a column by Dr. Carlos Montezuma, a Yavapai-Apache activist and a founding member of the Society of American Indians, in which he took aim at several "blockades to Indian civilization." On education, he wrote:

> . . . With a shake of my head I would say, very few Indian schools are needed in the United States. Or, I might go so far as to say, no Indian

school is necessary, especially when the public school is the Anchor of our educational system. To me to deprive the Indian children of this anchorage is an insult. You may as well say: 'You are an inferior race of children; we do not want you in our public schools.'

In Indian schools Indians teach Indians. When you allow their ignorant parents to decide for their children's welfare, you only encourage the blind to lead the blind, and Indians will remain Indians for ages to come. My plea is, if the public school is good enough for all races, who (sic) not for the true American children.

The *Arizona Sentinel* of Yuma, however, ran a brief item from the *Parker Post* of Arizona, on August 24, 1911, that showed many whites, even a decade later, weren't ready for Native Americans in public schools. It said:

At the public mass meeting held last Saturday night the question of admitting Indian pupils to the public schools is definitely settled in the negative. At least, it is hoped that the matter is settled, and no doubt is almost unanimous, and this ought to convince the department that it is useless to make further endeavor in this connection.

William H. Pfeifer, principal teacher at the San Felipe Day School in Pueblo Agency, New Mexico, had a letter in the *Coconino Sun* of Flagstaff, Arizona, on August 31, 1923, that called for accepting a race's "good things" and rejecting the bad. It said, in part:

Editor Coconino Sun:
. . . In all my teaching of the Indian children I have always urged them to hold fast to the good things of their fathers, but to discard the bad; to take and use the good things the white man had to offer him but to fling away the evil, wickedness and immorality that is sometimes held out to him by the worst classes of the whites, and above all not to try to be a white man, but try to be a good Indian.

The recent federal investigative report found that the Indian boarding schools that operated for 150 years still impact Native Americans' health, education and economic status, but that more research is needed.

Among its conclusions was for the Department of the Interior to "affirm an express policy of cultural revitalization — supporting the work of Indian Tribes, Alaska Native Villages, and the Native Hawaiian Community to revitalize their languages, cultural practices, and traditional food systems, and to protect and strengthen intra-Tribal relations."

In a letter in the *Pacific Commercial Advertiser* of Honolulu, Hawaiian Islands, on December 31, 1888, C.M. Hyde presented the perspective pointed out in the recent federal report regarding the teaching of native Hawaiian children. The letter said, in part:

> Mr. Editor:
>
> . . . The charge has often been made, unjustly, so any well informed observer would say, that those who came from the States to Christianize the Hawaiians, tried to make them over in a cast iron mould (sic) of New England pietism. It seems to me that our modern scientific humanitarians in the policy they are adopting, are trying to make over the Hawaiians after the prevailing standards of nineteenth century mercantilism.
>
> . . . If it be true that Hawaiians cannot be boss mechanics, or merchant princes, or leading lawyers — and who, that knows them, has any idea they ever will achieve such social distinction? — have they no right to life, independence and social activity in such fashion as may best suit their national peculiarities, even if this should be in a style not in accordance with our ideas of culture?

The *Daily Sentinel* of Grand Junction, Colorado, ran an article on January 26, 1907, on a speech in Salt Lake City, Utah, by former Idaho governor W.J. McConnell, who also served as an Indian inspector for four years, in which he ripped conditions generally in Indian schools and Secretary of Interior Ethan A. Hitchcock, specifically. McConnell said, in part:

> . . . My sworn reports of terrible cruelties practiced by Indian school agents upon the pupils in their charge were pigeon-holed time and again and the offending agents simply removed to another school or promoted to a better government position. President Roosevelt does not know of the terrible condition that prevails in the schools of the Indian reservations of this country.

... I know that Indian girls from 10 years old up are forcibly taken from their mothers, under the compulsory education law of the reservations, and are placed in the reservation schools where they become the victims of neglect and incompetent management.

... Every reservation school is badly overcrowded. The appropriation for these schools depends on the number of pupils each has, so that agents compel as great an attendance as possible, irrespective of the facilities of the school for caring for them.

I have seen Indian boys and girls whose bodies were covered with runnine (sic) tubercular sores made to sleep with healthy pupils. The linen of the sick and well washed in the same water.

In late July 2022, Pope Francis visited Canada, where he apologized to Indigenous people for the past role of the Catholic Church. By 2021, more than one thousand unmarked children's graves and remains had been identified at former Indigenous boarding schools in that country. What the pope said in contrition in Canada easily could have applied to other missionaries and the United States as well:

I ask forgiveness, in particular, for the ways in which many members of the church and of religious communities cooperated, not least through their indifference, in projects of cultural destruction and forced assimilation promoted by the governments of that time, which culminated in the system of residential schools.

In line with the pope's apology, more than a century earlier, the Reverend Carl E. Grammer, president of the Indian Rights Association, honored American Indian Day with a piece in the *Minneapolis Morning Tribune* of Minnesota, on May 13, 1916, that said, in part:

It is an admirable custom to dedicate a day to the American Indian. The second Saturday of May, which has been appointed, will probably serve well as the date for the future.

... Many friends of the Indians will improve the occasion — very truly and justly — to dwell upon the debt we owe this picturesque people. Without them our early history would be colorless indeed. The American schoolboy would be badly off without the story of Daniel

Boone and the Indians. The literature of the world must have suffered an appreciable loss had not Fenimore Cooper given to it the figures of Uncas and of Leatherstocking and his red men. One of the most original of our poems is Longfellow's Hiawatha.

The Indian's influence is written into every map of our country and the music of his speech is linked with our streams and our mountains.

. . . But the reverse of the shield, the picture of the influence of the white man upon the Indian, is the darkest page in our national annals.

. . . The rich possessions of the Indians have been always the object of the white man's cupidity. The children of the setting sun have been pushed steadily backward until today most them are in the West and the Southwest, making their last stand on government reservations, as individual communities.

In this long process of spoliation and attrition, it should be pointed out, many Indians have assimilated white civilization and customs and have been lost sight of as members of the tribes.

Much more recently, in the Termination Era from 1953-68, Congress decided to end the special trustee relationship that tribes had with the federal government. The 1951 Urban Indian Relocation Program, for instance, urged Native Americans to live in large cities. This led to severe unemployment and poverty, according to a Howard University School of Law report. This policy, in effect, upended the government's "legal obligations to provide for the health, education, and welfare of Native people," wrote Erik Stegman on the Aspen Institute's website.

As it happens, on May 29, 2024, *The Washington Post* published the results of an investigation by five reporters that detailed the abuse of Native children at Catholic-run schools in parts of the Midwest and Pacific Northwest.

The report found that more than 120 priests, sisters, and brothers at twenty-two boarding schools beginning in the 1890s sexually abused Indian children. Most of the cases, affecting more than one thousand kids, were from the 1950s and 1960s.

These days, about 90 percent of Native children attend public schools. The remainder go to one of the 180 schools operated or funded by the Bureau of Indian Education (BIE) and tribes or private schools. Many of the BIE-funded or -operated schools, as well as the tribal schools and even the public schools are under-resourced and lack culturally relevant curricula, notes Susan C. Faircloth, a member of the Coharie Tribe and a Colorado State University professor, in an article on the American Federation of Teachers website.

As The Red Road organization points out, only 70 percent of Native students who start kindergarten graduate high school, compared to a national average of 82 percent, according to the National Center for Education Statistics. Those attending BIE schools have an even lower graduation rate of 53 percent. And only 17 percent of Native students attend college, with only 13 percent of Native Americans holding a college degree. The organization states, "A lack of funding and resources coupled with geographic isolation can be a major obstacle for students who want to receive a quality education."

Chapter 4

Sad Legacy of Slavery, Lynchings, and the Klan

Nation states emerged in Europe in the fifteenth century, spurred by the transformation of political authority. One result was the creation of New Monarchies, which took the lead in the slave trade, beginning with the Portuguese, then the Spanish, and later the French and English. The Dutch also assumed a substantial role in the trafficking of humans.

In the book *The Transatlantic Slave Trade: A History, revised edition*, author James A. Rawley, with Stephen D. Behrendt, noted that this development was tied to "the Renaissance, the secularization of culture, the rise of capitalism, the revolution in prices, agricultural change, and the development of long-distance trade and transport."

The Atlantic slave trade existed for some two hundred years before it reached the shores of North America. When European explorers began arriving, they determined that the climate of the Americas was excellent for some crops that were popular on their continent, including coffee, sugar, tobacco, indigo, and cotton, according to author Andrew Frank. One obvious need was a sizable labor force to grow and harvest the crops.

The first twenty enslaved people from Africa were taken to the American colonies in 1619, a year before the Pilgrims landed at Plymouth. It wasn't long before many more were forced in from central and western Africa.

Eventually, more than 10 million Africans were kidnapped and shipped to the New World in the slave trade. Not only did the slaves endure inhumane hardships when they were forced to work, but they first had to survive the brutal Middle Passage ocean voyage of two to three months. Some 20-30 percent of the captives were believed to have died on board the ships.

When they got here, they faced unbearable cruelty—and no, regardless of what some in Florida might think today, slavery wasn't an apprentice program in any sense. Perhaps Mary Reynolds, a former slave who was interviewed in the late 1930s—when she was older than one hundred—for a Works Progress Administration project, summed up the experience universally when she recounted:

> Slavery was the worst days was ever seed in the world. . . . I got the scars on my old body to show to this day. I seed worse than what happened to me.
>
> I seed them put the men and women in the stock with they hands screwed down through holes in the board and they feets tied together and they naked behinds to the world. Solomon, the overseer, beat them with a big whip and Master looked on.
>
> . . . They cut the flesh most to the bones, and when they taken some of them out of stock and put them on the beds, they never got up again.

It wasn't until 1808 that the United States outlawed the slave trade, but Frank noted in the book *The Birth of Black America: The Age of Discovery and the Slave Trade* that people of African descent continued to be enslaved until 1865, when the Civil War ended and the Thirteenth Amendment to the Constitution was ratified. The amendment formally abolished slavery, except as legal punishment for a crime.

The struggle for equality for African Americans is ongoing, magnified by today's Black Lives Matter movement, which began in 2013 after the exoneration of George Zimmerman, who shot and killed Trayvon Martin, an unarmed Black teen in Florida. Black Lives Matter gained strength in 2020 following the death of George Floyd in Minneapolis, after a police officer knelt on his neck as the forty-six-year-old Black man was being arrested.

A major factor further complicating and threatening contemporary civil rights is the growing white supremacist movement.

On April 13, 1824, "Brissot" of Jackson County, Illinois—who apparently and ironically took the name of the Frenchman who was a vocal supporter of the French Revolution and founded the abolitionist Society of the Friends of the Blacks in the late eighteenth century—had an open letter in the *Edwardsville Spectator* of Illinois, advocating the spread of slavery in the cause of national unity. Brissot had requested that all Illinois newspapers publish the letter after it first appeared in that state's *Kaskaskia Republican*. It said, in part:

Fellow-Citizens —

. . . It is true, fellow-citizens, that the first introduction of negro slavery into these United States, was an error in its adoption which will ever be lamented by the friends of humanity; but it is an evil from which we cannot at present extricate ourselves, and it is one that had better (in my humble opinion) be extended to the whole than confined to a small scope of country.

The adoption of it into some of the states and its prohibition in others, has formed prejudices very discordant to that harmony which is necessary for the greatness and prosperity of this nation.

While the education and habits of the people of the non-slaveholding states has caused them to differ on this subject with those of the slaveholding, it is reasonable to expect that prejudice would exaggerate, and policy misrepresent the conduct of one section of the Union to the other . . .

"A Farmer" took exception to Brissot's letter with his own in the *Spectator* on May 4, 1824, that said, in part:

FOR THE SPECTATOR.

Mr Printer,

I have just read Brissot's labored defence (sic) of Slavery in your paper of April 13. The writer has begged all the printers in the state to publish his production; but whether this proceeded from a belief that it was a masterly argument, and calculated to make converts of all who might read it, or from a conviction that it was so utterly destitute of merit that no printer would publish it without a special request from the author, I am unable to determine.

Brissot, like all other advocates of slavery, runs at once into inconsistency.

. . . Here we are told that the introduction of slavery into the United States was an error; yet Brissot appears to think that it would be no error to introduce it into this state. Those who first introduced slavery into the United States had the same fallacious and ridiculous plea which is now urged in favor of introducing slavery into this state, viz. the evil exists in other countries, and by extending it, it will be decreased.

By the same course of reasoning it might be shown that all the murderers since the days of Cain, were not only innocent but entitled to applause. By the same rule, also, there is not a crime that has ever been committed, but the repetition of it might be justified.

In the name of common sense, if slavery is an evil, why is Brissot so anxious to introduce it into Illinois.

The *Anti-Slavery Bugle* of New Lisbon, Ohio, on August 22, 1845, ran a jaw-dropping letter by "T.H.A.," of Stratham, New Hampshire, that it had picked up from the Granite Freeman, of Concord, New Hampshire. The letter, headlined "Washington's Runaway Slave," said, in part:

There is now living, in the borders of the town of Greenland, New Hampshire, a runaway slave of Gen. Washington, at present supported by the county of Rockingham. Her name, at the time of her elopement, was Ona Maria Judge. She is not able to give the year of her escape, but says she came from Philadelphia, just after the close of Washington's second term of the Presidency, which must fix it somewhere in the first part of the year 1797.

. . . Washington made two attempts to recover her. — First, he sent a man by the name of Basset to persuade her to return; but she resisted all the arguments he employed for this end. He told her that they would set her free when she arrived at Mt. Vernon, to which she replied, 'I am free now, and choose to remain so.'

Finding all attempts to seduce her to slavery again in this manner useless, Basset was sent once more by Washington, with orders to bring her and her infant child by force. The messenger, being acquainted with Gov. Langdon, then of Pourtsmouth, took up lodgings with him, and disclosed to him the object of his mission.

The good old Governor, (to his honor be it spoken,) must have possessed something of the spirit of modern Anti-Slavery. He entertained Basset very handsomely, and in the meantime sent word to Mrs. Staines to leave town before twelve o'clock at night, which she did, retired to a place of concealment, and escaped the clutches of the oppressor. Shortly after this, Washington died, and, said she, 'they never troubled me any more after he was gone.'

The *Anti-Slavery Bugle*, which eventually was based in Salem, Ohio, published a letter on January 14, 1848, from "E.C." of Wadsworth, Ohio, appealing to "free" women to stand up for enslaved women. The letter said, in part:

> Free daughters of America, will you lend your ears a moment to the sad recital of a sisters woes?
> . . . You are taught the beauties of science and plunging into deep literary lore, may deck your brows with unfading laurels, while your African sister for no other crime than wearing an ebony skin, is forbidden to learn to read the name of God. The laws of your country protect you from wrong. But the female slave has no protection. The Christian people of this Christian country have enacted laws which place her beneath any protection save that of property.
> . . . In view of these frightful outrages upon her sex, how ought woman to stand affected. Let her arise in the dignity, and strength of her influence, and extend her hand to save. Your pleadings will not be in vain.

With the entrenchment of slavery and the accompanying racism came brutal consequences, most despicably lynchings, which began in the 1830s and extended into the 1960s. The NAACP estimated that just between 1889 and 1922, 3,436 people were lynched in the United States.

In his book *Blood and Politics: The History of the White Nationalist Movement from the Margins to the Mainstream*, author Leonard Zeskind noted that well-publicized and -attended lynchings solidified the second-class status of Black vis-à-vis white people. They also reinforced state and local Jim Crow laws that buttressed racial segregation in the South in the late nineteenth and early twentieth centuries.

Thus, the anti-lynching effort was a key component in combating legal segregation, Zeskind wrote.

Usually, newspapers noted lynchings of African Americans on their pages only briefly, and often casually. An example of such a brief was in the *Birmingham Age-Herald* of Alabama, on July 15, 1914, with a dateline of Lake Cormorant, Mississippi. It said:

> James Bailey, a negro, accused of the theft of three mules, was hanged today by a mob of about 20 masked men near Lake Cormorant. Bailey was taken from an officer while en route in an automobile to the county jail at Hernando. An investigation by a coroner's jury late today failed to establish the identity of any member of the mob.

This terse dispatch of October 24, 1897, with a dateline of Rockingham, North Carolina, ran in the *Pittsburg* (sic) *Post* of Pennsylvania, on October 25. It said:

> A negro brutally assaulted Miss Lilly Cole, a respectable young white woman, yesterday. Two younger sisters of Miss Cole were with her at the time. They gave the alarm, but assistance came too late, and the negro escaped. The country is being scoured for miles around, and bloodhounds were started on the trail. If caught the negro likely will be lynched.

The Equal Justice Initiative, in its book *Lynching in America: Confronting the Legacy of Racial Terror*, noted that almost one-fourth of the lynchings in the South were linked to sexual assault allegations. An accusation alone often was enough to precipitate a lynching.

A case in point involved the apparent attempted rape of a white woman in Atlanta in 1906. The *Atlanta Georgian* ran an editorial on August 21, 1906, headlined "The Reign of Terror for Southern Women." The editorial said, in part:

> . . . It is difficult to discuss with any tranquility or with any reason a crime like this. The mere suggestion of the slightest familiarity on the part of a black and filthy negro with a refined and gentle woman of the Caucasian race is enough to stir the blood to fever heat, but the monstrous and unspeakable horror of the more serious and brutal assault, simply wakes to a frenzy and will always stir to frenzy the Caucasian blood.

The caption on a *Puck* magazine drawing in 1899 says, "The Lynching Problem." (Courtesy of Library of Congress)

The editorial went on to lament that lynching didn't appear to be a deterrent to rape and called for an alternative punishment: "personal mutilation." It concluded: "Let it be understood in advance that every negro who commits this crime will be treated to this punishment and let us see at least for a twelvemonth what effect the new punishment will have upon the old and frightful offense."

On August 25, 1906, the newspaper ran a full page of more than a dozen letters of support, with one more venomous than the next. The following are snippets of a few of the letters:

J.L.D. Hillyer wrote:

> To the Editor of The Georgian:
> . . . I believe that you are right — unless some new and terrible penalty, quickly applied, may have the effect of deterring the black rapists, the alternative will be the driving of the blacks out of our country, or the extinction of their race in America.

After all, Lynch law is a crude application of the principle that justifies the killing of a man who is about to commit a deadly felony, or is caught red-handed in the act.

"Junius" wrote:

> . . . I say, let every Southern city and town and village and community call mass meetings. Let our men be there. Ask every negro to be there. Make them come. At these meetings talk to the negroes. Tell them our demands. Let them understand our ultimatum. Warn them. Then let the white men organize in a solid phalanx and give the negroes to understand that it is race war and death to every one if as a race they do not stop this crime.

And, B.A. Pugin wrote:

> . . . Your idea of personal mutilation is good, but it comes too late. Let's continue to kill all negroes who commit the unmentionable crime, and make eunuchs of all the new male issues before they are eight days old.

On July 13, 1885, a fifteen-year-old Black male was lynched on the site of the former Baltimore County Jail in Towson, Maryland. Howard Cooper had been accused of the assault and rape of a white woman. He was caught and transferred to Baltimore City as angry mobs threatened his life.

According to a historical marker placed at the site in May 2021, an all-white jury in May 1885 found the teen guilty in less than one minute, even though the victim did not testify that she had been raped. An appeal of the verdict was denied.

Two months later, a white mob stormed the jail and hanged the teen from a nearby sycamore tree. Later, pieces of the rope were handed out as souvenirs. Cooper's mother had her son buried in an unmarked grave, and no one was ever held accountable for the lynching.

On July 15, 1885, the *Baltimore American* editorialized that preventive measures to protect Cooper should have been taken:

> This man Cooper should have been defended by all the power of the county of Baltimore. It would have been easy to summon the good and

true men of the county to defend the jail, and it should have been defended at whatever cost of life. But no steps seem to have been taken.—
There was no real defence (sic) of the jail.

In response to the opinion in the *American*, the local *Baltimore County Union*
of July 18, editorialized, in part:

> In the American's view of it there would be great pleasure and profit in
> dying in defence (sic) of a jail or of a brutal wretch who assaults defense-
> less women, but 'the good and true men' of Baltimore county take a very
> different view of it, and they are able to manage their own affairs without
> any suggestions from the American.

On the same day that it editorialized, the *Union* ran a letter from "Nestor"
that was headlined "The Lynching of Cooper—A Lawyer's View of the Affair . . ."
The letter said, in part:

> Messrs. Editors: Howard Cooper, the abominable negro who has been
> confined in your jail for several weeks under condemnation and sen-
> tence of death for an assault of an outrageous character upon a highly
> respectable young lady, was taken from the jail on last Monday morn-
> ing and hanged to a tree until he was dead. Without saying much more
> upon so repulsive a subject or bringing it again before the public, I
> assert most heartily and emphatically that those engaged in avenging
> the wrongs upon one so innocent, so unprotected, so comparatively
> weak in physical nature, deserve all praise and commendation for what
> they did.
>   Whoever the lynchers were, without hesitation I say they were right
> and deserve high praise.
>   . . . I speak thus as a lawyer who has practiced before the bar in Balti-
> more and elsewhere for many years. Hence I speak whereof I know. The
> chief regret is that the offender could not have been made to suffer longer
> and more severely for his offense.

The *Savannah Morning News* of Georgia printed a letter from the Reverend
A.M. Williams on August 19, 1903, in which he advocated for a limited legal-
ization of lynching. His letter said, in part:

A large crowd watches the lynching of Jesse Washington, eighteen years old, on May 15, 1916, in Waco, Texas. (Courtesy of Library of Congress)

Editor Morning News:

. . . There is one thing perfectly sure, the crime of rape is segregated in the public mind from all other crimes.

. . . A crime so low, mean, dangerous as to remove the guilty out of human categories and reduce to that of the brute. A crime that forfeits all claims to civilization, and therefore its usual processes.

. . . My suggestion was that the simplest manner of dealing with this case was to segregate rape and legalize lynching for that crime alone.

The venerable Booker T. Washington, founder and initial president of the Tuskegee Normal and Industrial Institute, of Alabama, frequently spoke out and wrote about lynching. The *Age-Herald* of Birmingham, Alabama, on June 22, 1899, published a letter he penned that said, in part:

To the Editor of the Age-Herald:

Several times during the last few months, while our country has been shocked because of the lynching of negro citizens in several states, I was asked by many and tempted to say something upon the subject through the press.

At the time of these lynchings I kept silent for the reason that I did not believe the public mind was in a condition to listen to a discussion of the subject in that calm, cool manner that it would later, when there would be no undue feeling or excitement.

. . . In proportion to the numbers and intelligence of the population of the south there exists little more crime than in several other sections of the country, but because of the lynching habit we are constantly advertising ourselves to the world as a lawless people.

We cannot disregard the teachings of the civilized world for eighteen hundred years, that the only way to punish crime is by law. When we leave this dictum chaos begins.

The weekly *Cleveland Gazette*, an African American newspaper founded in August 1883, ran a letter from Caroline W. Jackson, with a dateline of Salem, Oregon, on July 30, 1910, that praised her state's handling of lynching crimes. It said, in part:

> Editor Gazette, Dear Sir: — The disease of lynching has at last reached Oregon but the remedy applied will doubtless have a tendency to check the spread of it . . . Lest you have overlooked it, I send the enclosed clipping:
> One of the five Grant county lynchers have been convicted of murder in the first degree and sentenced to be hanged, and another having been convicted of murder in the second degree, the other three pleaded guilty to second degree murder and all are already in the penitentiary. It was prompt, efficient work on the part of the Grant county authorities. The punishment is terribly severe — one to be hanged and four sent to the penitentiary for life for the murder of one man and he a murderer — but the lesson was needed. Lynching of a prisoner will be a very rare event in Oregon hereafter.

Some have the misconception that there was little to no large-scale pushback from Black people to the lynchings at the time. A contradictory account in the *Quincy Daily Journal* of Illinois, on March 10, 1892, detailed an incident in a mixed-race suburb of Memphis known as The Curve. It said, in part:

A mob of about seventy-five masked men broke into the Shelby county jail at 3 o'clock a.m. for the purpose of lynching the negroes that were concerned in Saturday night's trouble at The Curve. There were twenty-seven negroes in the jail, charged with assault with intent to kill, for the ambushing and shooting down of four deputies, who tried to arrest a negro Saturday night at 'The Curve' for a minor offense.

The men secured Calvin McDowell, Tom Moss and Will Stuart, the leaders of the gang, and rushing them out of jail quickly disappeared with them in the yards of the Chesapeake & Ohio Railroad Company, which lie back of the jail. Daylight disclosed the dead bodies of the three men about a quarter of a mile north of the jail.

. . . The bodies were taken to the office of Jack Walsh, and at 7 o'clock a crowd of negroes began to gather. It rapidly increased and soon 5,000 people surrounded the place where the dead bodies are. Further trouble is feared. The negroes were reported to be arming at 'the curve.'

As soon as Sheriff McLindon heard of the gathering of the mob at 'the curve,' he secured a posse of fifty men and started for the scene. There he found a large crowd of whites and negroes, whom he ordered to disperse. After considerable delay the crowd sullenly scattered.

A historical marker at the site includes the final words of one of the victims, Thomas Moss, a co-owner of the People's Grocery, who said, "Tell my people to go west—there is no justice for them here." Famous journalist Ida B. Wells, who was editor of the *Memphis Free Speech*, began an anti-lynching campaign both in the United States and abroad as a result.

On September 15, 1900, Edward E. Cooper, editor of the *Colored American* of Washington, D.C., responded with optimism to a letter from a reader on what the future held for Black people heading into the twentieth century. Cooper wrote, in part:

> . . . Granted that many rights heretofore accorded us in certain sections are now being withdrawn or denied; granted, that in certain other places heretofore regarded as cities of refuge, we are being smitten, as it were, in the houses of our friends; granted that many a former friend to us has joined the great majority, or is at least dead to us, yet not withstanding all this, the future for us in America is brighter than anywhere else for the reason that here character, brain, pluck, enterprise, accomplishments

The charred corpse of eighteen-year-old Jesse Washington after he was lynched on May 15, 1916, in Waco, Texas. (Courtesy of Library of Congress)

are achievements respected and honored when possessed by a colored man relatively as much as when possessed by a man of any other race or nationality.

. . . The white man who berates us should remember that if the United States currency he has in his pocket does not bear the genuine signature of a colored man, it is a worthless counterfeit; he should remember that every stamp that he uses to forward his mail throughout this country is issued by a colored man; he should remember that every real estate deed recorded in the nation's capital is recorded by a colored man; he should remember that the most indigenous and loyal citizen in this country is a colored man.

That same year, 1900, federal anti-lynching legislation was introduced in Congress. However, then and in subsequent years, bills were introduced and failed to pass nearly 200 times.

One account of the legislation's rejection by the Senate ran in the *Appeal*, an African American newspaper in St. Paul and Minneapolis, Minnesota, on December 9, 1922. The story from a century ago, which notes the use of the Senate filibuster, read, in part:

> Washington, Dec. 8. [Crusader Service]
>
> The Dyer Anti-Lynching Bill has been killed in the Senate. The motion last Monday to make this the unfinished business of the Senate started a filibuster conceded to be about the most perfectly organized the Senate has known since the Lodge force bill was brought up more than a score of years ago. Since Senator Shortridge made that motion the Senate has been in a complete deadlock. No business of any kind has been transacted, and the Democratic leaders announce that none will be transacted until the Republican leaders withdraw the measure.

The Senate filibuster also stopped anti-lynching legislation in 1934. Use of the filibuster became commonplace after Reconstruction. With post-Civil War Reconstruction, newly emancipated slaves could own land, vote, and hold office. But in 1891, the filibuster, which has generated much present-day controversy, scuttled a federal elections bill to ensure that Black men in the South could vote. In 1942, it thwarted poll tax legislation, and in the 1950s and 1960s, Southern senators used it to block civil rights reforms.

A letter, headlined "Law of Lynchers," from Walter H. Mazyke to the *Washington Herald* of the District of Columbia on August 12, 1922, promulgated the would-be federal role on anti-lynching legislation. It said, in part:

> To the Editor, The Washington Herald:
>
> . . . If the several States are unable or unwilling to protect the lives and property of American citizens, the Federal government can and should do so.
>
> . . . If any State does interfere with the right, this fundamental right of life of a citizen of the United States, the United States government can move to protect that citizen or the United States government is an empty name. Such a law should be enacted and statements regarding the constitutionality of the law should be left to the Supreme Court. The Federal government must demonstrate Its determination to rid the country of this menace.

Finally, a century later—in March 2022—Congress approved legislation making lynching a federal crime. The Senate's unanimous vote in favor of the Emmett Till Antilynching Act came less than a month after the House approved the measure. The bill was named after fourteen-year-old Emmett Till, who was lynched in 1955 in Mississippi.

Ku Klux Klan

Many of the lynchings and much of the intimidation directed at Black people over the decades resulted from the insidious efforts of the Ku Klux Klan.

The Klan started as a social club in Pulaski, Tennessee, on December 24, 1865. Its membership included many Confederate army veterans. By 1870, it was in most Southern states and formed the often-violent opposition to the Republican Party's Reconstruction policies, which benefited Black people economically and politically.

Klan violence led the federal government to adopt the Civil Rights Act of 1871, then known as the Ku Klux Klan Act. In response to the legislation, Klan leaders disbanded to circumvent federal actions, wrote Pete Simi and Robert Futrell in their book *American Swastika: Inside the White Power Movement's Hidden Spaces of Hate*. Local groups still met, however.

Over time, Klan tactics, targets, and membership ebbed and peaked; in the 1920s, it again had a strong presence in the United States. In its later iteration, its enemies list expanded to include Catholics, Jews, and other non-WASPs (White Anglo-Saxon Protestants), author Zeskind noted. In the mid-1920s, Klan membership reached more than 3 million, with a number of adherents living in the North and Midwest.

An account of the nascent original Klan from "Traveler," a correspondent in Columbia, Maury County, Tennessee, that ran in the *Nashville Union and Dispatch* of December 18, 1867, said, in part:

> Otherwise the town and county are quiet as usual, unless it be some general and undefined dread among the negroes of a secret order that has recently made its appearance, known as the 'Ku-klux Klan.' No one, as yet, states publicly who compose the 'Klan,' or what are its purposes.
>
> One singular feature in it is the unbroken silence maintained by them while on parade. They dress in long red gowns, red pants and red caps, with black face-cloths covering their features. They have extended themselves all over Maury and Giles counties.

Some of the negroes are wonderfully exercised over them, and some of the white Radicals have been heard to express the opinion that they were 'Rebel bush-whackers,' but as yet no one can say who or what they are.

Interestingly, sixteen men renounced their membership in the Klan of Alamance County, North Carolina, in the August 3, 1870, edition of the *Weekly Standard* of Raleigh, North Carolina, saying, in part:

> This organization in the outset, as we understood it was purely political and for the mutual protection of the members thereof and their families; but since joining, we have been pained to know that while the objects of the organization were to attain certain political ends the means used and resorted to were such as would shock a civilized and enlightened people.
>
> And we hereby publicly and independently dissolve our connection with this organization, and call upon upright law-abiding citizens everywhere to do the same thing, knowing as we do, that unless the crimes which have been committed by this organization can be put a stop to and the organization itself broken up, civil liberty or personal safety are at an end in this country, and life, property or any thing else will soon be at the mercy of an organized mob.

The *Home Journal* of Winchester, Tennessee, on February 20, 1868, published a directive from the "Grand Cyclops" of local "Ku Klux No. 38." It said:

> Be it Known:
> Resistance to Tyrants is obedience to God. Our Klan is in your midst. — We make war on no man who wars not on his fellow man. The heel of the oppressor only shall feel our wounds. Mystery is our cover — the right our power — let the tyrant tremble. Seek us not. If wanted you will be sent for. Let the Klan remember that Honor, Courage, Patriotism, are our bulwark.

The *Fayetteville Observer* of Tennessee, on October 22, 1868, printed the testimony of Richard Moore, a Black man, before the Military Committee of the Tennessee General Assembly on the "outrages committed by the Ku Klux Klan in Middle and West Tennessee." Moore testified, in part:

> On Saturday night last, two weeks ago, sixteen of this Klan came to my house and knocked me down with sticks and their pistols, beating me severely; and after they had cut my head to the skull in several places, took me from the house and stripped me, and whipped me with a strap of leather, with a buckle on its end, striking me 175 licks. The Klan asked me if I was a Radical.
>
> . . . They told me that I nor no other colored man should vote in the Presidential election.
>
> . . . I do not believe any colored or white Union man is safe in that county, or will be until there is better protection given.

In 1915, William J. Simmons, an Alabama native, founded the Second Era Klan in Stone Mountain, Georgia. Simmons called on every white American to join "The World's Greatest Secret, Social, Patriotic, Fraternal, Beneficiary Order" for the sake of white Anglo-Saxon Protestant preservation, Simi and Futrell wrote.

The upshot was that the KKK strengthened and became a powerful political organization.

Sam Cooke of Walthall, Mississippi, had a letter in the *Okolona Messenger* of Mississippi on September 15, 1921, that apparently ran initially in Memphis' *Commercial Appeal,* pointedly—and bizarrely—elevating the original Klan and castigating the newer version. It said, in part:

> To The Commercial Appeal:
>
> Futile, puerile and silly efforts to imitate the genuine, original Ku Klux Klan, that had their conception, generation and birth in 'the sweet sunny land of Dixie,' are, to a surviving member of that invisible, powerful and invincible organization, ridiculous, if not ineffably contemptible.
>
> Nothing but the horrible conditions existing in that fair land during the dark and bitter days of reconstruction could invoke the existance (sic) of such a mystic and mysterious body.
>
> . . . The true Ku Klux Klan were superlative in their irresistable (sic) influence and, as intended, the universal superstition of the negro in

every recess of his vivid imagination, intensified by the appearance of a Ku Klux Klan in his hedious (sic) regalia.

. . . The true Klan never even manifested any disrespect to women and never stooped to feathers and tar buckets as the modern Klan are reported to have done. The latter have no discipline.

In 1921, the Klan was making inroads in Seattle, Washington. The *Seattle Star* published a letter from resident W. G. Eden on August 17, 1921, that started out with the hope that the KKK "will not be allowed to function in the State of Washington."

It went on to say:

> The Ku-Klux-Klan, a secret American organization, which is said to have been founded in 1866 at Pulaski Tenn. for the purpose of amusement so called, soon developed into an association of dictators.
>
> . . . After fifty years they have revived these brutal tactics among the white and black. They have insulted the Declaration of Independence, ignored the 13th amendment to the Constitution.
>
> . . . Before any of your readers sympathize with this group, consider what has been done in the name of the Ku-Klux-Klan in the past and present. We have lots of judicial courts in every state, and all kinds of juries.

In a letter on August 22, 1921, "Reader" responded to Eden and referenced the 1866 date, saying, in part:

> . . . People could leave their homes unlocked at night or during their absence and they were not molested. Can you do it today? I do not know of either men or women who are straightforward or upright who have ever been bothered with or even fear either the law or Ku Klux Klan. I would like to see one or more Ku Klux Klan men residing in every city block in the city of Seattle.

A number of Klan "newspapers" in the early 1920s routinely published the "Ku Klux Kreed," which included a few measures designed to sound reasonable, such as vows to uphold the Constitution, freedom of speech, and "a free press uncontrolled by political parties or by religious sects," but also included:

Dr. H.W. Evans, Imperial Wizard of the Ku Klux Klan, leads his Knights of the Klan in a parade in 1926 in Washington, D.C.

- I believe in the prevention of unwarranted strikes by foreign labor agitators.
- I believe in the limitation of foreign immigration.
- I am a native-born American citizen and I believe my rights in this country are superior to those of foreigners.

The *Evening Public Ledger* of Philadelphia, Pennsylvania, ran a series on the Ku Klux Klan that spurred letters from readers on September 16, 1921. One such letter, from F.L. Moore, said:

> To the Editor of the Evening Public Ledger:
> Sir — After having carefully studied the ideals of Washington, Lincoln, Grant and others, who gave their best in defense of this country, I feel safe in saying nothing they could have done would have been of more value than the courage of the EVENING PUBLIC LEDGER in exposing the secrets of the Ku Klux Klan.

It deserves the appreciation of every one, regardless of race or creed, for its endeavors to preserve the ideals of the Nation. I sincerely trust its great work will go on.

The *Monitor*, an African-American newspaper in Omaha, Nebraska, on July 11, 1924, ran an address by James Weldon Johnson, secretary of the NAACP, that implored Blacks to make the Ku Klux Klan the main issue in the upcoming presidential election. Johnson said:

Colored Americans should not be lulled into a feeling of security by the fact that the Klan is seemingly no longer anti-Negro. The Klan is as much anti-Negro now as it was the day it was organized.

At present it is not spending much time in tarring and feathering or branding or mobbing individual Negroes. It is devoting its energies to a bigger job, the job of gaining political power, of gaining control of government. When it has done this, if it succeeds, it will again turn its attention to the Negro and it will then execute its policies not upon individual Negroes but upon the race as a whole.

The *Omaha Daily Bee* of Nebraska, on October 3, 1921, printed a letter from J. Braxton Garland in defense of the Klan that was reminiscent of today's rhetoric. It said, in part:

To the Editor of The Bee:

. . . I believe the Klansmen are marshalling the defensive forces of America into an integrate power of organization to save the republic from the domination of an alien civilization, the abject creature of politico-ecclesiastical autocracy, crawling upon its very belly in servility to its master, and now arises in bold effrontery to challenge supremacy within this republic."

Another letter, from Mrs. W.A. Collins, that mirrors contemporary fears regarding white supremacists, appeared in the *Indianapolis Times* on August 14, 1924. It said, in part:

To the Editor of The Times:

. . . The existence of the Klan is a damning indictment aglnst (sic) our claim to be an educated people. It may force us to ask if millions spent on schools have not been thrown away. It ought to teach us that Americanism is something that needs a clearer definition than has yet been given, since so many now confound it with that which would destroy us.

. . . If the Klan taught its members the truth about the Catholic church, there would be no Klan. Neither Catholic, Jew, negro nor any fair minded Protestant would consider it an American organization. Our Constitution say (sic) 'No State shall abridge the privileges or immunities of the citizens of the United States, nor shall any State deprive any person of life, liberty or property without due process of law.'

By the late 1920s Klan membership had dropped precipitously, following various scandals, including stories of terrorism and brutality that tarnished the organization's self-righteous image, according to Simi and Futrell. However, its violent activism resurfaced in the 1950s and 1960s in response to civil rights protests.

The authors wrote in their book, published in 2010, that the Klan still influenced "Aryan vigilantism and devotion to white power."

Chapter 5

The "Stolen" Election of 1876

In recent times, American society has been roiled by presidential election results, with the most contentious in 2020 with the election of Joseph Biden. Incumbent President Donald Trump and his followers falsely claimed widespread election fraud after he lost both the popular and Electoral College tallies.

Matters came to head with the rioting at the Capitol on January 6, 2021, by Trump's supporters who hoped to keep him in power. Eventually, a congressional select committee investigated the circumstances and produced a report that, among its conclusions, determined Trump "purposely disseminated false allegations of fraud related to the 2020 Presidential election in order to aid his effort to overturn the election and for purposes of soliciting contributions. These false claims provoked his supporters to violence on January 6th."

In November 2022, U.S. Attorney General Merrick Garland appointed Jack Smith as special counsel to oversee two investigations into Trump's actions. On August 1, 2023, Trump was federally indicted in connection with his effort to overturn the results of the 2020 election.

Additionally, Trump and eighteen others were indicted on August 14, 2023, in Georgia state court after Fulton County District Attorney Fani Willis brought charges that they tried to overturn the election result in that state.

More than two decades earlier, the 2000 election of George W. Bush wasn't determined until the U.S. Supreme Court voted 5-4 to halt a Florida recount undertaken after Bush won by just 537 votes and to reverse a ruling by the Florida Supreme Court for a selective manual recount. Bush became president

President Rutherford B. Hayes, left, Democratic presidential candidate Samuel J. Tilden, right, c. 1876. (Courtesy of Library of Congress)

although Gore won the national popular vote by 547,398, making the latter the first presidential candidate since Grover Cleveland in 1888 to capture the popular vote while losing in the Electoral College.

Subsequently, following complaints about voting irregularities in Florida, the U.S. Commission on Civil Rights conducted an investigation. Among its findings, the commission determined that roughly 14.4 percent of the state's Black voters cast ballots that were rejected for various reasons, compared with 1.6 percent for non-Black voters.

Prior to 2000, the most controversial presidential election likely was that of 1876, which had the highest turnout in U.S. history: 82 percent (by comparison, the presidential election of 2020 had turnout of 67 percent).

The voters, who had had enough of the corruption associated with President Ulysses S. Grant's administration, were expected to give Samuel J. Tilden and the Democrats the victory over Republican Rutherford B. Hayes. At the time, the Republicans were more generally supportive of Black people and had led progressive Reconstruction efforts that had given Black people a degree of political and economic power. Meanwhile, small farmers and shopkeepers in particular, along with working men and women, blamed bankers and other financiers for tariffs and taxes that were leaving them financially strapped. They viewed the federal government generally as infringing on their personal freedom.

Tilden, the governor of New York, in fact won the popular vote by 250,000 over Hayes and preliminarily garnered 184 electoral votes, one short of victory.

However, as Sheila Blackford wrote for the Miller Center at the University of Virginia, after the voting, the state "returning" or canvassing boards in Florida, Louisiana, and South Carolina tossed out enough Democratic votes to hand their nineteen electoral votes to Hayes, arguing that "fraud, intimidation, and violence" in some districts invalidated votes. The states were the last three in the South with Republicans in power as a result of Reconstruction. One other electoral vote, in Oregon, was also in dispute.

In early March 1877, after both parties put forth their own slate of electors, a divided Congress created a 15-member federal Electoral Commission to resolve the dispute. Meanwhile, influential backers of the Republican candidate secretly met with moderate Southern Democrats, who withdrew opposition to Hayes in return for the withdrawal of federal troops from the South. The troops had been sent to enforce Reconstruction, which began in earnest in 1865.

Thus, the Compromise of 1877 handed Hayes the victory, 185-184, while effectively bringing Reconstruction to an end.

Interestingly, Republicans at the time favored expanding the power of the federal government. Southern Republicans, in particular, viewed securing the voting rights of Black citizens as a key federal function and a symbol of the nation's "inherent goodness," noted author Roy Morris Jr. in *Fraud of the Century: Rutherford B. Hayes, Samuel Tilden and the Stolen Election of 1876*.

Northern Democrats, on the other hand, were tired of having their patriotism questioned by Republicans who accused them of copperheadism, or supporting the Confederacy in the recent Civil War, Morris wrote.

Author Michael F. Holt, in his book *By One Vote: The Disputed Presidential Election of 1876*, called the presidential elections of 1876 and 2000 "eerily similar," even beyond Republicans gaining Florida's electoral votes. He cited the resorting by both parties to state and federal courts, although in 1876 that action took place in South Carolina as well as Florida.

Black citizens, whose status was set back fundamentally after Reconstruction ended, continued to vote heavily for Republicans until the 1880s and 1890s.

As a result of the 1876 presidential election, the Electoral Count Act of 1887 was designed to address the rules that had led to the controversy. After the 2020 election, in which Vice President Mike Pence certified the election result—and made him the target of Trump and his supporters—GOP Representative Liz Cheney, of Wyoming, and Democratic Representative Zoe Lofgren, of California, proposed legislation to firm up contemporary elections. Passed by Congress in late December 2022, a revision to the 1887 act makes clear that a vice president isn't empowered to overturn the results of the presidential election.

Still, the presidential election of 1876 and its surrounding circumstances continue to reverberate today. Since the 2020 Census, Republican-controlled states have enacted laws restricting voting access, notes author Gerren Keith Gaynor in TheGrio. With the outcome of the 2024 presidential election potentially at stake, a number of voting rights cases have ended up in the courts. Also, in the lead-up to the election, concerns have been raised about the possible intimidation of voters by poll "observers."

Prior to the 1876 election, "Colored Voter" had a letter in the *Highland Weekly News* of Hillsborough, Ohio, on October 26, 1876, that said, in part:

> I notice the Hillsboro Gazette has become interested about us poor colored people. I do not know why it has become so all at once. The Gazette says Wm. Anderson was brutally assaulted by a band of negroes because he voted the Democratic ticket. Suppose he was. What has the Gazette to do with that? It was done by entirely his own race. What is the colored man assaulted for in South Carolina? Is that because he 'votes the Democratic ticket?' No! but because he will not vote it!
>
> Hold on, Mr. Gazette! 'It is poor rule that will not work both ways.' You do not say any thing about the colored men who are killed in the South because they will not vote for your party. But you are very sorry for poor Bill Anderson because he has lost a leg in Uncle Sam's army. What warm sympathy, to come from a Democrat!
>
> . . . I hope the boys will all wake up, so we can help elect Hayes in November, and then you Democrats will have to sing:
>
> 'We can here no longer stay,
> For Hayes's waves around us roll,

GRANT TO HAYES —I GUESS THAT REFORM BAIT WONT WORK THIS SIDE BETTER TRY AN ANTI-CATHOLIC WORM

An illustration in 1876 shows Democratic presidential candidate Samuel Tilden fishing with an unidentified man on the left bank of a river while on the right side, Republican Ulysses S. Grant is advising Rutherford B. Hayes that the "reform bait" is not working, so give an "anti-Catholic worm" a try. (Courtesy of Library of Congress)

And we must launch away.'

After the election, the *Memphis Daily Appeal* of November 9, 1876, had a large, front-page headline reminiscent of the infamous "Dewey Defeats Truman" headline in the *Chicago Daily Tribune* many decades later. It said: "Tilden Elected!" One of the sub-headlines said: "All Efforts of the Radical Party Managers to Turn the Popular Tide Prove Unavailing—The Democracy Has Triumphed."

The *Stark Democrat* of Canton, Ohio, on March 8, 1877, ran a long address that came out of a caucus of Democratic members of the House of Representatives. The caucus, held on March 3, unanimously adopted the address, including language that sounds similar to some nowadays.

It started by accusing the Republicans of the unconstitutional use of the army in South Carolina, Florida, and Louisiana, where President Grant had sent the federal troops "to see that the proper and legal boards of canvassers are unmolested in the performance of their duties." The elections in those states, the Democrats charged, "were held in the shadow of military power."

The address went on to claim:

Ballot Boxes Were Stuffed

... In the interest of Republican candidates, poll-books were falsified in some instances and then returned to the canvassing board, while in other cases returns, giving Democratic majorities, were withheld from the canvassers altogether.

Astounding Frauds of Louisiana Returning Board Reviewed.

... The members of the Board changed poll-books so that Republican officers appeared to be chosen when their opponents had in fact been elected. They forged the names of officers to certificates of election. They threw out votes of precincts upon affidavits which they knew had been fraudulently obtained.

Florida Frauds.

In Florida the same frauds characterized returns, and by the action of the Returning Boards, votes were thrown out with the same disregard of justice. Besides, in that State, it refused to recognize orders of courts of competent jurisdiction, and proceeded with a most defiant contempt of judicial authority. In this manner, more than one thousand votes were thrown out in Florida, and more than ten thousand in Louisiana. The votes of those States, in consequence of the conspiracy, which, in fact, had been cast for Tilden, were given to Hayes.

Dangers of the Intimidation Scheme.

We should not fail to call the attention of the people to the dangerous effect of the doctrine of intimidation in politics. Two persons may conclude to make a case of intimidation, and thereby cause a parish casting thousands of votes to be rejected. It makes elections a farce. It takes power from the people to rest in the Returning Boards. It enables the latter to impose the severest of political penalties, disenfranchisement, without giving to persons punished an opportunity of hearing or a trial. The public deserves to lose its liberties if it tolerates such outrage for an hour.

Leading up to the election, in a letter dated October 24, 1876, which a number of newspapers carried, Tilden responded to Republican assertions that the South was seeking compensation for the losses in the Civil War and the slaves. Invoking the Fourteenth Amendment to the Constitution, which deals with citizenship rights and equal protection under the law, he wrote, in part:

> Should I be elected President, the provisions of the fourteenth amendment will, so far as depends on me, be maintained, executed and enforced in perfect and absolute faith. No rebel debt will be assumed or paid. No claim for any loss or emancipation of any slave will be allowed. No claim for any loss or damage incurred by disloyal persons arising from the late war, whether covered by the fourteenth amendment or not, will be recognized or paid.

While the outcome of the election was still in doubt, the *Daily Kennebec Journal* of Augusta, Maine, on November 9, 1876, ran a brief letter from "L." that said:

> Mr. Editor: — Already may be seen the result of the ascendency of the democratic party, in the boldness and insolence manifested in flaunting the rebel flag before the loyal portion of the community, as is seen displayed from the office of the Maine Standard at this time.

A letter from Colonel John F. Dent in the *Prince Georgian* of Upper Marlborough (now, Upper Marlboro), Maryland, on December 26, 1876, made clear his feelings on the election, whose winner was still undeclared at the time. He wrote, in part:

> Dear Sir—I notice near the close of an editorial paragraph, in your issue of the 22d of December, you use the following language:
>
> 'We could rejoice still more in the promised prosperity, which the Democratic victory should ensure us, were we sure that we would not be forced, at the point of the bayonet, to relinquish the fruits of that victory.'
>
> Excuse me for suggesting that no such apprehension should be indulged in for a moment. They are reflections upon the manhood and patriotism of the people who elected Tilden and Hendricks by such an overwhelming majority, as well as upon the honest, conservative people of the whole country.—

In the issue at stake no frauds can defeat the will and rights of a determined people. The love of liberty and justice, which dominates in the American people, will never submit to such a fraud as that sought to be perpetrated upon them.

Instead of expressing apprehensions of such a character, the honest, patriotic press throughout the country should warn the conspirators of the consequences of their contemplated crimes, and seek to infuse (if such infusion be needed) into the hearts of the people the same spirit that led them to take up arms, under infinitely less provocation, against the encroachments of a hundred years ago.

Submission to the contemplated crime would be an abandonment of all the rights dear to an American Freeman.

The *Cecil Whig* of Elkton, Maryland, printed a letter from "J.H.P." on February 17, 1877, that mentioned the role of U.S. Supreme Court Justice David Davis in the continuing brouhaha. The letter said, in part:

Florida is for Hayes. That question is now settled beyond a doubt. And in losing Florida, it is conceded by prominent Democrats here, that they have lost their best case, and that it will be like fighting against fate through the rest of the struggle.

In fact, many Democrats last night conceded the election of Hayes as practically decided, and expressed their willingness to abide by the decision. There are others who are furious at the result, and go so far as to denounce Judge Davis for placing himself in a position to make his selection as the fifth Judge impracticable, claiming that if he had been selected be would have gone with the Democrats on all matters of dispute.

Justice Davis, having been appointed to the Supreme Court by President Abraham Lincoln, played a key role in Congress' instituting a federal Electoral Commission that was to determine the election outcome. He also served on the commission and was expected to be the deciding vote. But after the Democratic-controlled Illinois legislature selected him for the U.S. Senate in an effort to gain his vote for Tilden, he left the commission, resigned from the Supreme Court, and assumed the Senate seat. A Republican was appointed in his place, paving the way for Hayes' ascension.

After the election was certified for Hayes, the *Eaton Democrat* of Ohio, in an editorial on March 15, 1877, said, in part:

> The Presidential difficulty is now over. Hayes has been counted in by the partisan ruling of the Electoral Commission, and inaugurated. We, in common with every friend of reform, regret the defeat of Mr. Tilden, and more especially so as it was accomplished by the most outrageous, shameless and unblushing frauds and the blackest and darkest kind of perjury. We know that the condition of things is discouraging to us, and we have heard Democrats say, 'well, it is no use to hold elections and vote, and that henceforth they will refrain from attending either State or Presidential elections.'
>
> But this is all wrong, the Democratic party was never in a better condition than it is to-day. Having carried their candidate by a popular vote of 250,000, and 900,000 of the white voters of the United States, surely there is nothing to discourage them in this.

A letter from "Patriot" in the *Weekly Oskaloosa Herald* of Iowa, on March 8, 1877, defended Republican rule coming out of the election. It said, in part:

> Eds. Herald. — Our nation should be thankful that the presidential contest is at last decided in favor of Right. Now as our opponents complain of Republican rule, let us summarize some of our sins:
>
> 1st. We always held that amnesty to rebels was too cheap, and should have been granted more sparingly. Also, we think that the less honorable sympathizer of the North should have been kept at a suitable distance.
>
> . . . Further, Republicans should keep aloof from secret organizations, originated in southern minds and sent north to be hatched into Democrats. All lovers of our country should beware of giving aid or comfort so (sic) our country's enemies; especially we should never encourage those filthy rebel papers occasionally issued in our Northern States, as such sheets are as injurious to youth and ignorance as Voltaire or Paine's writing on the religious world.
>
> Moreover, the arm of the government should long since have stopped those atrocities in the Southern States, and we assert most emphatically, that if our government does not stop the killing and maltreating of our poor citizens in the South, regardless of color or previous condition, we

may as well send to Philadelphia, and have that old bell at Independence Hall thrown into the Schuylkill river . . .

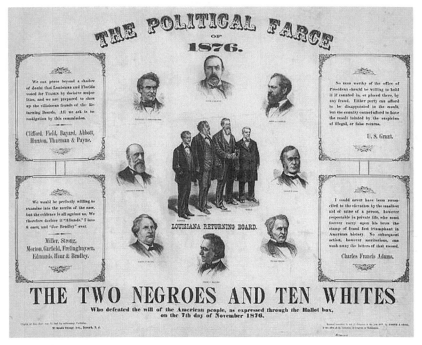

An illustration in 1877 ridicules the Louisiana "returning," or canvassing, board for its vote in helping determine the outcome of the 1876 presidential election. (Courtesy of Library of Congress)

A.B. Farquhar of York, Pennsylvania, in the *New-York Tribune* of March 13, 1877, expressed his joy at Hayes' victory. Farquhar's letter said, in part:

> To the Editor of The Tribune.
> . . . Every lover of his country must have read Hayes's inaugural with admiration, but truly to appreciate it, it was necessary to listen to its delivery and take in the full impression of the man; all those bronzed lineaments seemed to bear the legend of his country's welfare, and the words were audible with weight and integrity and meaning.

Samuel McGowan, a brigadier general for the Confederacy during the Civil War and later an associate justice of the South Carolina Supreme Court who served as an elector for the Democratic ticket in 1876, had a letter in the

Augusta Chronicle and *Sentinel* of Georgia that defended the role he and other Democratic electors played. The letter, which was picked up by the *Anderson Intelligencer* of South Carolina, ran on January 25, 1877, saying, in part:

> Editors Chronicle and Sentinel:
>
> . . . I was one of the electors at large for the State of South Carolina on the Democratic ticket, and as such, in association with other electors, had in charge specially the interests of Tilden and Hendricks. It was not only my duty to support their election and promote it in every honorable way, but I did it con amore. Having a strong opinion of the great importance of their election, I supported them earnestly as a matter of principle and patriotism.
>
> . . . Even under the 'peace and prosperity' policy, all the white people voted for Tilden and Hendricks, and it is most confidently believed that the large, colored vote polled for them was secured alone by that wise and just policy which was strictly in accordance with Mr. Tilden's letter of acceptance.
>
> We think these facts prove the sincerity, good faith and activity of the Democratic electors for the State of South Carolina in the late canvass, and that Tilden and Hendricks were not 'deserted.'

The *Anderson Intelligencer* of South Carolina solicited a letter from ex-Governor B.F. Perry on what actions—or inactions—the Democrats should take in the wake of the election outcome. The largely conciliatory letter of response, which was published on April 12, 1877, said, in part:

> Messrs. Editors: I am in receipt of your letter of the 7th inst., asking me to furnish you for publication my views in reference to President Hayes' Southern policy, and whether Democrats should accept office under his administration. I received, a few days since, a similar letter from the editor of the Augusta Chronicle & Constitutionalist, and I answered this letter very fully, stating that I saw no impropriety in Democrats accepting office under President Hayes if they still adhered to their Democratic principles.
>
> It is certainly a matter of the greatest importance to have all public offices well filled by honest and competent men. The great curse of the Southern States, for the last ten or twelve years, has been that all the

public offices, with few exceptions, have been filled with corrupt or incompetent officers. This evil must continue unless Democrats will consent to hold Federal offices.

A letter from "Citizen" to the *Daily Constitution* of Atlanta, which ran on
April 7, 1877, was much less accepting. In fact, its argument was similar to that
made by some Trump supporters at the time Biden's election was certified. The
letter said, in part:

> Editors Constitution — We all recollect the general feeling of disappro-
> bation which our people felt when the democratic representatives and
> senators in congress, seeing that they had been cheated, and that the
> electoral commission was a party machine, engaged in the perpetration
> of fraud upon the country, did not prevent its consummation, by delay-
> ing the count and preventing its completion till the fourth of March.
>
> This course would have prevented the fraudulent counting in of
> Hayes, and would have secured the inauguration of Gov. Tilden as pres-
> ident, as the house of representatives would have immediately elected
> him, and he would have been inaugurated; and we would to-day be
> under a democratic president, with the government administered ac-
> cording to old democratic usage.

And "Justitia," writing in the *Daily Memphis Appeal* of Tennessee on March
31, 1877, took aim at Hayes, saying in part:

> Editors Appeal —
> . . . I am unable to see how the country can expect any good from
> a man justly branded as the embodiment of fraud. Were he to equal
> Washington's administration, still the great crime of reaching the Pres-
> idency as he did should ever be held up, as stung with thousands of vi-
> pers, a terror to every future attempt of the kind, and let all the people
> say amen.

Washington correspondent "Nemo," in the *Louisiana Democrat* of Alexandria, on May 30, 1877, weighed in on speculation as to why Tilden was absent
from a meeting of the Chamber of Commerce in New York at which President
Hayes was a guest. Nemo wrote, in part:

Much is being said in Republican papers of the fact that Mr. Tilden declined to be present at the meeting of the Chamber of Commerce in New York on yesterday, at which meeting President Hayes was a guest. No remarks from Republicans as Republicans, are in order. The meeting was not, ostensibly, in honor of President Hayes, and Mr. Tilden may have had excellent private reasons for refusing to attend.

Business, health, or the mere disinclination to be present would be sufficient reasons. It is likely, however, that Mr. Tilden believes, with most of his countrymen, that Mr. Hayes was not elected President and is not, in either law or equity, entitled to the office. If he so believes, then that, also was a sufficient reason for his absence.

On March 16, 1877, the *Burlington Weekly Free Press* of Vermont carried a correspondence from Alton, in New York, that said the election controversy was in the past and that peace had prevailed. It said, in part:

> To the Editor of the Free Press and Times.
> . . . The inauguration is over, and Hayes is, as he should be, President. Tilden and Morrisey played a bold, daring game for very high stakes; they lost, and subside. All the talk of resistance has stopped, for it was never meant to be anything. It was intended to prevent the inauguration, if possible, but was not intended to go any farther.
>
> The business Democracy are as well pleased as the Republicans that the question is settled, and they will give the new administration a cordial and honest support. The Wall street men held a meeting, and resolved, and the Union League Club did likewise. Both bodies recognized Hayes as the legitimate President of the United States, and endorsed the policy shadowed forth in his inaugural as fully as he could have desired it.
>
> The Cabinet is entirely satisfactory to New York, and altogether there is a sort of political love-feast prevailing, that is not only pleasant but encouraging.

The *Juniata Sentinel and Republican* of Mifflintown, Pennsylvania, on June 20, 1877, ran a letter with a dateline of "Near Seven Star Tavern" from Barton Speak, whom the newspaper described as "an old Jacksonian Democrat of Greenwood Township." The letter, which reminded readers of the role of the Electoral College, said, in part:

Mr. Tilden laid it on heavy that he had been elected by the popular vote, and that the popular vote had been outraged because Mr. Hayes, who is the minority man, occupies the Presidency.

It would be beneath Old Andy, if he were living, to go before the people with such stuff as that, for it is well known to even people who do not read, or cannot read, that Presidents are not elected by the popular or majority vote; they are elected by what is called the electoral vote.

I have never heard that Mr. Tilden advocated a system of voting for the President of the United State by majority ballot. Since the rebellion they have not had an honest majority election in the Southern States.

Chapter 6

Women Get the Vote—Finally

On May 21, 1919, the U.S. House of Representatives passed the Nineteenth Amendment to the Constitution granting women the right to vote. Two weeks later, the Senate followed suit with approval in a 56-25 vote. Still, thirty-six states needed to ratify the measure for it to become an amendment to the Constitution.

On August 18, 1920, the Tennessee legislature's support pushed it over the top, and U.S. Secretary of State Bainbridge Colby certified the ratification on August 26, 1920.

Historian Ellen Carol DuBois makes the case that the importance of women's suffrage remains crucial, "as hopes and fears for American democracy rise and fall." She says issues affecting women in particular, such as abortion, are front and center in American politics. In fact, in the run-up to the 2024 presidential election, millions more women than men had registered to vote in recent cycles, as pointed out by Julia Manchester and Julia Mueller, writing in *The Hill*.

Even so, the patriarchy so artfully scrutinized in the 2023 hit film, *Barbie*, has been firmly ensconced in American life, and remains so today. As Cassie Miller wrote in a Southern Poverty Law Center publication on right-wing extremism in 2023, "White supremacy is central to the hard right, but so is a desire to maintain patriarchal society where people adhere to strictly defined gender roles and men act from a position of dominance."

A women's suffrage march in 1913 fills Pennsylvania Avenue in Washington, D.C. (Courtesy of Library of Congress)

Women's suffrage was a major issue in the United States—and elsewhere—for many decades prior to the constitutional amendment's ratification, as efforts for a federal amendment frustratingly failed.

Historian Faye E. Dudden in her book, *Fighting Chance: The Struggle Over Woman Suffrage and Black Suffrage in Reconstruction America*, pointed out that by the end of the 1850s, the struggle for women's rights emphasized political action at the state level.

A long letter by Annie Savery, of the Iowa Women Suffrage Association, that was published in the *Buchanan County Bulletin* of Independence, Iowa, on October 20, 1871, typified that strategy. It said, in part:

DES MOINES, Sept. 13, 1871.

The executive committee of the Iowa Women Suffrage Association, have requested me to take necessary steps to secure a full representation of the friends of woman suffrage at our next annual meeting, to be held at Des Moines on the 19th of October.

. . . The leading statesmen and thinkers of the age, those who lead the advance guard in letters, in law, in politics and religion, those who direct the march of events in both hemispheres, have conceded not only woman's right to exercise any and all avocations, but the justice of her claim

to political equality. — And political rights have been conferred upon
women in many parts of Europe and in two of our territories.

Therefore the time has past for the discussion of woman's right to the
ballot. It now only requires one more combined and determined effort
on the part of the women of Iowa to secure it.

During Reconstruction following the Civil War, those advocating for a
woman's right to vote often had a rocky relationship with those pushing for
the Black vote.

Activists Elizabeth Cady Stanton and Susan B. Anthony, both of whom were
abolitionists, opposed the fourteenth and fifteenth amendments to the Constitution, which gave Black men voting rights, in the belief that the right to vote
should be universal.

Author Dudden recounted that in 1854, Stanton coldly said, "We are moral,
virtuous, and intelligent, and in all respects quite equal on the proud white
man, yet by your laws we are classed with idiots, lunatics and negroes." Eventually, there was a divide in the women's suffrage movement.

Still, Stanton, Anthony, and other early activists had ensured their place in
history, as demonstrated by an editor's reply to Celia Thomas in the August 3,
1910, edition of the "People's Column" in the *Boston Daily Globe*. It offers a
timeline of key support for women's rights:

> Equal rights between men and women has been discussed for nearly 400
> years. Plato in his 'Republic' suggests they should have the same educa-
> tion as men . . .
>
> . . . Mary Woolstencroft published her 'Vindication of the Rights
> of Women' in 1790. At the time of the establishment of the American
> republic, Abigail Adams, wife of John Adams, asked that women should
> be recognized in the constitution, and Hannah Lee Corbin protested
> against taxation without representation.
>
> Many supporters of the cause of woman's rights were gathered during
> the antislavery agitation, the most prominent being Wendell Phillips and
> William Lloyd Garrison.
>
> The first women's suffrage convention was called at Seneca Falls,
> July 19, 1848. Mrs. Elizabeth Cady Stanton, Lucretia Mott, Martha C.
> Wright and Mary A. McClintock were prime movers.

. . . In May, 1869, the National women's suffrage association, with
Susan B. Anthony and Elizabeth Cady Stanton as leaders, was organized
and met in Washington every winter from that time till 1890. In that
year it united with the American women's suffrage association, established in Cleveland.

By the 1880s and 1890s, the women's suffrage cause had burgeoned, in
part from the growing influence of the Western United States, a re-emphasis
on amending state constitutions and from the temperance movement. Many
women joined the latter, which had spurred women's advocacy for the right to
vote, according to DuBois in her 2020 book *Suffrage Woman's Long Battle for
the Vote*.

One such letter, from "Voter," of Union Dale, Kentucky, addressed the troublesome combination of men and alcohol. It appeared in the *Breckenridge News*
of Cloverport, Kentucky, on August 30, 1893, and said, in part:

> Why civilized society or a community half-civilized submit to the barba-
> rous and demonizing rum traffic is beyond comprehension. Who is he
> that denies or does not positively know that the open saloon is an expres-
> sion of all the evils of which hell itself is heir to? These sinks of iniquity
> are opened wide in the name of liberty. Liberty for what?
> . . . That men with uncontrolable (sic) appetites and passions may in
> the name of personal rights, imbibe all the desires which fit him for the
> commission of every crime enumerated in the decalogue. Why should
> our nation bear even the name of a Christian civilization? There is no
> half-civilized or barbarous country on the face of the earth which is
> dominated and ruled by a greater curse than these United States, by the
> rum power.
> . . . Woman can only be liberated by the ballot and being free. By the
> exercises of it she will be in a position to cure her other half, man, from
> some of his contemptibly bad habits, which he says by his imbecile na-
> ture, he is too weak to resist.

A letter from J.F. Durant, addressed to the "Kickers" Column in the *Quincy
Daily Herald* of Illinois, on October 13, 1894, also made the case for the female
vote in terms of equality to men. The letter said, in part:

Editor Kickers' Column: — The question of the right and propriety of women exercising the same right as men at the polls is just now being much discussed.

Cardinal Gibbons says that if women go into politics he is sure they will 'carry away with them some of the mud and dirt of political strife.'

Now we are of the opinion that the use of the ballot by women would tend to do away with political 'mud and dirt.' Men speak of home as women's natural sphere as though the world was anything but a world of homes.

. . . The bugaboo of political defilement as urged against woman's participation in legislative affairs is all bosh. The fact that a woman is a mother is an argument for, not against, her right to citizenship. I say let her vote; let her have all the privileges man has. Politics and morality should know no sex, and the same consequences should attend the departure of man from the paths of moral rectitude as the departure of woman.

Another letter, from "Alma" in the *Fresno Morning Republican* of California, on May 8, 1895, took up the cause of women, saying denial of the right to vote was just another misguided form of discrimination against females. It said, in part:

Editor Republican

. . . As for the reasons why woman should not vote, there are none. But some timid souls believe if a little slack were allowed, they would take the bits in their teeth and capsize the whole business. The sentiment that now discriminates against her in politics but yesterday discriminated against her in the drama, in literature, in every vocation of independence; discriminated against her in the privileges of education.

. . . There is a great deal said about woman's lot here being on the retiring and 'patient' order, which, of course, carries the influence that her lot hereafter will be something very different. Of the latter I know nothing. But, this I do know, we are here, man and woman, with interests inseparable, and to share alike the possibilities of earth as they are worked out, either in splendor or ignominy.

She will lose no womanliness, but will exemplify in her perfect development, that beauty in its highest form rests upon and grows out of intellectual and moral values, that its foundation is strength, not weakness.

Members of the Congressional Union for Woman Suffrage picket outside the White House in 1917. (Courtesy of Library of Congress)

Editorials and letters at the time on the contentious topic ran in newspapers throughout the country, both prior and subsequent to ratification.

"A Hungry Husband," in a letter in the *Star* of Newark, New Jersey, on November 22, 1909, had no use for women's suffrage:

> To the Editor of the Star:
>
> As a married man I wish to protest against this suffragette business. A man comes home and finds a wifeless home and a supperless table. What does he do? Angry, he patronizes the corner cafe; result, a probable domestic quarrel.
>
> I appeal to the people. Can you not see the train of misfortune following in the wake of this? Divorces, broken homes, and think how much worse it will be if they ever get the ballot. Oh! Women of Newark, save us.

"Visitor" had a backhanded criticism of women in a letter complimenting the prowess of men in the kitchen in a letter that ran on June 10, 1896, in the *Dalles Weekly Chronicle* of Oregon. It said:

> The coming woman can don masculine continuations, tie her four-in-hand around her stand-up collar, pull down her vest, straighten her hat and sail in to take the business responsibilities from the weary shoulders of her henpecked 'hubby' just as soon as she pleases, for it was fully demonstrated last Saturday evening at the basket social, held in the hall of The Dalles Lodge No. 2, 1. O. G. T., that the rising generation of young men are fully capable of caring for the culinary department of the household.
>
> In fact, the lunches brought by the boys when compared with those which the girls prepared two or three weeks ago — well, we won't compare them, the girls might get offended — but they were works of art, every one.

As passage of women's right to vote inched closer early in the twentieth century's second decade, a letter from Josiah Bond of Alto, Arizona, that appeared on October 19, 1912, in the *Border Vidette* of Nogales, Arizona, raised concerns that many men shared. It said, in part:

> Editor THE BORDER VIDETTE:
>
> Sir: The men of Arizona have been called upon to think about allowing the women to vote in this State. I have read considerable in regard to the matter but it has unfortunately been almost altogether appeals to vote for women, without a particle of argument as to the effect of giving them this right and how it has worked in the places where the experiment has been tried.
>
> As a matter of fact the only argument I have yet seen, was directed against the women. This stated and brought forward an array of facts to prove it, that wherever the women had the right to vote, a lower tone of law-making was immediately perceived, even in the laws affecting woman and children, where it has been confidently asserted that progress would surely follow female suffrage.

However, male opposition to the female vote certainly was far from universal. Chris B. Foltz of Two Buttes, Colorado, had a colorful letter in the *Weekly*

Eagle of Wichita, Kansas, on May 24, 1912, that lauded his wife and mother in making the pro-suffrage case. It said, in part:

> Editor Weekly Eagle: —
>
> . . . About sixteen years ago where the thriving town of Holly is located now, then it consisted of the Double S Ranch, I overheard a group of men discuss the election held there the day before. The topic was about how the women cast their first ballot and how it displeased a few of the old politicians who could not carry out their plans in the presence of the ladies.
>
> One old duffer, who could not see good in women voting, let his pent up emotions give expression in a few foul-mouthed oaths just to show his authority. This acted like a boomerang on him. The strangled laugh of his chums and disgusted looks from the rest made him hide out like a whipped cur.
>
> . . . My sainted mother was and my wife is in judgment far superior to myself, and so there are others like Mrs. Sangster and ye editor of the Weekly Eagle. Why I could not for the life of me deny them the rights that Indians, negroes and fools enjoy.
>
> Whenever I hear any one argue against Woman Suffrage I look at the color of their hair and cannot help but think about the dark ages.

And, an unsigned letter in the *La Crosse Tribune* of Wisconsin, on February 10, 1912, argued on behalf of women, while raising issues about corporate pricing that sound relevant today. The letter said, in part:

> Mr. Editor:
>
> Last evening I attended the meeting of the Woman's Equal Suffrage association and I was proud of the earnest women I found there, who have undertaken the task of promoting woman's suffrage in the state of Wisconsin.
>
> I know many arguments have been advanced against giving women the right to vote. Here are some I have heard advanced in these last few weeks:
>
> 'Women suffer enough without woman's suffrage,' 'Women do not know enough about politics to vote,' 'Women as a mass, do not want to vote,' 'It is only the idle who have nothing to do who want to dabble in

"ALL TOGETHER NOW! STOP HER!"

An illustration in *Puck* magazine on May 2, 1914, shows several women and men hanging onto the robe labeled "Woman Suffrage" and the sandal of a large woman striding forward; a placard on the ground says "Anti-Suffrage." (Courtesy Library of Congress)

politics,' 'Women should stay home and tend the babies and wash the dishes.'

All such arguments appear to me to be simply nonsensical.

. . . The women will want to know why the absolute necessities of life are soaring so high in price, why our foodstuffs are so expensive. Why did sugar go up to $7 a barrel at canning time? Why did the Standard Oil trust and the cotton and wool trusts raise the prices of their products? Did they proceed from natural causes such as scarcity of the products, a greater demand than there was a supply or an advanced cost in manufacture? Or did these prices come into existence to swell the immense campaign fund which is spent at every election to aid to office a friend and protection of 'the moneyed interests?'

Eight years prior to ratification of the federal legislation, a number of states moved to change their constitutions regarding the female vote. One such state was Michigan, which held a referendum on the issue in the November 5, 1912, election. As the votes came in, it appeared that suffrage had won. Mrs. Bessie Whipple, of Detroit, wrote a thank-you letter that appeared in the November 11, 1912, edition of the *Detroit Times* and said, in part:

> To the Editor of The Times:
>
> The election is over. Suffrage has won in Michigan. Women are now citizens, having a voice in affairs of state. The battle is over and the victory won, thanks to the justice and loyalty of good men whose will has prevailed.
>
> . . . In conclusion I wish to say that The Detroit Times deserves the thanks of every woman in Michigan for the attitude your paper has taken all through the suffrage campaign.

It turns out the letter was premature. A story on the vote in the *Detroit Times* of November 12 included this sentence: "It now appears that in five counties — Ingham, Genesee, Emmett, Presque Isle and possibly one other — the constitutional amendment giving women the right to vote was not printed in full on the ballots, as is required by the constitution." Ultimately, the ballot question was defeated by the razor-thin count of 248,135 to 247,375.

In Tennessee, which was the thirty-sixth state—and final one needed—for ratification, a front-page story in the *Chattanooga News* on August 19, 1920, quoted House member Harry Burn, who cast the deciding vote.

He said, ". . . I know that a mother's advice is always safest for her boy to follow, and my mother wanted me to vote for ratification." He went on to say, "I appreciated the fact that an opportunity such as seldom comes to moral man—to free American women from political slavery—was mine."

But the same news story noted that there was immediate blowback to the ratification vote. It said:

> There are persistent rumors in circulation that charges will be made on the floor of the house by anti leaders that the bribery of a member of the house by suffrage forces was responsible for yesterday's ratification.
>
> . . . Legal steps are already being taken to prevent Secretary of State of Tennessee Stevens from certifying to the federal secretary of state the

fact of ratification. In event the antis fail to block suffrage by reconsideration, papers will immediately be filed in some state court to tie up the amendment.

. . . There is no diminuition (sic) of the intensity of the struggle. The antis have arranged to have hundreds of telegrams sent to every member who voted for ratification, protesting against his vote. On the other hand even a greater number is coming from friends of suffrage throughout the state to the men who aided them.

Apparently, the suspicions of bribery were aimed at Burn, whose mother said in an interview in the next day's *Chattanooga News*: "To be honest and true to his convictions is Harry's motto, and I am sure he wasn't paid to vote for the suffrage amendment, as been charged in some of the Tennessee papers."

The interview story said Mrs. J.F. Burn received many telephone calls asking if she had wired her son to vote for suffrage, but she had sent him only one letter in which she said she hoped he would vote for the amendment.

"I am glad that he loved me enough to say afterward that my letter had so much influence on him," she said. "I don't think anyone over there was better posted on suffrage than Harry," Mrs. Burn added, noting that her son subscribed to at least thirty-five magazines.

Subsequently, despite some legislative and legal attempts to rescind the vote, the attorney general and governor Albert H. Roberts announced that Tennessee's ratification of the amendment couldn't be undone. Even though ratification of the Nineteenth Amendment became official, lawyers opposed to ratification filed fruitless legal challenges for two years.

Later in 1920, Vermont and Connecticut voted for the suffrage amendment, making the Tennessee legal fight moot in any event.

On August 26, 1920, the *Connecticut Western News* of Litchfield County ran an editorial that said, in part:

VOTES FOR WOMEN

The inevitable has happened. The legislature of Tennessee has ratified the eighteenth amendment (sic) granting equal rights at the polls to women which marks the end of a fight by prominent women throughout this country extending over a period of more than sixty years.

The battle is over and they who have used suffrage as a means for diversion may now turn their attention to the political side of it, whereby we shall expect to vote for 'our leading woman' in place of commonplace man. This is not sarcasm, as we fully expect that women officeholders will be a common occurence (sic) during the next few years.

A letter from a woman with the initials "O.B." that ran in the *Crossville Chronicle* of Tennessee, on September 8, 1920, pulled no punches regarding the amendment. It said, in part:

> The fact that I am a southern woman has always been a matter of pride to me, and until just recently have (not had) a cause to be ashamed of it. The cause is the present wrangle concerning the suffrage amendment, and the fact that women all over the state are waging war against a step towards higher and better womanhood, which also means a better manhood and a better nation.
>
> I do not believe there is a county in Tennessee where there are not women taxpayers, and women who have become proficient in some kind of work, and thereby supporting themselves.
>
> . . . The remark so often made that, if allowed to vote women would merely repeat their husbands' votes, is too obselete (sic) for this day and time. The woman of today is a thinking, intelligent being (for) whom marriage means comradeship and not slavery.
>
> Would it not be more sensible to say that, if women could help make the government of their country it would be an incentive to them to keep abreast of the times, and they could themselves be better guides to their sons and daughters?

Ratification led to logistical issues in some places regarding voter registration—for white women, that is.

Fred W. Bynum, chairman of the Democratic Executive Committee for Richmond County, North Carolina, had a front-page letter on voter registration on September 9, 1920, in that county's *Rockingham Post-Dispatch*. It said, in part:

> Editor Post-Dispatch: Just a word about registration of voters. Whatever may have been the individual wishes of any person in this county, we are now confronted with the fact that women are entitled to vote on the same footing as are the men.

. . . I want to see all the white women in the county register between September 30 and October 23rd and to that end the men should lend every assistance.

For Black women, although active in the suffrage movement for decades, their political engagement increased following ratification of the Nineteenth Amendment in the hopes of countering anti-Black violence and the disfranchisement of Black men after World War I, according to an article by Sharon Harley, an associate professor at the University of Maryland, College Park, that was published on the National Park Service website. Still, Black women had to overcome the same obstacles, such as poll taxes and literacy tests, that Black men would continue to encounter in trying to vote in the South.

Following ratification of the Nineteenth Amendment, consumer fraud was a concern, as indicated in a brief item, headlined "Women 'Voters' Stung," that ran in the *New Britain* (Conn.) *Herald* on August 27, 1920:

Pittsburgh, Aug. 27. — Many Allegheny County women have been defrauded by a bogus tax collector who went into action shortly after Secretary Colby signed the suffrage proclamation yesterday, according to an announcement today by H.H. Rowan, district attorney.

The bogus agent visited homes, informed women they must pay him a poll tax if they wanted to vote In November, collected the money, handed out a receipt and then disappeared.

A letter from Anna B. Lawther in the *Telegraph-Herald* of Dubuque, Iowa, on March 27, 1923, referencing Sheppard-Towner federal legislation aimed at reducing maternal and infant mortality, pointed to the positive role the female vote could play in society. The letter said:

Editor, Telegraph-Herald:

In the issue of your paper of March 23 there is an editorial that is clever and amusing. Your statement of the purpose of the Sheppard-Towner bill is so delightfully vague that the reader would have to be a member of the League of Women Voters to recognize the bill.

I feel a real sympathy for our members of the legislature whom you refer to as 'uncertain' and 'lacking in backbone.' The members of the present legislature know that they are representatives of the people, and 'women is people.'

You have paid an indirect compliment to the women voters by show-ing that their organized efforts have been so effective. You have con-firmed my belief in the power of the ballot in the hands of women.

As it happened, though, women's groups were disappointed that only about 26 percent of eligible females nationwide voted in the 1920 presidential elec-tion, the first for which they could cast a ballot, as noted in *Decade of American History: America in the 1920s*, by Michael J. O'Neal. Women tended to mirror the male vote along party lines, giving the election to Republican Warren G. Harding.

A letter from C.A. Dagley, of Dania, Florida, in the *Chattanooga News* of Ten-nessee, on January 13, 1923, addressed political parties vis-à-vis women. It said:

Editor The News:

Mrs. Bernice S. Pyke, democratic national committeewoman from Ohio, is quoted as saying at the recent Jackson banquet: 'Women are going to join the party that convinces them of its usefulness and they are now asking where lies the greatest good to the greatest number.'

That sounds good, and, to me, it seems quite reasonable. However, Mrs. Pyke had better be mightly (sic) careful talking about 'the greatest good to the greatest number,' or some of the self-appointed advisers of all the parties which I know anything about, will be telling her to 'go away back and sit down.'

Perhaps if they could only find just such a party more men, as well as women, would permanently 'join the party that convinces them of its usefulness,' and that it was constantly seeking to do 'the greatest good to the greatest number,' instead of flopping from one party to another — out of the frying pan into the fire — as evidently they did in 1920 and in 1922.

And many women activists were discouraged by the fact that the 19th Amendment did not lead to more widespread advancement in general. For example, over the next decade, female employment grew by only about 1 per-cent and most of the jobs were lower paying in the service sector, according to O'Neal.

A letter in the *Newark* (N.J.) *Sunday Call* of October 31, 1920, signed by "One Who Advocates Women's Service with the Colors," touched upon the evolving—but obstacle-filled—landscape for women in American society. It said, in part:

> Sir — Has the government in planning for reorganizing the army and navy to a peacetime basis included in their plans the enlistment or enrollment of women as 'yeomen' in the navy, naval reserve or marines, and in the army as clerks?
>
> If not, why not? Did not thousands of women serve in this capacity throughout the war? Was not their service rendered with intelligence and efficiency? Was it not rendered with the same alacrity as was displayed by our boys?
>
> In view of the fact that women have been given the right to vote, does it not seem 'only right' that they be given the privilege to serve with 'the colors?' Does not this privilege belong to them for their war service?

An editor's note after the letter responded: "No plans for the enrollment of women in the army or navy are contemplated."

Even the incremental advances women were making displeased some, as this letter from "Free Lance" in the *Buffalo Express* of New York on January 10, 1923, showed. It said:

> Editor Buffalo Express: — I still insist that women should not sit on juries. A woman should be the mother of five or six children and should be content with the duties of governing her home and looking after the welfare of her children. She should have everything in comfortable order for the coming home of the breadwinner, who has been laboring through the day for money to support his family in comfort. His wife and children with happy faces and extended hands should welcome him home.
>
> The father of such children should be a happy man, and the family supper should be an enjoyable feast. The father in a happy temper; the mother and her children full of joy.

A number of letters further touched on the balancing of home life and employment affecting both women and men in the early 1920s. For many, day-to-day living remained a struggle.

For example, "Miserable" had a desperate letter about her marital plight in the *St. Louis Star* of Missouri on January 6, 1923. It said:

> Editor The St. Louis Star: I am a married woman with three children, the youngest 6 months old. My husband does not work. He has not worked for a year. He goes away every morning. On Monday he goes away and says he is surely going to work and will get paid on Saturday and when Saturday comes it is not so. It is getting so now that the furniture company wants their furniture back and the landlord wants his rooms, but he still does not work.
>
> Is there any place where I could report this and see that he is made to provide for his family? I would be very thankful to know. I would surely like to see something done as many a day we have hardly anything to eat and not any too much clothes to wear.

Mrs. J.M. Cloverdale of Casper, Wyoming, had a letter in the *Casper Daily Tribune* on June 17, 1922, that advocated for young women seeking employment—at the expense of working married women. It said:

> Editor Tribune: — I sincerely hope you will allow me space in your paper in regard to employment for young girls that have just finished school. What are we going to have them do for a living?
>
> I know of young girls walking the streets looking for honest employment that can't be found with a search warrant, simply because our married women are holding down the jobs.
>
> These women have husbands able to support them and are working too. Investigate some of the offices, laundries and stores, etc., etc., and find out for yourself. I think it is high time the married women were staying at home and sewing some buttons on Bill's trousers and ceasing to feed him out of paper sacks and tin cans, and let the girls have a chance to work.

If the future banks on the aspirations of young people, then this letter from Belinda Riemenschneider, a "farmer girl of 16" from Wahpeton, North Dakota, held out hope for both women and the country at large. It appeared on July 22, 1918—shortly before Tennessee's deciding vote in favor of the

A charcoal and chalk drawing in 1917 shows a suffrage supporter holding a banner quoting one of President Woodrow Wilson's speeches.

nineteenth Amendment—in the national edition of Fargo's *Nonpartisan Leader* and said, in part:

> Editor Nonpartisan Leader:
>   . . . I think if women are capable of being president and the people elect one, she has the right to govern the United States as well as a man.
>   Many women are as capable and more so of voting and holding office as some men. Some women are better educated. My opinion is that equal suffrage would help America.
>   Too many youths and men pay no attention to what their government is doing. If women voted, they would be afraid that the women and girls would know more about it than they. They would read up on

the actions of their government, as would women. Democracy means equality of opportunity, does it not?

As something of a postscript, historian DuBois wrote that the right to vote certified the independence of women, whether single or married. Without the vote, she said, "all women's other aspirations would have been even more hobbled and halted than they were."

To take it a step further, a record number of female candidates ran for federal and state office in the 2022 midterm elections, according to the Center for American Women and Politics at Rutgers University.

Chapter 7

Abortion and Birth Control Over the Years

Birth control methods appeared thousands of years ago, with the earliest condoms believed to have originated in Crete and Egypt around 3000 BCE. The crude devices were made of animal and fish bladders, intestines, and linen sheaths, according to the *Our Bodies Ourselves Today* website. In roughly 1850 BCE, Egypt created one of the first spermicides out of crocodile dung and fermented dough. In 1855, the first rubber condoms were introduced.

Abortion, meanwhile, dates back over five thousand years, when the Emperor Shennong supposedly prescribed the use of mercury to induce abortions, according to the *Orlando* (Florida) *Women's Center* website.

An Egyptian medical text in 1550 BCE described the insertion of a plant fiber covered in honey and crushed dates as an abortion method, according to "History of Abortion" on the *Britannica ProCon.org* website, which added that abortion was accepted practice in ancient Greece and Rome.

Birth control and abortion have remained thorny issues for the many decades in the United States, particularly as they were tied to the evolving women's rights and feminist movements. In the nineteenth and early twentieth centuries, the pages of American newspapers were filled with accounts of arrests and trials involving abortion.

For example, *The Evening Star* of Washington, D.C., on May 6, 1864, reported on a trial surrounding the death of a young woman named Maggie

Duvall. A witness said she had taken sick, "the result of an endeavor to procure an abortion." However, the story included testimony that the woman's right lung was "totally diseased." A Dr. Burrows testified that "no medicine could be administered to produce an abortion that could possibly bring on a violent acute pulmonary disease."

The *Pantagraph* of Bloomington, Illinois, on January 19, 1880, ran a brief that said:

> — Dr. Little and John O'Neil were discharged on Saturday, at the termination of the examination into the charge that they had procured an abortion on Miss Whalen. The case was first set for Lawrence's court, and then taken by change of venue to Esquire Pancake. Dr. Little was entirely exonerated by the evidence, and this was plainly stated by Esquire Pancake.

A one-line item in the *Montana Post* of Virginia City, Montana, on September 21, 1867, said: "Fifty prominent physicians of Indianapolis have been indicted for procuring abortion."

By the middle of the nineteenth century, reports stated that American women were aborting at least one in five pregnancies, according to *Abortion: Statutes, Policies, and Public Attitudes the World Over*, by professor Rita J. Simon.

Until 1860, the "quickening" doctrine, under which abortion wasn't indictable until a fetus showed movement, was in place in every jurisdiction in the United States.

As far back as 1140 AD, quickening, according to Canon Law, was considered to occur forty days after conception for the male fetus and eighty days for the female fetus, Simon wrote.

In 1869, Pope Pius IX declared that quickening took place at conception and Roman Catholic women would be excommunicated if they aborted a fetus.

Under the landmark Roe v. Wade decision in 1972, the U.S. Supreme Court permitted abortion prior to fetal viability, which was defined as occurring from twenty-four to twenty-eight weeks of gestation. The Roe decision was overturned by the Supreme Court in June 2022 via its ruling in the Dobbs v. Jackson Women's Health Organization case.

Following the Dobbs decision, a number of states passed restrictive abortion measures. For example, in August 2022, Idaho approved a law that bans abortion except if the mother's life is endangered or in cases of rape or incest, but is restricted to the first trimester and only if there is a police report that has been given to the doctor. In April 2023, Florida Governor Ron DeSantis signed legislation that bans abortions after six weeks, unless the woman's life is in danger or in cases of rape or incest, under certain conditions. The law took effect on May 1, 2024.

A number of states have held referendums, starting with Kansas, since Roe was overturned, and in every case to date abortion rights have been preserved.

Looking back, by the end of the 1800s, performing or trying to perform an abortion was punishable by fines and imprisonment in almost all states in the country, according to *The Abortion Rights Controversy in America*, edited by N.E.H. Hull, Williamjames Hoffer and Peter Charles Hoffer.

An editorial in the *Chicago Daily Tribune* on August 29, 1880, typified newspaper commentary on abortion. The editorial, in the context of the arrests of two doctors, said, in part:

A HIDEOUS CRIME.
During the past week there have been two arrests in this city for the commission of one of the most hideous crimes in the calendar, — attempt at pre-natal murder resulting in the slaughter of the mother. In the one case the accused is an old offender, who has been arrested several times upon a similar charge and was once convicted. He is a professional butcher. In the other case the evidence points to an equally incompetent, unscrupulous, and callous practitioner, with previous experience in this worse than brutal pursuit.

Years before, the *Shasta Courier* of California, on July 6, 1867, ran a front-page story on abortion, headlined "The Slaughter of the Unborn," addressing a paper by Dr. Morse Stewart, "an influential physician of Detroit, Michigan," in the *Western Medical Review*. The hyperbolic story, picked up from the *Republican* of Springfield, Massachusetts, said, in part:

. . . Dr. Stewart declares that the statistics, confirmed by the observation of physicians, prove that there is no crime more surely punished in the persons of those committing it than that of abortion, and that more lives are lost by it than by childbirth. Of those who survive the operation, the majority are made invalids for life by a complication of incurable disorders that break down the constitution and often produce insanity. When the attempt fails the child that escapes the fate plotted for it and often the succeeding children will be deformed, idiotic or diseased in various ways.

The crime is never safe, and when the evil consequences of the unnatural act are apparently evaded at the time, they are certain to be developed later and to bring terrible retribution upon the mother.

On May 21, 1867, the *Chicago Tribune* ran a brief, pointed letter, headlined "The Alleged Abortion," from Dr. H.K. Stratford that said:

> To the Editors of the Chicago Tribune:
> I was surprised to see in your issue of Sunday last, a statement in which I was mentioned as the physician who had given medicine to a young woman for the purpose of procuring an abortion. I know not what prompted the statement ...
> ... I certainly have no knowledge of the case in question.
> I would simply say that my practice is free from such features, and that I court an investigation of the case, well satisfied that a thorough investigation would show me to have had nothing to do with the transaction.

A long letter from "Le Medicin" to the *Hartford Daily Courant* of Connecticut on September 12, 1871, indicated that public support for abortion, while kept under wraps, was, in the author's opinion, unfortunate but widespread. The letter references Jacob Rosenzweig, a New York City saloon owner who later operated five abortion offices and who was found guilty of second-degree murder in the death of a woman whose body was found in a trunk. Abortion in New York at the time was legal until quickening, according to the *Murder by Gaslight* website. Le Medicin's letter said, in part:

> To the EDITOR of THE COURANT: —
> . . . I think I am safe in making the following assertions, based on personal observation and knowledge; those exceptions which are supposed to prove a rule being conceded.
> The majority of abortions are produced upon married women!

The crime is as common in society, and among well-to-do people as among the lower classes, and is no bar, according to my observation as far as individual experience is concerned, to church membership.

It is impossible to obtain conviction for the crime unless the woman dies from the effect of the operation, and almost impossible then unless the public is shocked by concealment of the body, as in the Rosenzweig case: witness the Bottsford case in Hartford, and others.

The clergy will not take up the matter, as being too delicate, save in the way of private admonition, for which they have, of course, no opportunity. A woman does not consult her spiritual adviser when she wishes to prevent offspring. The press fights shy of it because — because — I will let the press answer.

On March 11, 1899, Chicago's newspaper *Lucifer, The Light-Bearer*—described in its masthead as standing for "Light against Darkness" and "Science against Tradition," etc.—reran an article from the *Medical Council* of Philadelphia that discussed medical ethics in two abortion cases. It said, in part:

> . . . Dr. Playfair contended that he had a right to do as he had in the interest of his family. During the trial the judge asked the following question of one of the medical witnesses: "Suppose a medical man were called to attend a woman, and in the course of his medical attendance he discovers that she attempted to procure an abortion. That being a crime under the law, would it be his duty to and tell the public prosecutor?" The reply was, "The last legal opinion upon that very question, obtained by the Royal College of Physicians, is 'Yes.'" "Then," said the judge, "all I can say is that it will make me very chary in the selection of my medical men."
>
> The second case cited by Dr. Raymond occurred in the city of Brooklyn and is given anonymously because won by the defendant. A physician and midwife were accused of performing an abortion by the intra-uterine injection of warm water. At least the woman was so accused, whilst the physician was held liable as an accessory because he had not notified the authorities when called into the case. One of the leading surgeons of the city stated upon the stand that he would have notified the authorities, but that he readily saw that one with less experience would be liable to

overlook this in the anxiety to save the patient. The jury rendered a verdict of acquittal.

The *Reporter and Farmer* of Webster, South Dakota ran a story on February 27, 1896, on the death of a woman believed to have had an abortion. The story, which included testimony by a Dr. Skaro, said, in part:

> Dr. Skaro was next sworn. He testified — I was at post mortem; Sullivan called me to the barn; he said she died from an attempted abortion; she had taken oil of cedar, tansy, and penny-royal; the post mortem showed the heart flabby and empty, lungs highly congested; foetus taken from the dead woman about 4 months; in his judgment death was caused by choloform (sic) or ether.

The *Falls City Daily News* of Nebraska published an item from the *Columbus Telegram* of the same state on April 26, 1907, that took potshots at the *Omaha World-Herald* newspaper. It said, in part:

> . . . in another column of the same paper appears the advertisement of a quack who offers for sale to the women of Omaha his sure-cure abortion pills.
> . . . Humanity looks with a low eye upon an abortionist, and gentle humanity should give no better look to the newspaper which encourages the crime by printing the advertisements of the abortionist.

In fact, many newspapers ran abortion ads, some subtle, in those days and in decades prior. For example, the *New York Herald* published a column of such ads on September 22, 1842, including one from "Madame Restell."

Women's roles in society and family, including toward birth control and abortion—as well as sexuality generally—began to shift considerably in the first thirty years of the twentieth century. Between 1914 and 1916, contraception entered the societal political debate when Margaret Sanger, a pioneering birth control advocate, was arrested twice for violating the Comstock Act, an 1873 amendment to the U.S. Postal Code that banned the shipping of obscene materials, which included information and devices that could prevent conception.

MEDICINES.

MADAME RESTELL,

FEMALE PHYSICIAN, Office and residence, 148 Greenwich street, between Courtlandt nd Liberty streets. where she can be consulted with the strictest confidence on complaints incident to the female frame.

Madame Restell's experienca and knowledge in the treatment of obstinate cases of female irregularity, stoppage, suppression, &c., is such as to require but a few days to effect a perfect cure. Ladies desiring proper medical attendance during confinement or other indisposition, will be accommodated during such time, with private and respectable board.

"Preventive Powders," for married ladies, whose delicate or precarious health forbids a too rapid increase of family, will be sent by mail to any part of the United States. Price $5 a package. All Letters (post paid) addressed to 'box 868, New York. Boston Office, No. 7 Essex street."

A classified advertisement from Madame Restell in the New York Herald on September 22, 1842. (Courtesy of Library of Congress)

(Curiously, the century-and-a-half-old Comstock Act was invoked by Texas federal judge Matthew J. Kacsmaryk when he ruled on April 7, 2023, against the Food and Drug Administration's approval of mifepristone, a pill used in abortions. The case ended up at the U.S. Supreme Court.)

Needless to say, Sanger and her push for birth control clinics generated much controversy. The *Coshocton Morning Tribune* of Ohio, on May 31, 1916, penned an editorial that said, in part:

> Mrs. Sanger advocates birth control. Better that babies be not born at all, she says, than that they should be born to inevitable squalor, misery and degradation. Women, she says, should be mistresses of their own bodies, not mere vessels of the lust of men. They should refuse to have children they do not want. They should not kill the children after the children have been conceived. That would be murder. They should prevent conception. Because Mrs. Sanger proposes that women should be told how to do this, she is subject to prosecution.
>
> Now, the distinction between contraception and abortion is extremely fine. It pushes murder back but a step. Moreover, the theory of

birth-control will not end human misery. Fewer people is not the remedy for social ills.

Birth-control advocate Margaret Sanger in 1922. (Courtesy of Library of Congress)

From 1916 to 1945, the birth control movement succeeded in legalizing contraception and making it available in more than 800 clinics in the United Sates, according to *Birth Control Politics in the United States 1916-1945* by Carole R. McCann.

Even today, pro-choice advocates question why anti-abortion supporters don't encourage more availability of birth-control means.

The growth of clinics coincided with the rise in availability of pessaries, or occlusive diaphragms. There were at least fifteen varieties and fourteen sizes of the devices in the 1910s and 1920s, and they needed to be properly fitted, McCann wrote.

The *Oregon Daily Journal* of Portland, on July 4, 1916, printed a letter, headlined "Birth Control and Morality," from R.A. Bohlcke. The letter, in response to an editorial in another local newspaper, references Margaret Sanger, saying, in part:

> To the Editor of The Journal —
> . . . Do we stand for abortion? We have shouted from the housetops that our aim is to discourage that evil practice of today. Some claim that

the first pages of Mrs. Sanger's booklet sanction abortion. She simply states what may be done in certain cases of suppression, on the theory, I suppose, that simple things that physicians do in cases of this kind, and which they have succeeded in monopolizing in the past, it will do the average woman no harm to know.

But it is unreasonable to suppose, even if there were room for supposition, that a woman will suffer the pain and anguish of abortion and all its attendant evils, when she is possessed of knowledge to prevent conception.

. . . I am deeply concerned with the morality of future generations, but cannot bring myself to believe, that one who is not competent to decide which method a woman would choose to use, abortion or prevention, provided she chose to use either — is competent to reason out abstractly a safe moral criterion for posterity.

A few months before, on November 30, 1915, the *Ottawa Evening Journal* of Kansas picked up a piece written by Sanger that addressed the advantages of birth control for working-class women. It said, in part:

I saw the women of wealth, the masters' wives, obtain birth control information with little difficulty.

I saw that if the working man's wife refused to have more children, she was compelled to resort to abortion. Over 150,000 abortions are performed in the United States each year, and 25,000 deaths occur as the result of them.

I saw that it is the working women who fill this death list, for though the master's wife may resort to abortions, too, she is given the best care and attention which money can buy . . .

The *Catholic Union and Times* of Buffalo, New York, expressed editorial outrage on February 9, 1922, about Sanger's upcoming speaking engagement in that city. The commentary said, in part:

The morning papers of this city give us, today, (Wednesday) the unpleasant information that the malodorous Margaret Sanger is on her way to Buffalo to ventilate her mephitic ideas on the subject of 'birth control.' The unholy activities of this female, whom 'society' now seems disposed

Men and women with baby carriages sit outside Margaret Sanger's clinic in Brooklyn, New York, in 1916. (Courtesy of Library of Congress)

to take to its sterile breast, almost tempt us to express the regret that her parents did not practice her teaching on the accursed day when she began to exist.

The *New York Tribune* of September 2, 1916, published a letter from Adelma H. Burd, secretary of the National Birth Control League, on the arrest of three citizens for violating the state's penal code as it pertained to birth control. The letter, which addressed class differences, said, in part:

> To the Editor of The Tribune.
>
> Sir: Three reputable citizens are under arrest in this city for violating Section 1142 of the penal law of this state. All three are lawyers and well acquainted with the statute in question.
>
> . . . Section 1142 above referred to is entitled 'Indecent Articles' and prohibits the dissemination in any form or manner of information concerning birth control. Every intelligent person knows that contraceptive methods are the only means of overcoming the terrible practice of

abortion and are the greatest help to humanity. In Holland, where clinics to teach these methods are given government encouragement, prosecutions for abortion and infanticide have almost entirely disappeared.

The law which prohibits the giving out of information concerning contraceptive methods is archaic and outrageous. We all know this knowledge can be obtained by the favored few for a price from physicians; we all know the cultured and the rich are or less acquainted therewith; but when some one undertakes to give this information to the poor and uninformed, to those who need it most, then he or she is seized under this law and arrested . . .

Quite a few newspapers nationwide ran the syndicated "Cynthia Grey's Letters" column. A letter from "A Mother of Two" in the column, which appeared in the *Seattle Star* of Washington state, on April 1, 1916, supported birth control, although clearly from an elitist perspective. It said, in part:

Dear Miss Grey: Looseness of thought characterizes the discussion of birth control in the article signed 'A Woman.'

It opposes birth control, yet states that 'self-control is the only right and true way to control birth.' This last is what the advocates of birth control really seek, the question being as to what constitutes self-control.

No proof supports the statement that more women approach death from controlling birth than from bearing children. Even were this true, it would be an argument favoring the open dissemination of information regarding harmless methods of birth control. Cannot these deaths resulting from ignorant attempts at prevention be laid at the door of the doctors who are financially interested in maintaining general confusion on the question, and also to the religious moralists who confuse ignorance with sanctity?

. . . The statement that 'every woman who indulges in sexual association, but frustrates the possibility of becoming a mother, is a prostitute,' is to say that 'morals' in society rest mainly with the degraded tenement dwellers who make a yearly addition to their bedraggled brood of mental inefficients.

If the views of 'A Woman' represent the only opposition to birth control, the case for family limitation is a clear one.

James Waldo Fawcett, associate editor of the *Birth Control Review*, responded to a derogatory editorial on birth control and abortion that ran in the *Morning Examiner* of Bartlesville, Oklahoma, on January 14, 1917. Headlined "We Are Called Down," his letter said, in part:

> Dear Sir: An editorial 'Birth Control' from the Examiner of December has my attention.
> . . . You say 'Birth Control means nothing more or less than a legalization of abortion.' This is untrue. Birth control is not to be confused with child-murder in any form, for it is an entirely different philosophy. Birth control is directly opposed to abortion, and is engaged in a vast struggle with it. It is a gross misrepresentation to confuse the two.
> Birth control, rightly understood, means happier homes, finer children, better social conditions and a firmer country and better organized race.
> . . . Birth control is a fact; hundreds of thousands of American parents have come into possession of the facts in the case and they are happier and better people today for having this knowledge.

An amusing wire item that appeared in the *Evening Herald* of Klamath Falls, Oregon, on February 7, 1917, with a dateline of Los Angeles, said:

> Owing to the interest in birth control created here by last week's meeting, a newspaper man conceived the idea of interviewing all members of the council to get their views on the matter. President Betouski was the most pronounced in his view:
> 'It's all bunk, I tell you; just plain bunk. If it's going to be a girl nobody can change it. There's no such thing as birth control.'

Also on February 7, 1917, *The Evening Sun* of Baltimore, Maryland, published a letter from "John Doe" in response to a previous article in the newspaper, in which he basically called birth control un-American. The letter said, in part:

> To the Editor of The Evening Sun:
> Sir —

. . . Let me say right here that it is not the capitalists as a class, not the laborers as a class, not the middle class of people who are opposed to the dissemination of birth control literature, but the American nation, as a class, that is opposed to its dissemination. The straight-limbed, clear-cut, clear-thinking American man and woman of today have no place in their lives for such meditations.

. . . Any woman who would circulate such information and take the platform and deliver lectures regarding the theory of 'birth control' (mental abortion, I call it), has sacrificed her standing and her sex. She is not a man, but she is not a woman as we have known women.

The *Daily Northwestern* of Oshkosh, Wisconsin, on February 22, 1917, printed a letter from Julia Riddle, an Oshkosh physician, that took a very conservative position on birth control. It said, in part:

(To the Editor)
. . . There is no reliable scientific preventive means of birth control. All honest physicians will agree upon this point. All known remedies are unreliable and harmful to the mother. It matters not what they are. For this reason it is entirely a woman's question. (Man can only study it from a selfish viewpoint.) But when woman decides to practice birth control, she takes her own life in her hands to hasten the day when a Mrs. No. 2 takes her place in the race of life.

However, "A Physician" defended birth control in a letter in the *St. Louis Star* of Missouri, on March 4, 1922, calling the practice safe. It said, in part:

Editor The St. Louis Star: If the drastic laws against birth control information were to be repealed it would not force anyone to practice any of the methods unless they cared to. A man and woman wanting a large family could still have it if they desired, and those desiring no or few children could practice it.

. . . Some people in letters to this column express the opinion that birth control is injurious. There are harmful and harmless methods in this process as in anything else, but those methods known and advised by professionals are absolutely harmless.

The Seattle Star on March 1, 1918, published a letter from "An Old Sub-scriber" arguing for an, um, interesting alternative to birth control. It said:

> Editor Star: A letter recently appeared in your columns from a certain physician of Seattle urging birth control. It is only a year or two ago that such a movement was started In New York, I believe, but was quelled by the proper authorities. What we need is not birth control, as he would make it, thru surgery, for our population is not increasing too fast, and where is the woman who cannot bear three or four children if she lives according to the laws of nature?
>
> Therefore, what we need is man control. Impress that in the minds of men. If man leads a clean life he will save a lot of wasted energy, have better health, and therefore will have cleaner and healthier offspring.

In the *Nebraska State Journal* of Lincoln, on November 26, 1921, Charles Kuhlman of Billings, Montana, responded to a letter that had run the previous week from John P. Sutton, who had written regarding an editorial in the *State Journal*. Kuhlman's letter, propounding an argument frequently heard nowadays that anti-abortion advocates care little about babies after birth, said, in part:

> To the Editor of the State Journal:
> . . . In the fourth place Mr. Sutton cites the horrible example of France. He seems to think that the French are a degraded and degenerate lot. This is an idea 'made in Germany' from which most of the instruments of abortion and sexual debauchery are imported into France.
> . . . The French race is not committing suicide. It is simply accommodating its population to its resources, using humane foresight to avoid general wretchedness. We could do much worse than follow the example of France. We might follow that of Germany and Japan where, supposedly they do not practice 'pre-natal murder' but kill their victims after they have reached manhood.

In 1921, Congress passed the National Maternity and Infancy Protection Act, known as the Sheppard-Towner Act. Under the legislation, states instituted prenatal and infant welfare programs. Through the act, thousands of prenatal care clinics were established and infant care seminars and home visits by nurses were funded. Certain aspects of the act generated opposition. The Sheppard-Towner Act was repealed in 1929.

William D. Chapman, councilor of the Fourth District Illinois State Medical Society, had a long letter in the *Rock Island Argus and Daily Union* of Illinois on December 6, 1921, dissecting the Sheppard-Towner Act and warning about parts of it that pertained to Illinois. Chapman's rather hyperbolic letter said, in part:

> . . . Federal aid in general is a socialistic innovation born of the unreasoning hope that maybe some good might be accomplished by rearranging whatever has become established.
>
> . . . The children's bureau of the department of labor will, in the language of the amended bill, 'study, investigate, and report' such things as may 'promote the administration of the act.'
>
> . . . They have advocated birth control with abortions, compulsory registration of pregnancy (early) with a public health officer or his deputy, together with various other unique features also of soviet origin, all as outlined in Madame Kollontai's Russian Maternity System, which has been characterized as 'the greatest crime of modern times and the ruin of an entire Russian generation.'
>
> These measures are not contained in the bill; certainly not; but they have been openly advocated by the people who will administer the bill and they have clearly indicated why they wish to be the teachers of the public. Their power is absolute.

On March 4, 1922, the *St. Louis Star* of Missouri printed a letter from "One of the Latter" that ripped those who both failed to think for themselves and invoked God to oppose birth control. It said:

> Editor The St. Louis Star: I have found that most of the letters denouncing birth control, or any other step towards enlightenment and progress, are obviously written by persons who do not understand the matter at issue, and who unfortunately do not care to understand it.
>
> These individuals are in the majority fanatics who object to the dissemination of knowledge, claiming that it is unnatural and against the will of God.

According to these people, all that is conceived by human brain, tending to freedom of mind and seeking comfort and happiness, is against God, and artificial.

If God would listen to prayer, we could ask Him to recreate us, asking Him to exclude from our new form brains; for I know (not believe) that it is useless in the heads of these law-abiding people; and they believe (not know) that it is a dangerous means for contamination, in the craniums of men and women who seek the light and have nothing to fear.

The *Star* also published a letter from "Anti-Birth Control" on September 11, 1922, that did invoke God, saying:

> Editor The St. Louis Star: Birth control is the very foundation of evil, a sin against home, God and country.
>
> It is a mystery how any God-fearing, home-loving people can say the 'Our Father,' and the phrase, 'Thy will be done,' and then hypocritically commit the greatest sin against flesh and blood — murder.
>
> Murder it is when God creates and man takes away the life that is born into the world. God is life, yet the politicians would legalize murder.

Mary Ware Dennett, director of the Voluntary Parenthood Association, responded to "Anti-Birth Control"'s letter in the October 2, 1922, edition of the *Star*. Her reply said, in part:

> Editor The St. Louis Star:
>
> . . . People who protest against birth control as murder are probably ignorant of this fact and they assume that what is meant by birth control is abortion.
>
> One of the strongest reasons for making preventive contraceptive knowledge available for the use of those who need it, is that it will tremendously lessen the extent of abortion, which is one of the appealing and disgraceful characteristics of life at present.

The *National Leader* out of Minneapolis, Minnesota, ran a series of letters on birth control in its issue of April 17, 1922, with most opposing the practice. One such letter, from A.C. of Watonga, Oklahoma, said, in part:

I am the mother of 13 children. All the wealth on earth would never touch one of them.

. . . I am opposed to birth control. God made women to bear children and when they practice birth control it is against our creator's will and they will surely be punished. Any woman that would rather nurse a poodle dog than her own flesh and blood — let her do her own murdering at the risk of her own life.

Another letter, from G.D.C. of Huerfano, Colorado, was more measured, reflecting on birth control in terms of family expenses. It said:

Should we discuss birth control? It seems to be quite a question, but the younger generation are settling it. Perhaps when they see their mothers' cares, and troubles, under the present system, and see how they have themselves been denied of education, it will not look so fine to bring children into the world to suffer for clothing, food and shelter.

. . . We should have proper government and in this way encourage our younger generation to bring children into the world with the prospects of having enough to eat and proper care.

I'm not for birth control, but we can't expect to encourage our sons and daughters when they have had the experience in a family of eight or nine children to care for, with no rest from 6 o'clock in the morning until 9 at night.

S.J. Worley of Ardmore, Oklahoma, penned a letter that appeared in the *Oklahoma Leader* of Oklahoma City on September 25, 1925, linking birth control and feminism—and went on to disparage women. The letter said, in part:

Editor Leader:

. . . Feminism is an idealistic theory concerning the capabilities of women, and 'birth control' is a means to enable her to avoid bearing children that she may be able to engage in occupations that childbearing would interfere with and mostly to escape the duties of motherhood. Some men as well as women do not want any children.

Since the active teaching of feminism began, discontent has become so common among women and abortion so common among them that many doctors are advocating the teaching of birth control as a lesser evil.

Margaret Sanger and Dr. Charles V. Drysdale attend the opening of the sixth International Neo-Malthusian and Birth Control Conference on March 25, 1925, in New York. (Courtesy of Library of Congress)

> . . . For over two thousand years among the higher classes the women have received the higher instruction in music and painting, yet she has never painted a master picture nor composed any great piece of music nor been a master performer on any kind of instrument. Though she has had the care of the children she never invented a toy to amuse them.

S.R. Stewart of Clay Center, Kansas, also had a letter in the *Leader* on September 4, 1925, which made a strong case for birth control, saying, in part:

Editor, Leader: Men being concerned, birth control is not a 'feminist fad.'

That women would not bear children is proven false by statistics where scientific contraceptic knowledge is available. Holland's birth rate dropped one-fourth; baby death rate dropped one-half; increased ratio of population became one-seventh greater. New Zealand did better, having the lowest baby death rate in the world — 50 per 1,000; Holland's the lowest in Europe, 90 per 1,000, against 180 formerly.

All marriages should have the best scientific knowledge of contraception. If some find life well worth living and are too selfish to pass it on to children, humanity is better off without their kind.

. . . You who call abortion murder, don't lay the blame on the mothers, but on those misguided humans who oppose birth control and who are responsible for laws keeping such knowledge from mothers. Church teachings, enslaving the minds of men and more especially of women, are largely responsible for such laws and for present birth and baby death rates.

Incredibly, birth control isn't quite the settled matter that it appeared to be many years ago. A Washington Post story on June 5, 2024, detailed how some on the far right have been spreading misinformation in an effort to conflate birth control with abortion.

Since 2022, a *Post* analysis determined, Republicans have blocked efforts in at least 17 states to approve legislation safeguarding the right to birth control. And that same June day, U.S. Senate Republicans blocked a bill introduced by Democrats to guarantee access to contraception nationwide.

Chapter 8

Wealth and Capitalism Glorified, Vilified

In contemporary society, income inequality is one the main issues leading to discontent and division.

In a tweet on October 4, 2022, university professor and former Secretary of Labor Robert Reich wrote: "745 billionaires now hold more wealth than half of American households."

As political commentator, author, and radio host Thom Hartmann noted in one of his daily reports, for most of the twentieth century, the top tax rate on income above $5 million annually was 74 percent to 91 percent. Typically, CEOs made twenty or thirty times what their employees earned and lived near them.

"Today's CEOs make hundreds to thousands of times what their workers make (depending on the industry) and live in 30-room mansions with servants['] quarters, yachts, and private jets," he wrote.

The Pew Research Center, in a 2020 paper titled "6 facts about economic inequality in the U.S.," pointed out that in 2018, the top 5 percent of income earners (making at least $248,729 a year) held 23 percent of all income, while in 1968, the top 5 percent had a 16 percent share.

The Pew study also concluded that the wealth gap between the richest and poorest families in the United States more than doubled from 1989 to 2016, the income gap between Black and white Americans has persisted, and 61 percent of Americans say there is too much economic inequality in the country today.

The Trump administration's tax cuts in 2017 were a source of controversy then and remain so for the 2024 presidential election. In early April 2024, Trump told wealthy fundraisers that he plans to extend the tax cuts, which reportedly benefited the rich disproportionately and increased the deficit. An article by the nonpartisan Center on Budget and Policy Priorities said that in 2025, the top 1 percent of income earners will receive a tax cut of more than $60,000 while the bottom 60 percent of households will average tax cuts of less than $500, based on Tax Policy Center figures.

Besides tax cuts, part of the explanation for income inequality—which has moderated slightly in recent years probably due to exceedingly low unemployment and some minimum wage hikes around the country—rests with financial deregulation, technology, and globalization. But the decreasing power of unions over the past few decades also has played a major role.

A paper by economists Florence Jaumotte and Carolina Osorio Buitron published by the International Monetary Fund in 2015 basically concluded that unionization's decline has led to the rich getting richer.

By 1919, more than one-third of U.S. industrial wage earners worked in factories, noted David Brody in his book *Workers in Industrial America: Essays on the Twentieth Century Struggle.* Between 1935 and 1940, union membership rose from 3.8 million to 9 million, but by 2010, only 7.4 percent of private-sector workers were unionized.

Nevertheless, unionism seems to be making more recent gains. Starbucks and Apple employees have been leading the charge among younger workers and, significantly, 73 percent of Volkswagen factory workers in Chattanooga, Tennessee voted in April 2024 to join the United Auto Workers union. The fact that the vote was in a Southern plant made it especially noteworthy.

In the nineteenth and early twentieth centuries, capitalism, wealth, labor unions, and socialism all frequently found their way into newspapers' letters to the editor. The struggles of coal miners, in particular, was a hot topic at the time. There were defenders of the capitalist system and those who rejected it as an evil, and many of the letters, including those on taxation, were understandably impassioned.

Coal Mining

The Cumberland Plateau, located in southeastern Tennessee, was a large coal mining region in the late 1800s. Over the years, clashes between unionized and nonunion miners escalated.

A letter from "Jolly" in the December 21, 1905, edition of the local *Sequachee Valley News* that glorified the benefits of being a "scab" said, in part:

> My man was once a union man but now he is a scab, and all that I hate is that he didn't go to work the first morning that they started. You can just say what you want to say about the union, but you can't tell me a thing about it.
>
> They say that they get plenty to eat but a union woman told me the other day that they didn't get enough to keep a cat alive.
>
> . . . You can talk about having a good time Christmas, but you will see who has the good time. We are the ones. We have got the money to have a good time with. We are going to have some whiskey and plenty of everything we want. We can have the phone to order our grub hauled to our doors.

A letter in the paper on December 28 from "Morning Star" responded to Jolly, saying, in part:

> . . . Well, Jolly, I want to know who that poor union woman is who don't get enough grub to keep a cat alive. I will sure climb the mountain to bring her something to eat. We have always plenty to eat and to feed our friends on, 'and then are not out on' draw day.
>
> No, Jolly, if you had as much grub ahead as I have you wouldn't work any more for a year. You think we don't know you, but we do. I have known the whole generation as far back as I can remember.

A letter from "Faraway David" in the December 21 edition of the newspaper exalted the power of the United Mine Workers of America union, saying, in part:

> . . . I notice from an official report that there is a paid up membership of 304,000 United Mine Workers at the close of November, 1905. Taking in consideration those who are a month or so in arrears there are approximately 95 per cent of the eligible persons in good standing.
>
> . . . I am working at a place where before the miners were organized we received 65c per ton for coal run over an 1 3/4 inch screen, and now we receive from 83 1/3c per ton to 93 1/3c per ton run over an 1 1/4 inch

screen. Now, to take into consideration the differences in the screens we are receiving over one dollar per ton for coal that we got 65c for before, or in other words, we are working at an advance of 35c per ton, if not a little more.

A United Mine Workers of America membership certificate, c. 1899. (Courtesy of Library of Congress)

On the same day that the *Sequachee Valley News* ran a front-page story saying that on April 1, 1906, 550,000 members of the United Mine Workers planned to strike over wages, the newspaper ran a letter from "An Old Scab" that said, in part:

> I am a scab in full cloth. I am for law and order in day light, but when night comes I am for trouble, and I am for laying it all on the union. I consider it the duty of a strikebreaker to make things so unpleasant that all men who are contending for better condition will have to leave a hunt a more congenial clime.
>
> I am for corporations dictating everything and I am interested in them saying what a man shall work for and I want them to have all the luxuries of life, occupy all the high offices and control our government. I am opposed to Pres. Roosevelt because he lent his sympathy to organized labor.
>
> . . . I believe the law should be enforced on the union, and as far as is possible, the scabs should be shielded from prosecution.

Needless to say, "An Old Scab"'s letter didn't go unnoticed or unanswered. The following week, "Hunting John" was one of those who responded with a letter that said, in part:

> . . . 'Mr. Scab' says he is for law and order in the day time but when night comes he is for trouble and laying it on the union.
>
> . . . Brethren, let us union people pray lest we enter into temptation for the company will get their portion in due season. They have condemned the just who have not resisted them unlawfully. We have fought an honest fight and we aim to keep fighting as long as we can fight.
>
> Go to now, ye rich men. Weep and howl for your miseries shall come upon you. Your riches are corrupted.

SOCIALISM VS. CAPITALISM

Letter writer John Busch of Clark, Wyoming, had a testy exchange with the editor of the *Northern Wyoming Herald and Garland Irrigation Era* of Cody, Wyoming, on November 17, 1911, over the nature of the newspaper. The letter and the editor's response (shown here in parentheses) said, in part:

Editor of The Herald,

Dear Sir: —

Your masters, the little capitalists are very persistent — they presume that I need their paper. I am a Socialist, am a party member of the socialistic organization. I am for the co-operative commonwealth.

. . . You are owned body and breeches by the capitalist. Your existance (sic) depends upon the capitalist. You are their mouthpiece and FOR THAT REASON I do not want your paper. I never ordered your paper. You will do me a favor If you will stop it.

(Mr. Busch will STILL read The Herald, though he may not be on the list — he will religiously BORROW it each week, from his neighbor, as does another man in Park County. We have seen hundreds of Mr. Busches in our newspaper career. He is not even original. That WOULD help some.)

On June 30, 1919, the *Chicago Daily Tribune* of Illinois, included a vituperative letter from local resident Roy S. Anderson headlined "Fighting Bolshevism." The Bolshevik Revolution in Russia had taken place in 1917. The letter said:

[Editor of The Tribune.] — I think it is about time to page Ole Hanson or Judge Landis. Why permit bolsheviks to gather and plan strikes, etc.? If you keep the people well scattered I am sure you would not have very much trouble.

As the old saying goes, 'United we stand, divided we fall.' Well, why not divide them? Maybe the fall will bring them back to earth. Instead of feeding them candy and ice cream on a spoon, they ought to be fed poison in a cup.

The Day Book, an experimental, ad-free newspaper in Chicago, ran a letter from Theodor Johnson on December 30, 1914, that took direct aim at capitalists, saying, in part:

Editor Day Book— Despite all their talk of 'business efficiency,' 'economy,' 'safety first,' etc., the capitalists of the United States have proven themselves inefficient, nay, absolutely incapable, to manage the country's industries and business life.

. . . Industrial depression and panics, shortage of money, failures in business, overproduction, no markets for the products, thousands of men employed in useless and harmful industries, millions of men unemployed, starvation in millions of homes, millions of health, (sic) hungry children without food, hundreds of thousands of women and girls working at starvation wages all this is the order of the day under the capitalists' mismanagement of the productive forces of the country.

. . . Surely, if any worker or foreman in any shop or office performed his work as badly as the capitalists do theirs he would soon be discharged on account of inefficiency and carlessness. (sic) Why, then, should not the capitalists be discharged?

The *Nonpartisan Leader* of Fargo, North Dakota, was the official newspaper of the Nonpartisan League, a left-wing political party founded in 1915 in the state by Arthur C. Townley, a former organizer for the Socialist Party of America. The league's platform called for reforms ranging from women's suffrage to state ownership of banks, mills, and insurance, among other industries.

On June 17, 1918, the *Leader* published a letter from L.F. Greenup of West Fork, Montana, about the boycotting of a local newspaper. It said, in part:

Editor Nonpartisan Leader:

Some of the deluded small-town business men of Valley county are aligning themselves against the farmers from whom the bulk of their business is received. We have a county paper here, the Valley County News, whose editor has a habit of boosting for what he thinks is right.

He has investigated the Nonpartisan league and approves of its principles. He has therefore been boosting for the League. It is needless to state that he has been drawing considerable of his income from advertising and job work from these small business men, who have flatly demanded that he refrain from printing anything favorable to the League.

The business men of Glasgow, or part of them, have told the editor of the Valley County News that if he continued to print anything favorable to the League they would withdraw their support of the paper.

. . . There are about 4,000 League members in Valley county and I do not think they will allow this editor to become financially embarrassed on account of printing articles favorable to the farmers' cause. They will also remember the Glasgow business men when purchasing goods."

A cartoon in 1914 titled "Ammunition" depicts capitalists shooting human bodies from large cannons. (Courtesy of Library of Congress)

A letter from "Sociologist" in the *Sequachee Valley News* of Tennessee, on July 25, 1912, took issue with socialism's perceived take on religion. It said, in part:

> Editor News:
>   Whenever anyone offers the objection against socialism that it is opposed to religion, at once some well primed socialist is heard to reply: 'Oh, no, it is not.'
>   . . . According to it we have no duty to God because no God exists but we have a duty to wipe out the religion of Jesus Christ. This is Socialism and if this be christianity applied it is surely a queer application. Does anybody really think that socialism is Christianity applied?

An April 16, 1912, letter in the *Norwich Bulletin* of Connecticut, signed by Fred Holdsworth, William Kellas, and Daniel Polsky of the Press Committee of the Socialist Party of Norwich, Connecticut, addressed the electoral defeat of Milwaukee's socialist administration. It said, in part:

> Mr. Editor: Amongst those who take an interest in politics, the question is now frequently asked: 'What happened in Milwaukee that caused the defeat of the socialists?' The Bulletin in its editorial comments said that it was from the old parties combining in the interest of good government.
>
> . . . The Milwaukee election has demonstrated what the socialists have always claimed that there is no fundamental difference between the republicans and democrats — they both stand for the same thing: Capitalism and exploitation, and when their profits are in danger they will combine to save them.

A letter from "Grumbler," of Buffalo, New York, in the *Buffalo Sunday Morning News* on March 24, 1878, made the case for how capitalists could assist workers. It said, in part:

> Editor Sunday News:
>
> . . . There is plenty of dormant capital in the city to replace with fine buildings the little wooden tinder-boxes and low brick structures which are wedged in between some of the better edifices all along Main street. Our leading business thoroughfare could be made one of the stateliest on the continent.
>
> . . . Building materials are low; labor is cheap and its necessities are great. Now is the time for capitalists to invest their money in building enterprises which will ultimately be profitable to themselves, and will immediately assist the industrial classes, and thus accelerate the return of good times.

W.G.H. Smart of Ashton, South Dakota, an elderly socialist, authored a long letter complaining about socialists of the day but that expressed contentment with his own lot. The letter, which appeared in the *Minneapolis Journal* of Minnesota on March 18, 1906, said, in part:

> To the Editor of The Journal.

. . . I feel justified in stating that if the western miners are socialists at all, they are undeveloped socialists and do not act at all in accordance with the socialist principles or socialist policy. It seems to me that they act more like such anarchists as precipitated the tragedy at the Haymarket in Chicago a few years ago, who were all good, earnest men, but whose foolish methods, induced by semiknowledge (sic) of socialism, sent them to the scaffold.

I am now an old man — a veteran socialist on the retired list, living on a Dakota farm; 80 years of age, nearly; poor as a church mouse, but taken care of by loving children and grandchildren; of some mind but infirm of body; happy in my old age, in my books and papers and in reminiscences of the past — as radical and revolutionary a socialist as ever.

C.N. Durand had a letter, headlined "Socialism and the Rich," in the *Denham Springs News* of Louisiana on October 14, 1915, that defended the accumulation of wealth, saying, in part:

One of the most pleasant past-times of some popular reformers is to abuse the rich. It does very little harm; absolutely no good; but does please the public and is quite a harmless way to kill time. It is quite characteristic of Mr. Roosevelt to say: 'The predatory rich and wicked wealthy are responsible for the deplorable conditions that exist in this country, and they should be put in the penitentiary and dressed in stripes.'

When he delivers this bit of wisdom and emphasizes it with a snarl, the grasping audience makes the air vibrate with applause. But nobody is benefitted and nobody is harmed, though the crowd is tickled and Mr. Roosevelt is pleased. Just as though those men and others of their financial standing were not merely human beings like the rest of us.

Just as though the only difference between them and the rest of us did not consist of the fact that they have simply taken what has been given them. They will continue to take as long as we permit them. The best of the reformers would do the same if they had the opportunity.

In a similar vein, J. Murphy M'Farland had a letter in *The Atlanta Georgian* of January 28, 1914, that said:

Editor The Georgian:

Railroad workers stand on a crank handcar in a photograph taken between 1850 and 1860. (Courtesy of Library of Congress)

Some one has suggested that Vincent Astor should donate his enormous estate to the community. Others would forcibly, by means of legislation, confiscate such fortunes as are enjoyed by Mr. Astor and others. In effect these are proposals of robbery — legalized robbery of the rich by the State.

If the people have an ax to grind, if the people have grievances, the money of the rich will not answer the purpose. If the people have wrongs to right they can not right those wrongs by wronging the rich.

Paul M. Mulford of Buffalo, New York, clearly a "globalist" of his day without being a socialist, served up a plea in the *Buffalo Express* of January 16, 1923. It said:

Editor Buffalo Express: — Educate the people to reason and wars will cease. Teach them the folly of their ancestors, the mistakes of Alexander the Great, the faults of Sargon of Babylon and the foulness of the policy of that Austrian Metternich.

Show them the contributions to science of the Mohammedans, the contributions to religion of the Egyptians and the Hebrews, the contributions to philosophy of France, and the contributions to civilization of Greece and especially of Athens. Emphasize the disasters of Bonaparte, of Cortez, of Ali Pasha and of Darius the Great. Stress the victories of Chaucer, of Saint Paul and Saint Augustine and Saint Gregory, the work of Shelley, of Raphael and of Lincoln.

Every man should profess his loyalty to the cause he represents, but it should not be a narrow loyalty. It should be a loyalty that is international, but not socialistic or anarchistic. Be a national, but have an international spirit.

The *Beatrice Daily Sun* of Nebraska, on January 14, 1923, published a letter from Mrs. I. M. Palmer on the pursuit of wealth that said, in part:

Nothing perhaps more surely foreshadows calamity than certain fixed ideas. Germany was possessed of a fixed idea, the idea of her superiority and her ability to conquer anything.

. . . From her experience we can learn much or little according as we are so minded. America's fixed idea is wealth. It makes no difference if we own a million, nay even a billion we are pushing on for more. It is leading us to destruction as surely as Germany was led. We come into the world with nothing, we depart likewise.

. . . Observation has taught us wealth does not essentially lead to happiness, neither can it always purchase happiness. Happiness comes from within, and not from a surplus of material possessions.

Three days later, the same newspaper ran a humorous letter from "H.A.S.," headlined "Not All That Glitters," that said, in part:

Editor Daily Sun:

Some of the Sunday papers seem to have gone on a mental debauch and are indulging in an insufferable amount of puffery anent a female who, while returning from a 'social function' where she had indulged in 'poker' was robbed of two hundred and fifty thousand dollars worth of jewelry. This happened in an eastern metropolis where no doubt a half million babes are put nightly to bed hungry and where perhaps that many souls are exploiting garbage cans for food. She is lauded as being a philanthropist. Imagine a female struggling down Court street under the weight of a quarter million dollars worth of jewelry. What a picture this presents to the mind.

Among the plunder were five bracelets. What need had she of five bracelets? Had there been six one might suppose that she had worn three on each arm to keep her hitched to the center of gravity.

The *St. Louis Star* of Missouri, on January 6, 1923, printed a letter from D. Cooley about mechanical advances—and their dangers for workmen—arguing that capitalists won't make the machinery safer. The letter said, in part:

> Editor The St. Louis Star:
>
> . . . My contention is that the introduction of new machinery not only causes as much to be produced as before with fewer workmen, but it also increases the danger to life and limb for the workingman. The machine system fetters him to a monster that moves perpetually with a gigantic power and with insane speed.
>
> Only the closest, never-fagging attention can protect the workingman, attached to such a machine, from being seized and broken by it. Protective measures cost money; the capitalist does not introduce them unless he is forced thereto.
>
> . . . Workingmen are cheap, but large, airy workshops are dear.

A letter from "Long Distance" on November 14, 1918, in *The Evening World* of New York, addressed the plight of telephone operators specifically. It said, in part:

> To the Editor of The Evening World:
>
> . . . Due to the many complaints made by the public in regard to the present telephone service, we wish to say, in behalf of the long distance operators, that the public cannot and will not receive better service while the present conditions prevail. One menace to the service is the constant resigning of operators capable of handling the business. They are unable to live, or even exist, on the small salary paid by the telephone company.

. . . An operator is supposed to work eight hours per day, every other holiday and every third Sunday. We also are supposed to have a fifteen minute relief in the morning and the same in the afternoon. Do we get it? No.

. . . In the Washington, D. C., section of our playground, as Mr. Burleson called it, we have eighteen operators. These girls handle twelve to thirteen hundred calls a day. Eighty per cent of these are Government calls. Does the public realize the time spent in trying to locate the party called?

Harvey J. Swann, of Boys' High School in Brooklyn, New York, had a letter in *The New York Times* on May 4, 1919, that took aim at the city's teacher's union, a familiar target nowadays. It said, in part:

To the Editor of The New York Times:

From some of the reports of the controversy of the Teachers' Union with the Board of Education the impression might be gained that the union is supported by a large proportion of the teachers of the city. I should like to correct this impression. Nothing of the kind is the case. The great majority of the teachers stand solidly behind the board in opposing the union.

. . . They do not think, as apparently do those on whom the union lavishes its support, that there is any necessity of applying in America the doctrines of Russian Bolshevism. They do not believe that the violence of revolution is the method of political development suited to conditions in the United States. They do not believe in fanning class hatreds, nor in instituting a class dictatorship. In short, they do not sympathize at all with the ideas of the protégés of the union.

The *St. Louis Star* of Missouri, on January 6, 1923, ran a letter from "A Victim of Circumstance" that complained about the system being rigged against the worker. It said, in part:

Editor The St. Louis Star:

I wonder if you could find space to print this, to show the people of St. Louis to what small means a big soulless corporation will go to keep down wages of their open-shop employes. (sic)

. . . We have a labor board which is supposed to fix conditions, wages, etc. We also have a signed contract to adjust wages every six months according to the cost of living. It is arrived at by an index figure, by taking the average cost of food, coal, furniture, etc., but no savings item. If it rises five points above this figure, we get a raise; if it goes under five points, we get a cut.

This last date for figuring this puzzle showed a raise of more than five points. The labor board voted for it and had the figures to show for the vote. The company's efficiency expert comes along and says some picture show reduced its price of admission and therefore lowered our index figure below five points, and presto, we won't get a raise, in spite of the increase of food this fall and winter. The raise would have been $2.50 on the month.

And then they say corporations have a soul and come out with New Year thanks for our hearty cooperation in our work tell us our E. M. B. A. is a wonderful thing to get the company and employes together. What a huge joke.

Taxes

Benjamin Franklin was credited with the well-worn quote: *"In this world nothing can be said to be certain, except death and taxes."* Well, if the quote holds sway, so does the fact that letters addressing various taxes have been a fixture in American newspapers for two centuries.

For example, the *Charleston Mercury* of South Carolina published a letter from "One of Fifty" on August 21, 1830, lauding a new tax law and taking a potshot at the "Northern Monopolist." The letter said, in part:

[For the Mercury.]

Fellow Citizens — 'A Shop keeper' in the Courier complains of the new Tax on sales, in place of a Tax on stock; now listen with attention to the profound reasoner — Why is this — in 1829 he paid $7.50, and in 1830 $3.90; therefore $3.90 is $15.60, and $3.90 is also twice as much as $7.50. Dont (sic) laugh, 'tis only a ruse de guere. I have no doubt but he sold $50 worth of goods a day, and cleared on that $20; now poor I only sell from $5 to $10 worth per day, (which is the average sales of half the shop keepers in the city.) On this there is about $2 profit, which, by great economy, supports my family, and pays all my debts.

Now I paid in 1829 Taxes $4, but according to the new and most humane and equitable law I only pay $2 now. But this does not suit the Northern Monopolist.

No! no! he realizes a profit of from $20 to $100 a day, and 'tis only JUST, according to his notions, that I and my fellow poor honest shop-keepers should pay as much as he. 'Tis shameful.

A "Tax Payer" took issue with what City Hall in New York was spending on office furniture. The letter, which appeared in the *Brooklyn Daily Eagle and Kings County Democrat* of New York City on October 4, 1848, said:

Mr. Editor — I was struck with astonishment yesterday afternoon, at hearing the presentation of a communication in the common council chamber, from a respectable furniture dealer in Fulton street, stating that a bill had been presented to that body for $257.00 for 25 arm chairs, and the Brooklyn dealer offers to supply a much superior article, for $150.00.

It seems to me, Mr. Editor, that there is something very singular, if not very wrong in this conduct; whether done by whigs or democrats; the guilty persons should be held accountable and exposed, and to say nothing of the injustice of purchasing furniture from New York dealers for our City Hall, this enormous bill of $257.00 should be well exam-ined before being audited and paid.

"Max" had a letter in the *Weekly Register* of Point Pleasant in Mason County, West Virginia, on May 11, 1887, in which he railed against a proposed new jail. It said, in part:

Mr. Editor: — It is unquestionably very apparent from the tone of var-ious articles in the State Gazette, more especially in the last issue, with an expensive extra, that certain individuals are determined to build the 'new hotel jail' even should it pauperize the taxpayers of Mason county.

Do these chief agitators expect to be individually benefitted, by this new jail being forced upon the people?

. . . Is it public spirit to rob the poor by excessive taxation, to keep at ease, murderers, thieves, drunkards and vagrants, and the off-scourings of the earth, many of whom, if you do build this new jail, will only be too glad to commit some depredation in order to be given a good home, kept in idleness and fed at the expense of the taxpayer.

Similarly, years later, a brief letter from "Interested" to the *Bakersfield Morning Echo* of California on January 7, 1923, made the case for subsidizing a public hospital:

> Editor the Echo:
>
> Why is it that some taxpayers will point with pride to the finest home for criminals in the world, much more comfortable than many Kern County taxpayers can afford, and then 'holler' about spending a like amount for a county hospital to care for those whose only offense against society is that they are poor?

A drawing by Charles Lewis Bartholomew in 1898 takes a dig at proposed tax increases. (Courtesy of Library of Congress)

The Day Book of Chicago had a letter from "J.H.M." on September 19, 1914, on combating tax dodging that raised a pertinent question. It said:

> Editor Day Book: Sometime ago a big noise was made regarding the intention of State's Att'y Hoyne to force rich taxdodgers (sic) to pay their just taxes. Now everything is as quiet as the grave. I have heard it said 'That case was settled like all the rest,' which, of course, means that it was hushed up through the use of money.
>
> I do not like to charge Mr. Hoyne with resorting to dishonest practices, and I feel that there must be some good reason for silence after such a blare of trumpets. Will you kindly investigate and present your readers with the facts in this case?

The *Oregon Daily Journal* of Portland ran a letter from O.F. Neal on October 10, 1914, concerning laborers and taxes. It said, in part:

> To the Editor of the Journal — I ask space for the following, in reply to Mr. Wilson of Corvallis:
>
> You infer that the poor laboring man doesn't pay any taxes. You had better brush the standpat Republican wool from over your eyes and take a good look at your surroundings. Doesn't the poor devil, when he pays the landlord his month's rent, pay taxes on the property he occupies?

A letter from "Taxpayer' in the *Lawrence Daily Journal-World* of Kansas, on January 8, 1923, took on the oil companies, with an argument often heard today. The letter said, in part:

> Editor Journal-World:
>
> The writer has observed with a great deal of interest the issue of a Topeka daily of January 1, on the first column of the first page of which is a detailed record of issues of stock dividends aggregating two billion dollars, that have been declared within the last three months. This list indicates that 13,059 million dollars represents stock dividends declared by oil companies, and natural gas companies.
>
> It is most assuredly a hair-raising, breath-taking affair when one thinks about it — that the 'dear public' has enhanced the surplus accounts of these large corporations so as to enable them to distribute these

enormous earnings as stock dividends. Surely if any profiteering is going on, these oil companies are in a class by themselves, as no other industry is comparable with them.

In a letter of March 9, 1922, in the *Albuquerque Morning Journal* of New Mexico, resident A. Fleischer called for the city to take over services from contractors to save money. It said, in part:

Editor Morning Journal:

I desire to bring forward for public discussion an issue which many of us consider of vital importance, and which ought to have some influence in the selection of three city commissioners at the election on April 4. That is the suggestion that the city do its own paving in the future, rather than let it by contract.

. . . I can conceive of no valid objection to this plan under our present form of city government, which is absolutely non-partisan, and therefore qualified to conduct the city's affairs on a strictly business basis.

I am convinced that the city could do this work for a great deal less than any contractor, however benevolently inclined he may be. The experience of other cities bears this out.

"Tax-Payer" had a letter in the *Leavenworth Weekly Times* of Kansas on February 22, 1877, that called for an institution that remains untouchable to this day to pay its fair share. It said, in part:

Editor Times: While we rejoice to see the subject of taxation discussed in the columns of The Times as thoroughly as is now being done, we think it worth while to direct attention to another great evil which has been grafted upon the American system of government, viz: The non-taxation of church property.

It is a truism of the American people that all property shall bear its just proportion of the burden of taxation. This has been carried out to its fullest extent as regards property of every description, excepting such as is under the control of the churches and schools of our state.

. . . In Kansas, alone, there was in 1875 no less than $1,912,600.00 worth of church property, which escaped its just proportion of the burden of taxation. In the United States there is not less than $250,000,000.00

worth of church property, and none of it taxed, to assist in lightening the oppressive burden of taxation under which our people are struggling.

A tax levy of three per cent on this large sum would yield an annual revenue of $750,000.

. . . While discussing the subject of taxation, let the people get at the root of the evil and see that all classes of property — probably excepting schools — shall be equally taxed, and the tax faithfully collected.

A letter from H.R. Schneck in the *Omaha Daily News* of Nebraska, on October 17, 1925, argued that certain taxation was burdensome. The letter said:

Editor Omaha Daily News:

When a man buys a farm or city property for, say $12,000, he pays, say $3,000, down and gives a mortgage for the rest. For so many years he owns only one-fourth of the land, yet he is compelled to pay taxes for the entire tract.

That is unfair and unjust, and is not permited (sic) in any other civilized country. Reformers, please see to it that this unjust law is repealed when the legislature meets again.

Chapter 9

Technological Marvels

In Kurt Vonnegut Jr.'s 1952 novel, *Player Piano*, Bud Calhoun is out of work because his job classification has been eliminated. Paul Proteus, who is approached for help, is surprised because he knows Bud had invented an impressive "gadget."

> Paul could see the personnel manager pecking out Bud's job code number on a keyboard, and seconds later having the machine deal him seventy-two cards bearing the names of those who did what Bud did for a living — what Bud's machine now did better. Now, personnel machines all over the country would be reset so as no longer to recognize the job as one suited for men.

In the twenty-first century, we've witnessed an impressive, nonstop array of technological advances, many of which have altered how people live. The list includes smartphones; electric cars, and eventually self-driving vehicles; 3D printing; augmented reality; blockchain, first used in 2008 to create cryptocurrency; and, of course, social media, with Facebook established in 2004 and two years later, Twitter. By 2013, the latter platform had more than 200 million active users, according to the *New York Times*.

Much focus now is being placed on artificial intelligence; newspaper stories are appearing almost daily on AI's positive applications, such as personalizing learning for students, diagnosing health care problems or forecasting the weather months in advance, etc., etc.

In 2004, the late professor John McCarthy of Stanford University's Computer Science Department answered basic questions about AI on John McCarthy's original website, noting, "The effort is to make computer programs that can solve problems and achieve goals in the world as well as humans."

In May 2023, Congress began hearings on how to regulate the emerging AI industry, with an eye on the harm it could potentially do, especially if AI is eventually able to outsmart humans. And on May 15, 2024, a bipartisan group of senators unveiled a "road map" on how Congress might address AI in the future. The plan, which calls for $32 billion in annual spending on AI research and development to stay ahead of rival China, considers the impact AI could have on the military, employment, health care, and elections, among other issues.

More immediately, job-retention fears over AI surfaced during the Hollywood writers' strike that ran from May until September 2023. One concern for the writers was the role artificial intelligence might play in creating script content.

Also, AI is likely to eventually alter the nature of media coverage, Buzzfeed CEO Jonah Peretti pronounced one week after he laid off the internet company's news team.

"Broadly speaking, I believe that generative AI will begin to replace the majority of static content," he said, as addressed in the *Hollywood Reporter*. "Audiences will begin to expect all content to be personalized, interactive and dynamic with embedded intelligence formats that were developed before the AI revolution. And many other formats and conventions of the media industry will need to be updated and adapted or begin to feel stale and outdated."

If the scientific and engineering developments of today are staggering, imagine what it was like for humans in the nineteenth and early twentieth centuries, coming through the Industrial Revolution into a world of profound technological advances that set the stage for the way men and women navigate today's world.

Among the game-changing inventions were the locomotive, the telegraph, the telephone, the electric light bulb, the automobile, the airplane, the radio, the phonograph, and the motion picture camera. Even the most rudimentary computers were developed in the early nineteenth century, although Stanford University said the first "large-scale automatic general-purpose mechanical analog computer" was invented in 1931, according to Timothy Williamson on the *Live Science* website.

THE TELEGRAPH

The first electric telegraphs were invented around the same time by Brits Sir William Fothergill Cooke and Sir Charles Wheatstone and American Samuel F.B. Morse, who became interested in the possibility of electric telegraphy in 1832.

Cooke's and Wheatstone's system, patented in 1837, employed six wires and five needle pointers. Letters of the alphabet were arranged on a diamond grid, and two needles, controlled by the operator, directed the needles by pressing buttons, according to Allison Marsh, associate history professor at the University of South Carolina, writing on the *IEEE Spectrum* website.

Morse, meanwhile, obtained a patent on an electromagnetic telegraph in 1837. His device employed a sequence of short and long electrical pulses to represent letters and numbers, wrote Trevor English on the *Interesting Engineering* website. The pulses later became known as dots and dashes.

In 1843, with government backing, Morse erected a thirty-five-mile telegraph system between Washington, D.C., and Baltimore, Maryland. Wires were attached by glass insulators to poles alongside a railroad. On May 24, 1844, he transmitted his first message, the famous line, "What hath God wrought!"

With the telegraph, people, remarkably, could now communicate almost instantaneously over great distances. On May 30, 1844, the *Martinsburg Gazette* of West Virginia ran an account of that first transmission that it reprinted from the *Baltimore Patriot* of May 25. It said, in part:

> Morse's Electro Magnetic Telegraph, now connects between the Capitol at Washington and the Railroad Depot in Pratt, between Charles and Light streets, Baltimore.
>
> . . . A large number of gentlemen were present to see the operations of this truly astonishing contrivance. Many admitted to the room had their names sent down, and in less than a second the apparatus in Baltimore was put in operation by the attendant in Washington, and before the lapse of a half minute the same names were returned plainly written.

The *Litchfield Enquirer* of Connecticut, on July 10, 1845, ran an extract of a letter datelined Alton, Illinois, that it picked up from the *Weekly National*

Intelligencer of Washington, D.C. The extract, from a Washingtonian who was traveling out West, said:

> You can have a little idea how much there is felt all through this country in that astonishing invention, Morse's Magnetic Telegraph. Men are excited about it, and are talking now of ordering their goods for this immense West through the Telegraph. They say they must have it.

On May 31, 1845, the *Weekly National Intelligencer* carried an extract of a letter from "an intelligent scientific American gentleman in London" comparing Wheatstone's telegraph to Morse's. It said, in part:

> Dear Sir: Having some spare time yesterday, I visited the Telegraphic office, where I remained in conversation with the Director during the afternoon. The Telegraph (Wheatstone's) is really as pretty a failure as I ever saw. Positively, it requires an hour for them to transmit a sentence which you could transmit in five minutes.
>
> . . . I gave the man the poetry you gave me, (sent by telegraph from Washington;) also a copy of the alphabet, and Morse's report. He manifested great surprise that the American Telegraph could transmit as rapidly as we could talk, and still more surprise that it printed the communication, for their's (sic) does not print. In a word, I consider Wheatstone's Telegraph worth nothing compared with Morse's; and you may congratulate yourselves on having by far the best Telegraph in the world.

The issue of governmental involvement in electromagnetic telegraph operations grew over time. At one point, Morse had to shut down operations for lack of funding.

By late 1845, the telegraph was under the supervision of the postmaster general. Cave Johnson, who was appointed to that position by President James K. Polk, was asked to study the device's efficacy. In his letter to the president, which the *Southport Telegraph* of Wisconsin, published on December 23, 1845, he expressed the view that the telegraph wouldn't be financially profitable for the government, but could be a powerful tool depending on who controlled it. It's an argument that many make nowadays regarding social media companies. Johnson said, in part:

Students practice transmitting messages at the Marconi Wireless School in New York, c. 1912. (Courtesy of Library of Congress)

. . . In the hands of individuals or associations, the telegraph may become the most potent instrument the world ever knew to effect sudden and large speculations — to rob the many of their just advantages, and concentrate them upon the few.

If permitted by the government to be thus held, the public can have no security that it will not be wielded for their injury; rather than their benefit. The operation of the telegraph between this city and Baltimore has not satisfied me that, under any rate of postage that can be adopted, its revenues can be made to equal its expenditures.

. . . But, as an agent vastly superior to any other ever devised by the genius of man for the diffusion of intelligence, which may be done with almost the rapidity of lightning, to any part of the republic, its value, in all commercial transactions, to individuals having the control of it, or to the government in time of war, could not be estimated. The use of an instrument so powerful for good (or) evil cannot with safety to the people, be left in the hands of private individuals, uncontrolled by law.

Telephone

On March 7, 1876, Scottish-born Alexander Graham Bell patented the telephone. Needless to say, inherent tension developed between the telegraph and the arrival of the telephone, although at least at first, the two devices were seen as complementary. A small item ran in the *Newberry Herald* of South Carolina on the first anniversary of Bell's patent that said:

> This is a new invention by Mr. A. Graham Bell, of Massachusetts. The word Telephone comes from the Greek, tele, afar, and phonos, sound. By means of this instrument sounds can be transmitted over wire many miles. A few evenings ago parties in Salem and Boston, Mass., twenty miles apart, communicated with each other.
>
> 'Hold the Fort' was sung at one end of the wire, and was distinctly heard at the other. Conversation was carried on between the parties at each end of the line. This is undoubtedly a wonderful invention, but not more so than telegraphy was before the days of Morse.

In the pantheon of inventions, a brief editorial comment in the *Emporia News* of Kansas on February 23, 1877, encapsulated where the telephone was positioned for the ages:

> . . . All sorts of sounds can be transmitted, even music, as well as any kind of language. This is the most wonderful of all modern achievments, (sic) and beats all of Shakespear's (sic) prophecies.

The *Daily Astorian* of Oregon also glorified the telephone in a piece on September 13, 1877, saying, in part:

> It is still wonderful, notwithstanding the increasing commonness of the telephone, to hear a superintendent or head of a house in the city making inquiries and giving orders to his foreman out at the mill or factory twenty miles away . . .
>
> . . . So large has the demand become that the price for the use of the telephone which the patentee does not sell, has just gone up from $10 to $30 a year.

H.B. Smith Jr., writing from "the desert, 125 miles East of San Diego," gave a personal account of the telephone's effectiveness in a letter to the *Los Angeles Herald* of March 12, 1878. Smith said, in part:

> Editor Herald:
>
> . . . I impart the following information, viz; At every camping place we cut the telegraph line and (talked) with the telephone to parties and friends in San Diego.
>
> To-day we have talked with friends in San Diego through it, and, as wonderful as it may seem, we could hear them distinctly when talking in a moderate tone as well, almost as if they were in the room with us, and in some cases we could recognize by the voice the party talking to us.
>
> I will also state, for the benefit of any of our Los Angeles friends who may wish to establish a line to the residence of some friend in a distant part of the city, or from the store to their residence, that this wonderful instrument — the Bell telephone — is within the reach of all, as a complete set can be leased for the very reasonable sum of $5 per month, and that I will impart information to those feeling interested in them upon my return to Los Angeles. . .

By March 1, 1880, an item in the *Fall River Evening News* of Massachusetts noted: "The Bell Telephone Company has now in use 50,000 telephones of its own manufacture, and 100,000 additional will be put out during this year. The instruments are rented at a royalty of about $5 per year."

ELECTRIC LIGHT BULB

Thomas A. Edison patented the first electric light bulb in 1879 and then, again, a year later, although British inventors had been working on electric light for decades. The first constant such light was displayed in 1835, according to the U.S. Department of Energy.

Edison's work concentrated on upgrading the filament in a bulb, and by October 1879, his researchers developed a carbon filament that could last fourteen and a half hours, according to the department. As with any invention, the pathway to success wasn't always smooth.

The *Mendocino Coast Beacon* of California picked up an account from the *Sun* of New York that the former ran on May 10, 1879. It began with Edison sitting in his office in Menlo Park, New Jersey, looking over specifications for patents. It continued that a letter by a New York correspondent of the *Times* of London, stating that the inventor's electric light was a failure, was laid before him. In response, Edison said:

> I have seen the letter before. It is a mass of misstatements, and is evidently made up in the interests of the gas men. The writer is totally at sea.

The January 22, 1880, edition of the *Chicago Daily Tribune* published a letter by Chicago resident George H. Bliss, who apparently owned a telegraphy company, about his meeting with Edison and his team in which they demonstrated their light bulb. His long account said, in part:

> To the Editor of The Chicago Tribune.
> NEW YORK, Jan. 17. —
> . . . I reached Menlo Park after dark, and, on mounting the long flight of steps leading from the station to the high ground on which the town is built, found myself confronted by two electric lamps. They were mounted on wooden posts of about the ordinary hight (sic).
> . . . The claim that Edison's light is so fragile as to fall to pieces on the slightest provocation occurred to me, and to test this I gave the post a vigorous shaking without inflicting any damage.
> . . . Subsequently I had the satisfaction of handling the glass bulbs containing the horseshoe carbons. They can be turned sideways, upside down, and a sharp jar does not destroy them. They have been dropped on the floor without injury.
> . . . The flame from a gas-jet is larger than the incandescent surface of an Edison light, and the first impression on seeing the street-lamps is that it yields less light. A careful examination convinced me that both lights are practically the same in illuminating power.

Edison's light bulb went through a number of iterations and refinements. He had experimented with a platinum filament but ended up where he had started, with a carbonized one, although improved. The *New York Times* published a long-winded letter from F.G. Fairfield, of the New York College of

Veterinary Surgeons, on that subject on February 16, 1880. It questioned the worthiness of the newer bulb and the scientific diligence of Edison's team and said, in part:

> To the Editor of the New-York Times:
> . . . The work of the laboratory appears to be carried on by Mr. Edison and his assistants with a conspicuous disregard of exact measurement and registration of results, optical and electrical, as well as economical.
> . . . Taking all the factors into consideration, therefore, Mr. Edison's new lamp is by no means superior to his former one, in which platinum was substituted for carbon. The exaggerated descriptions of it may serve a speculative purpose for those who hold stock in the company he represents; but it by no means solves the question of the practical application of electricity to house illumination.

However, Edison had clearly captured the public's imagination, as this item in the *Sun* of New York, on January 3, 1880, demonstrated, although bizarrely. It began:

> So many people visited Menlo Park on New Year's Day that fears were at one time entertained that their weight would break down the second floor of the frame building, which is Edison's laboratory and workshop, where they all congregated. And some of them behaved very badly. Eight electric lamps were stolen. One clumsy fellow got his feet entangled in the rubber hose constituting a part of the delicate apparatus for obtaining a vacuum in the bulbs, and blundering his way out, tore down and destroyed the apparatus.
> A malicious rascal was caught trying to destroy the current and put out the lights by putting a piece of metal across the exposed connecting wires. When he was bounced out, he or other fellows of his kind tore down some of the connecting wires outside and stole the lamps.

A letter from "Veritas" on November 12, 1886, to the *Morning News* of Wilmington, Delaware, signified, at least indirectly, how the electric light bulb had secured its place in mankind's advancement. It said, in part:

To the Editor of The Morning News — Sir:

...The electric light has already accomplished such wonders that the public are ready to believe almost anything that may be claimed for it.

PHONOGRAPH

Edison's work on perfecting the telephone and the telegraph led to the invention of the phonograph, according to the Library of Congress. Basically, sound vibrations from talking into a mouthpiece made an indent on a cylinder (metal was substituted for paper tape early on). Edison applied for a patent on December 24, 1877.

The Jackson Standard of Ohio, on June 27, 1878, printed a long letter from Cornie McG. Baker of Chicago praising the invention and, in effect, pointing to the eventuality of audiobooks. It said, in part:

To the Editor of the Standard:

For the past three or four months as you are aware, the papers have been full of accounts of the phonograph, Edison's wonderful talking machine. There is one on exhibition in this city at the present time. Yesterday morning I met a lady friend down town, and we determined to see this great invention, which has been setting the scientific world in a whirl, and which, had it been made in the dark days of Ignorance and superstition, would have been called the work of Satan. We saw a machine that was not so complicated in its construction as a sausage-mill, and but little larger.

...The operator recited a well-known rhyme into the machine, imitating several animals at the end of it. The phonograph repeated it after him as deliberately and solemnly as though the fate of the whole world depended upon it: 'Ma-ry had a lit-tle lamb it's (sic) fleece was white as snow, And ev-ry where that Ma-ry went The lamb was sure to go. Dow, wow, wow, meow, meow.'

...For twenty-five cents you could buy an electrotyped copy of one of Dickens' works, put it into your phonograph, start the clockwork, lean back comfortably in your easy chair, and hear your favorite author read by the finest reader of the day.

The *Topeka Weekly Blade* of Kansas had this pithy note on May 16, 1878, taken from the *Norristown Herald* of Pennsylvania:

Thomas A. Edison poses with his early phonograph, c. 1878. (Courtesy of Library of Congress)

Edison's phonograph can whistle, sing, howl and jaw, but it can't throw a stone at a yowling cat on the back fence, or kick a chromo agent off the front stoop. There is still lots of room for improvement.

Wilson Strong of Brooklyn, New York penned a letter that appeared in the *Brooklyn Daily Eagle* of February 16, 1886, looking to future possible adaptations of the phonograph. It was quite prescient, saying:

To the Editor of the Brooklyn Eagle.

In your paper of this date there appears an editorial regarding the renewal of Mr. Edisons (sic) experiments upon the phonograph in order to adopt it for practical use. About a year ago, being interested in the development of this instrument, I wrote to Mr. Edison and suggested that he should combine it with his telephone in such a way that messages secured by the latter might be retained on the foil of the former by the use of a microphonic or extra sensitive diaphragm. I received from him a reply stating that he had already thought of the combination and that I might find such in his exhibit at the Electrical Exhibition in Philadelphia, which I did.

. . . Why could not the ante mortem statement of a person who had been assaulted or injured by accident be really phonographically taken? Think of the value of such evidence in a case where there were no witnesses to an assault or where there was 'no one to blame,' being given in the words and tones of the victim.

. . . Instead of a noisy gong on an energetic and seemingly vicious Yankee clock to waken us in the morning could we not have a sweet female voice to slug an awakening hymn, or a rough male one to point out the punishment prepared for the laggard, and to tell of the blessings of early rising?

Lastly could not phonographic primers and automatic lullaby singing, self rocking cradles be invented on behalf of the many poor mothers who are compelled to attend to their house hold duties and take care of their little ones at the same time?

Radio

A timeline on wireless research that ran in the *Redwood Gazette* of Redwood Falls, Minnesota, started innocently in the year 1827 with: "It was found that the magnetic discharge from a leyden jar would magnetize a steel needle." In 1831, English physicist Michael Faraday discovered electromagnetic induction between two separate circuits.

Cambridge experimental physics professor James Clerk Maxwell in 1865 predicted that electromagnetic energy could travel outward from a source as waves moving at the speed of light, according to David Herres, in a piece on the *Test & Measurement Tips* website. In 1886, German physicist Heinrich Hertz validated Maxwell's prediction over short distances by discovering and then writing that "discharging a Leyden jar into one of a pair of coils would induce an electrical spark to jump across an air gap connected to the other coil." Thus, the basis for radio transmission was formed.

Skipping ahead to 1907, radio stations were opened for limited public service in Ireland and Nova Scotia. In 1912, radio distress signals emanating from the Titanic were received. In 1914, Guglielmo Marconi and officials started testing wireless telephone between vessels of the Italian fleet. In 1916, President Wilson and the Mikado of Japan exchanged messages over a new trans-Pacific radio service.

In 1920, several radio stations began operating in the United States, including Pittsburgh's KDKA, which transmitted the nation's first commercial broadcast on November 2. By the next year, numerous stations were broadcasting.

The *Evening Journal* of Wilmington, Delaware, ran a news item on September 15, 1922, with a prediction by William Dubiller, identified as "radio inventor and manufacturer, who has made the new science a hobby since its early days." Dubiller said that with radio, civilization would make greater strides than ever before.

> 'Six months ago,' said Dubiller, 'probably 100,000 receiving sets were in use. Today it is conservatively estimated that more than a million homes are being entertained and educated by means of the radio telephone. 'I know of no science which has advanced civilization in such a short period to an extent equal to the promising outlook of the radio-phone.'
>
> Distances will be annihilated. Dubiller believes, time will be shortened, nations will be united and even languages will intermingle through the universal use of radio.

Some newspapers began running programming schedules and the frequencies of out-of-town stations for readers eager to make greater use of the new mass medium. And some papers even created radio editor positions. Readers began sending letters to newspapers indicating which out-of-town stations they could pick up on their sets. An example was this letter from "A.E.F." to the *Evening Star* of Washington, D.C., on January 5, 1924, which said:

> Radio Editor:
>   . . . I have a three-tube set, using a bedspring for an antenna. In three days I caught WRC, WCAP, NAA, KDKA, WCBD, WGY, WIP, WJAX, WOAW, WFI, WDAR, WLW, WORK, WJZ, WSAI, WDAP, KFKX and in four days with an outside antenna have caught these stations: WTAS, WBZ, WBAK, WJY, WCAD, WOO, KOP and 2XZ testing.

A brief item in the *Perth Amboy Evening News* of New Jersey, on March 22, 1924, showed how popular radio was becoming worldwide. It said:

Radio apparatus exported to other countries amounted in value last year to $3,448,112, an increase of more than 20 per cent over the exports of 1922. Most of it went to Argentina, Quebec, Ontario, Austrial, (sic) Panama, Mexico and England.

As the public became more engaged with radio, letters started being more specific and inquisitive. For example, W.H. Brooks of Birmingham, Alabama, had a letter in the *Birmingham News* of January 9, 1923, bemoaning the congested radio airwaves and offering a partial solution. It said, in part:

To the Editor The Birmingham News:

As the interest in radio is increasing each day, both from the standpoint of telegraphy over long distance with small power and in the good concerts being broadcasted all over the country, there is a jumble in the air each night which makes it almost impossible for any one to really enjoy it.

. . . Why not call a meeting of the operators using transmitting stations and ask them to split fifty-fifty with those who want to listen to the concerts. That is, ask them to operate their stations only every other night and leave the air clear at least three nights a week for those who want to listen to the concerts.

On March 26, 1925, the *Indianapolis Times* of Indiana ran a bunch of letters complimenting the broadcasts of Indiana's favorite sport. One such letter, from Frank P. Novell, of Shelbyville, Indiana, summed up the sentiment:

Radio Editor Times:

We certainly appreciated your broadcasting of the State basketball tournament. We received all of the games play by play and the neighbors came in to get the finals Saturday night. It was sure some service. Of course, we want The Times to broadcast it again next year.

It didn't take long for monopoly concerns to arise regarding the radio industry. A story in the *Indianapolis Times* of January 29, 1925, began:

WASHINGTON, Jan. 29.—The Federal trade commission has announced it will begin taking testimony March 18 at New York City on its complaint against the General Electric Company, American Telephone and Telegraph Company, Western Electric Company, Inc.; Westinghouse Electric and Manufacturing Company, the International Radio Telegraph Company, United Fruit Company, Wireless Specialty Apparatus Company and Radio Corporation of America. The hearings will be conducted by Attorney Edward L. Smith of the commission's staff.

Complaint charges in substance these companies 'have combined and conspired for the purpose and with the effect of restraining competition and creating a monopoly in the manufacture, purchase and sale, in interstate commerce, of radio devices and apparatus and other electrical devices and apparatus and in domestic and trans-oceanic radio communication and broadcasting.'

LOCOMOTIVE AND TRAINS

On February 21, 1804, in Wales, a steam locomotive built by Richard Trevithick and Andrew Vivian carried ten tons of iron. It was the first time a steam locomotive saw action, two years after the two men received a patent, according to the *American Rails* website.

Prior to the invention of the steam locomotive, wagons carried along rails, usually made of wooden stringers, were used in European coal mines for several hundred years, according to author Anthony J. Bianculli.

In 1807, the Swansea and Mumbles Railway in England was the first passenger-dedicated railway, although it used horse-drawn trains until 1897. The first modern public railroad, in 1825, was that country's Stockton and Darlington Railway. It combined the three necessary components: rails, wagons, and a steam locomotive, Bianculli wrote in his book *Trains and Technology: The American Railroad in the Nineteenth Century; Volume 1, Locomotives.* The first American locomotive, built by Peter Cooper, was tested on the Baltimore & Ohio Railroad in 1829.

By the 1850s, train use was widespread, according to *American Rails.* Locomotives propelled passengers seeking to travel distances and carried freight around the country.

"By routinizing movements of raw materials, goods, and people, railroads orchestrated the growth of the national economy," wrote H. Roger Grant in his book *Railroads and the American People.*

On January 12, 1830, the *Republican Compiler* of Gettysburg, Pennsylvania, printed a brief extract from the *Baltimore American* of a letter "written by a gentleman of high respectability in Liverpool to his friend in this city" about the performance of one of the new locomotive engines in England. The extract of the letter from W. Brown, Esq., to his brother, dated November 6, 1829, said:

> Mr. Winans and George A. Brown have just returned from this city, on the Liverpool and Manchester Rail-road, where they have been amusing themselves riding on Mr. Stevenson's Locomotive Engine, at the rate of twenty eight miles per hour — drawing about 30 passengers. She is represented to have gone one mile in a minute and sixteen seconds (about forty-eight miles an hour) — but this Mr. Stevenson himself can scarcely credit.
>
> . . . New Rail roads are projecting over the country — a meeting is to be held on Wednesday to create a company to carry one to Birmingham.

Later in the century, on November 2, 1871, a flowery editorial with religious overtones in the *Nebraska Advertiser* of Brownville exclaimed that this exciting form of mass transit could be transformative for remote regions of the country. It said, in part:

> Now that this section of Nebraska is hopeful of the speedy advent of the iron horse, which will, with lungs of steam, breath of fire, muscles of iron, and sinews of steel go prancing over our commonwealth, with scores of cars freighted with the products of our soil, and material fashioned by the hands of our enterprizing (sic) men and women, rattling at its heels, to return to us with the products of the East and South, it may not be amiss for us to say a word as to the power of the railroad as a civilizer.
>
> . . . The railroad, as a civilizing power, may be said to be fast taking the place of the priestly office and missionary element, at least it is operating as a sovereign aid to the former and entirely extinguishing the necessity of the latter.

Jumping ahead to August 24, 1901, the *Superior Times* of Wisconsin printed a confounding letter from Pearce Bodley of Louisville, Kentucky, who apparently authored a book titled *Home Rule Money* that touted little Superior's potential as a bustling metropolis—with the railroad as a key element in the unlikely scenario. It said, in part:

> Gentlemen: You are solidly correct advocating Douglas county farming development — Superior will become one of the largest cities in the United States; but with Canada brought into the Union, as Jefferson would have done long ago, by simply inviting all adjoining people like Canada and Mexico, to come in and sit at the table as brothers, not colonial subjects, and the people of those countries would organize annexation parties that would bring them in without our firing a gun.
>
> With Canada, Mexico and Alaska in the Union, Superior would be the natural point for the Capitol of the United States of America — Capitol of 'Continental America,' as the original 'Continental Congress' designed.
>
> . . . Let us do as Russia alone has had practical sense enough to do — want territorial soverignty (sic) only over land held together by steel railroads.

But as remarkable as the industry's growth was in advancing mass transportation and commercial and industrial development, there was an unseemly side that, for better or worse, grabbed the public's attention—fatal accidents, some spectacular. The public was both appalled and fascinated by the tragedies.

From the mid-1890s until the 1930s, spectators would pay to watch staged train wrecks at state fairs and festivals. On September 15, 1896, in Waco, Texas, two people among the 40,000 watching such an incident involving two locomotives were killed, Justin Franz wrote on the *Atlas Obscura* website.

Unsurprisingly, the *Free Dictionary* defines the idiom "train wreck" as "a major or total failure, disaster, or catastrophe."

While some members of the public in the nineteenth century had obvious fears about riding the rails, others were concerned about something more nebulous.

"From the dawn of railroad travel, some riders worried about their personal well-being, exclusive of the possibility of an accident that might bring injury or death," Grant wrote. "Before advances in medical sciences, there existed the belief that a lengthy train trip could cause 'American Nervousness,' a particular malaise common to the United States."

An example of an early letter describing an accident involving a New Jersey train and raising the question of whether train speed should be regulated by legislation was published in the November 14, 1833, edition of the *Lancaster Examiner* of Pennsylvania. The unsigned letter, reprinted from the *American Daily Advertiser* of Philadelphia, said, in part:

> Mr. Editor. — The authors of this paragraph were two of the passengers in the Camden and Amboy Rail Road line when the dreadful accident occurred on Friday, and were in the unfortunate car letter A, which upset, and were of the few who providentially escaped without injury. The scene was appalling beyond description. —
>
> One gentleman, viz: Mr. Steadman of North Carolina, died on the ground. He lived about half an hour after the accident. Another gentleman was left at Highstown, supposed to be in a dying state. A child, it was also supposed, would not live. Others had their limbs broken, and were otherwise dreadfully bruised; and some of them, if they survive, will probably be maimed for life.
>
> . . . The train was unquestionably at that time proceeding at the rate of above 30 and near 40 miles an hour. To this many witnesses will testify.
>
> . . . But it is a solemn question put to the proprietors of rail roads and especially of the one on which the dreadful scene of Friday took place, whether the lives and limits of those who venture to travel with are to be thus put in jeopardy by such velocity; and it is a solemn question whether our Legislatures and especially the Legislature of New Jersey, ought not to pass such laws in relation to travelling on rail roads, as will effectually prevent the recurrence of such another awful scene.

The *New York Herald* of May 7, 1853, ran a letter about a fatal New York and New Haven Railroad accident the previous day. The letter writer, identified as "from the scene," said, in part:

> Norwalk, May 6, 9½ o'clock, P. M.,
>
> I came up in the first cars after hearing of the murders here — in the 5 o'clock train — and reached the station house a little after 7. Ten miles below, we heard that forty-nine dead bodies had been taken from the water, and as members of my family and dear friends were among the passengers it was with the most fearful apprehensions that I entered

the morgue where the dead — the murdered — lay in ranks, their faces gleaming horribly, as lamps were carried along to enable the newly arrived strangers to discover whether their wives and children, or parents, or brothers, or sisters, were among them.

An unsigned letter in the *Herald* three days later said:

> To the Editor of the New York Herald.
>
> I would suggest that instead of imposing a penalty upon railway accidents, the Legislature should compel two directors to accompany each through train, one to sit on the front seat of the front car, and the other on the back seat of the rear car. We shall then hear of no more collisions from front or rear.

On February 23, 1875, the *Chicago Daily Tribune* reported that according to the *Railroad Gazette*, in the month of January, 131 train accidents occurred in the U.S., resulting in ten deaths and ninety-six injuries.

The worst disaster in U.S. history involving trains was the Malbone Street subway wreck on November 1, 1918, in Brighton Beach, Brooklyn, New York, in which 102 people died. The four sub-headlines in the *New York Tribune* story of November 2 read:

"Coney Train, With Green Motorman, Crushed in Tunnel"

"Heavily Loaded, Speeding Cars Jump Switch in Cut on Brighton Line Near Lincoln Road and Dash Their Human Freight to Death"

"Men and Women Fight for Lives As Debris Catches Fire and Burns"

"All Officials of the B. R. T. Have Been Ordered Arrested as Police Search for the Missing Motorman — Hard to Identify Dead."

The train's motorman, Anthony Edward Lewis, was arrested following the crash. It was determined that Lewis had taken a curve at too high a speed. Following the crash, New York City Mayor John Francis Hylan, a former motorman himself, traveled to Kings County Hospital and visited its morgue, according to an account in the *Sun*, of New York on November 3. The newspaper's story went on to say:

> Several bodies there are not identifiable. After a moment or two Mayor Hylan said, 'I cannot stand this' and left the place. In the yard the visitors met a man who was crying over and over 'She is dead; she is dead.'

Letter writer W. MacNicholl had an impassioned letter that appeared in the *Brooklyn Daily Times* five days after the incident, saying, in part:

> . . . Nearly all, if not all, the transportation companies in Greater New York show a culpable disregard for the safety and comfort of the public. Old shacks of cars are kept in commission, green hands are put in charge, cars are crowded during rush hours to suffocation, and all to satiate the greed of corporations.
>
> . . . We are the veriest slaves and barbarians to tolerate such execrable conditions even for one week. Why has the outraged public not raised a protest that could be heard all the way to Albany?

AUTOMOBILE

As far back as the fifteenth century, Leonardo da Vinci drew up designs for a vehicle that could transport people, according to John Fuller on the *HowStuffWorks* website. In a slow progression over the nineteenth century, various inventors created versions of wheeled vehicles.

Leading up to the automobile, crude wheeled vehicles such as roller skates and bicycles generated their own stir in mid- and late-nineteenth century America. For women, in particular, skates and bicycles were somewhat liberating.

A brief item on April 16, 1877, in the *Oshkosh Daily Northwestern* of Wisconsin noted: "A gentleman just returned from the east says that roller skating has become very general in that section and that roller skates are used there quite extensively by the young ladies in skating to and from school."

Bicycles, especially, exploded in popularity. Some late-1860s models, made of iron and wood, resembled today's bicycles, according to the Division of Work and Industry of the Smithsonian's National Museum of American History. "Rubberized wheels" were patented in 1868, and high-wheel bicycles that allowed riders to move faster gained traction in the 1870s and 1880s.

As letters to the editor and news items demonstrated, however, the march of technology in the form of the bicycle often clashed with old standbys, especially the horse and buggy. Sharing the road made for uneasy coexistence, with frequent consequences.

For example, this brief letter from "An Eye Witness" appeared in the *Buffalo Evening News* of New York, on May 22, 1888:

Editor Evening News:

Messrs. Brown & Clarke of the Clarke Oil Co., while out trying their new and beautiful horse, Black Jack, met with what might have proven a most serious accident. Going out the Humboldt parkway, the horse took fright at an approaching bicycle and turning suddenly, upset and totally wrecked the buggy, dragging the occupants for some distance, and only through the good management of Mr. Clarke and cool-headedness of Mr. Brown, they managed to save themselves and the young son of Mr. Clark, (sic) who was with them.

Pressure mounted for legislation to regulate bicycling. On March 10, 1880, the *Daily Kansas State Journal* of Topeka printed a letter from Fred W. Wood that took exception to a local law. It said, in part:

Editor State Journal:

The one or two unlucky owners of Bicycles in this city were astonished and disgusted yesterday morning to find that the City Council had passed an ordinance prohibiting 'bicycling' upon the streets, alleys or sidewalks of Topeka.

. . . Bicycling is not a nuisance. Timid horses may be frightened at first sight of these machines, but ask any citizen of Topeka to furnish evidence that these peculiar carriages (for such the Court of Queen's Bench, England, has decided they are) have caused a runaway or incommoded a single person.

In the east, man, youth and boy alike join in 'bicycling,' as it affords exhilarating exercise, fine amusement and (in many cases) practical utility.

The Supreme Court of New York decides, 'all persons may travel on the street or highway in their own common modes of conveyance; the use is general and open to all alike,' and this broad and reasonable opinion has been cited and approved by the highest courts in other States.

If the bicycle made a societal impact, the automobile eventually dwarfed it by a metaphorical mile. German Karl Benz, in 1885-86, is generally credited with producing the first automobile powered by gasoline in an internal combustion engine.

American brothers Charles Edgar and Frank Duryea—who were initially bicycle makers—built their first successful gas-powered automobile in 1893, and founded a "motor wagon" company in 1896 to manufacture the 700-pound vehicles that could carry eight gallons of gasoline and operate at up to 20 mph.

By 1900, there were about eight thousand cars in the United States.

Unfortunately for a curious and receptive public, the early automobiles were quite expensive. This reality was addressed in a letter from Israel G. Howell of Hopewell, New Jersey, to *The New York Times* of July 10, 1899. It said, in part:

> To the Editor of The New York Times:
>   We are living in the age of inventions, and one of the greatest things to be brought out yet is the horseless wagon.
>   . . . So far the horseless wagon is very crude. First it takes a small fortune to buy one; second, the weight is about four times what it should be; third, the complications are entirely too great; and as yet, none but the rich can buy one.

The biggest boost for automobiles came with the founding of the Ford Motor Company by Henry Ford and eleven investors in 1903. Ford had built his first car in 1896; the four-wheeled, gas-powered Quadricycle topped out at about 20 mph. The company sold its first Model A car on July 23, 1903.

Ford's famous Model T, built for the general public, debuted on October 1, 1908. The 20-horsepower, four-cylinder engine vehicle at first sold for $825, according to the *History* website.

Not long after automobiles took to the roads, various state bills were proposed to regulate them. "A Farmer" of Massapequa, Long Island, addressed one such New York State bill in a letter to the *Brooklyn Daily Eagle* on January 13, 1902. It said, in part:

> To the Editor of the Brooklyn Eagle:
>   On January 10, under the heading of 'Curbing the Automobile,' there appeared in your editorial columns an article relative to the proposed automobile legislation at Albany.
>   . . . The law empowers the Board of Supervisors to regulate the speed of automobiles at not more than eight miles an hour through villages and not more than fifteen miles an hour through the country sections,

Cars come off the assembly line at the Ford Motor Co.'s Highland Park Plant in Michigan, c. 1913. (Courtesy of Library of Congress)

and provides that they may fix a 'penalty' not greater than $25 for each offense.

This is all very well, so far as it goes, but it does not go far enough. The law does not declare the offense to be a misdemeanor, but simply provides a penalty.

The result is that the man who is speeding his machine at a forbidden rate, cannot be legally arrested, for he is committing no crime.

Angus Sinclair, president of the New Jersey Automobile and Motor Club, took issue with a proposed amendment to a law in that state. His letter to the *Evening Star and Newark Advertiser* on July 13, 1907, said, in part:

To the Editor of the Star: A cloud of false witnesses is passing over the State of New Jersey, striving by most disreputable means to work up sentiment against automobilists and the use of automobiles. The particular purpose of this movement at present is agitation in favor of an amendment to the Frelinghuysen Automobile Law requiring automobiles to pay an annual license of $10 or $15. There are a variety of excuses given for proposing this new imposition, but when they are carefully examined nothing is left but the desire to punish automobilists for owning or operating their motor cars.

Automobiles as a new cultural phenomenon also became the target of satirical pieces, such as this unsigned one, apparently penned by the "Anti-Auto Protective Society." It appeared in the *Washington Times* (and other newspapers), on July 12, 1908, under the headline "Unwritten, Perhaps, But Enforced Too Oft, Is Drivers' Experience," and said:

The following is the new code agreed upon for the season of 1908 by the constable of a little village in northern Michigan.

1. On discovering an approaching team, the automobilist must stop off side and cover his machine with a tarpaulin painted to correspond with the scenery.

2. The speed limit on country roads this year will be secret and the penalty for violation will be $10 for every mile an offender is caught going in excess of it.

3. In case an automobile makes a team run away, the penalty will be $50 for the first mile, $100 for the second mile, $200 for the third mile, etc., that the team runs, in addition to the usual charges for damages.

4. On approaching a corner where he cannot command a view of the road ahead, the automobilist must stop not less than 100 yards from the turn, toot his horn, ring a bell, fire a revolver, halloo, send up three bombs at intervals of five minutes.

5. Automobiles must be seasonably painted —that is, so they will agree with the pastoral ensemble and not be startling. They must be green in spring, golden in summer, red in autumn, and white in winter.

6. Automobiles running on country roads at night must send up a red rocket every mile and wait ten minutes for the road to clear. They may then proceed carefully, blowing their horns and shooting Roman candles.

7. In case an automobile comes up behind and wants to pass, the farmer will affect deafness until the automobile calls him a hard name.

8. All members of the society will give up Sunday to chasing automobiles, shooting and shouting at them, making arrests, and otherwise discouraging country touring on that day.

9. In case a horse will not pass an automobile, notwithstanding the scenic tarpaulin, the automobilist will take the machine apart as rapidly as possible and conceal the parts in the grass.

10. In case an automobile approaches a farmer's house when the roads are dusty, it will slow down to one mile an hour and the chauffeur will lay the dust in front of the house with a hand sprinkler worked over the dash board.

The *United Opinion* of Bradford, Vermont, on June 10, 1910, ran a report from its "special correspondent" in Washington, D.C. that said preliminary indications were that the Official Census had found property values rising throughout the country. "Real estate men attribute this largely to the automobile," the correspondent wrote. "People can live farther out in the country than they could before the automobile came into general use."

The report went on to say:

> The automobile has become an essential part of the complex life of today, and it is absurd to regard it as purely a pleasure vehicle. It has revolutionized the delivery service of the cities and has proven a potent factor in the world's progress.

AIRPLANE

"To fly was to achieve mastery and control over the environment, to taste ultimately freedom, to escape earthly restraint," wrote Walter J. Boyne in his book *The Smithsonian Book of Flight.*

Manned flight technically had been possible dating back at least 2,000 years to the invention of the kite in China or Southeast Asia, Boyne noted, adding that all the materials needed for a modern-type hang glider were available in ancient Egypt.

In 1890, the efforts of German Otto Lilienthal, who became known as the "flying man," likely led to the new, serious era of aviation. Lilienthal constructed what amounted to a hang glider, directly influencing Orville and Wilbur Wright in the process.

The Wright brothers, who operated a bicycle repair shop in Dayton, Ohio, read an article on Lilienthal's exploits in 1894 and became intrigued with the possibility of human flight, according to authors Ron Dick and Dan Patterson in their book *Aviation Century: The Early Years*. But the brothers really didn't get serious about flight until five years later.

In the interim, the Wrights studied bird flight, concluding that buzzards regained balance by "a torsion of the tips of the wings," the authors wrote. Eventually, the Wrights built gliders in 1900-2.

On December 17, 1903, Orville won a coin toss and was credited with the first manned flight at Kitty Hawk, North Carolina.

Quite a few newspapers offered written accounts by the brothers about that fateful day in aviation history. For example, a story picked up by the *Watchman and Southern* of Sumter, South Carolina, on January 13, 1904, said, in part:

> Dayton, O., Jan. 6. — The Wright brothers, inventors of the flying machine which has attracted such widespread attention, have prepared the following, which they say is the first correct statement of the successful trials made by them:
>
> 'In the morning of Dec. 17, between 10.30 and noon, four flights were made, two by Orville Wright and two by Wilbur Wright. The starts were all made from a point on the level and about 200 feet west of our camp, which is situated a quarter of a mile north of Kill Devil Sand, in Dare county, N.C.
>
> . . . 'Into the teeth of a 25-mile gale the "flyer" made its way forward with a speed of 10 miles an hour over the ground and 30 to 35 miles an hour through the air.
>
> 'It had previously been decided that for reasons of personal safety these first trials should be made as close to the ground as possible.
>
> . . . 'The succeeding flights rapidly increased in length and at the fourth trial a flight of 59 seconds was made in which the machine flew a little more than half a mile through the air and a distance of more than 852 feet over the ground.'

Henry Helen Clayton, of the Blue Hill Observatory in Massachusetts, penned a piece on the Wright brothers' extraordinary achievement and its place in history that was picked up by the *Williston Graphic* of North Dakota, on August 9, 1906. The write-up said, in part:

> . . . Profiting by the accumulated experience of those who had previously tried and by the very light motors which have been developed for automobiles and boats, an engine for driving their machine was built and a successful but brief preliminary flight was made in December, 1903.
>
> . . . After centuries of effort, successful flight is at last accomplished. After hundreds of failures, the loss of many lives and of many thousands of dollars, one of the greatest achievements in history, the conquest of the air, has auspiciously begun.

The Wrights' work suffered a heavily covered setback in September 1908—the same year in which they completed a thirty-two-mile flight—when a crash of their plane took the life of Lieutenant Thomas E. Selfridge and severely injured Orville Wright. The lead front-page story in the *Evening Star* of Washington, D.C., on September 18, though presented a strong defense of aviation from the U.S. War Department. The story began:

> Crumpled into a scarcely recognizable mass of muslin, wood and iron, the wreck of the Wright aeroplane lies this morning in the shed at Fort Myer waiting the verdict of the army board as to how the accident yesterday really occurred. Whatever is the verdict there is no question in the minds of army officers that the flying machine experiment will be continued, and that the ultimate development of the machine will be successful.

In 1908, Wilbur Wright held the distance, altitude, duration, and speed records documented by the Fédération Aéronautique Internationale, according to author Boyne.

On July 4, 1909, the *Pittsburg* (now Pittsburgh) *Press* of Pennsylvania glibly noted: "There's one advantage the Wright brothers have over the man in an auto. They don't have to get out and push."

The *New York Times* solicited letters from prominent people on what they believed was the most significant event of 1908. On December 27, it ran a series of letters. D.P. Kingsley, who headed New York Life insurance company, wrote:

Orville Wright flying on July 1, 1909, at Fort Myer, Virginia. (Courtesy of Library of Congress)

To the Editor of The New York Times:

The conquest of the air by Orville and Wilbur Wright was in my judgment the most important and significant event of 1908. The 'conquest' is not complete, but these men have literally 'flown' for a sufficiently long time to make it certain that fuller conquest is coming.

The consequences which will follow we can as yet only speculate over; but the event was not only the most significant of the year, it was one of the most significant events of all time.

In 1912, Wilbur Wright died at age 45 of typhoid fever, leaving Orville without his trusted partner.

On June 22, 1919, the *New York Tribune* ran a letter in its *Children's Tribune* from thirteen-year-old Israel Eisenstein of New York City about the future of aviation and Orville's likely role. It said, in part:

... The original machine was not more than thirty feet in its longest dimension, while a machine of to-day, such as the NC-4, is over two hundred feet in width.

But the inventor is not yet satisfied. As he has performed wonders in the past so shall he perform them in the future with this already remarkable piece of mechanism. And we may yet hope to see all our traffic and commerce carried by the aeroplane.

A letter from John Allen Winkler appeared in the *Dayton Daily News* of Ohio on December 1, 1918, making the case that the planned recognition of the hometown Wright brothers should be appropriate and respectful. It said, in part:

> Editor The Daily News.
>
> Dear Sir:
>
> . . . Suggestion has been made that Main street be called Wilbur Wright street. Mr. Editor, all Daytonians are proud of the Wright brothers and there are those who believe their fame should be reflected, not by a towering plinth, or a busy street, but in a splendid memorial building.
>
> The writer believes that for such a structure thousands of dollars would be contributed by admirers of the Wright brothers, all over the world, but the writer as sincerely believes that a movement to change the name of Main street to Wilbur Wright avenue or street, would not meet with the approval of the surviving members of the famous family.

Orville Wright's last project before he died of a heart attack at age seventy-six on January 30, 1948, was preserving the 1905 Wright Flyer III for Carillon Historical Park in Dayton. While he died before the sixty-five-acre park opened in 1950, Orville helped design Wright Hall, the building housing the Flyer, according to the *Dayton History* website.

Chapter 10

Clarion Call for Renewable Energy

The push for the development of alternative energy sources in the face of climate change has taken on increased urgency in the past few decades. The temperature of the Earth has gone up by 0.14° Fahrenheit (0.08° Celsius) each decade since 1880, but the rate of warming per decade has been more than twice that since 1981—0.32° F (0.18° C), wrote Rebecca Lindsey and Luann Dahlman on the *NOAA Climate* website. The years 2013 through 2021 were among the warmest on record.

A story in the *Guardian* in October 2021 stated that "scientific consensus that humans are altering the climate has passed 99.9%." Still, climate change denial remains firmly entrenched in some quarters in present-day America.

Nevertheless, for centuries humankind has been fascinated by and employed so-called alternative energy sources. Those sources are primarily water, wind, and the sun. In the nineteenth century, in particular, some scientists and inventors were driven by an understanding that fossil fuels—coal, specifically—were finite resources.

Water power—eventually developed into hydroelectric power—was used as far back as 202 BCE to 9 AD in the Han Dynasty in China, according to the *TRVST* website. A vertical trip hammer powered by a water wheel was employed to ground grain. The Chinese also applied water power famously to make paper.

An illustration from "Grist Wind-mills at East Hampton" in New York in 1872. (Courtesy of Library of Congress)

One of the first known applications of hydropower was in eighteenth-century England, where Richard Arkwright spun cotton in his mill using water.

As pertains to wind power, as far back as 644 AD, Umar ibn al-Khattab, the second caliph of Islam, was killed by Abu Lu'lui'a, a Persian technician who aspired to construct wind-powered mills and supposedly was angry about taxation, according to *Power from Wind: A History of Windmill Technology*, by Richard L. Hills.

On the European continent, Flanders and the north of France reportedly had windmills by the first half of the thirteenth century. The area around Ypres, in West Flanders near the French border, had 120 functioning windmills in the 1200s.

By 1847, France had 8,700 windmills—and 37,000 water mills—with 90 percent of the windmills in use for grinding corn, Hills wrote.

In North America, the settlers employed water and windmills to grind corn and saw wood. Most windmills were in use for farmers on the tops of tall towers, but they also operated on the tops of buildings and even in towns to supply water.

In England, the first windmill specifically designed to generate electricity was installed in 1899. The electricity was stored in cells that could supply 109 lights of between eight and twenty-six candlepower for eight days in winter, according to Hills.

More recently, the 1973 oil crisis, which drove up gas prices, once again sparked intense interest in wind energy.

Washington Post reporters Josh Dawsey and Maxine Joselow reported that in April 2024, presidential candidate Trump, during a fundraiser with oil executives, excoriated wind power while vowing to undo dozens of President Biden's environmental rules and policies. In dismissing climate change as a "hoax," Trump for years has harshly criticized wind power development. He bluntly declared to the oil executives, "I hate wind."

The Greeks were the first people to record a simplistic use of solar power in the fourth century BCE, according to Lucy Cogan, in a paper in the book *Fueling the Future: Solar Power*. They understood that building houses with south-facing walls took advantage of sunshine. The Greeks and Romans also used solar energy to heat water. The Chinese and Anasazi, or Pueblo, Indians applied direct sunlight as well.

It wasn't until the nineteenth century that initial measures toward controlled solar generation were taken. In 1839, Edmond Becquerel, a French physicist, determined that a certain material would conduct a small amount of electric current when exposed to light—the photovoltaic (PV) effect, Cogan wrote.

Later, selenium PV cells produced electricity at 1-2 percent efficiency. And in 1941, Russell Ohl, an American, invented a silicon solar cell.

The *Dupuyer Acantha* newspaper of Montana picked up an unsigned piece on wind power from the *Boston Herald* that it ran on August 15, 1901, and that could have been written three hundred years ago—or today, for that matter. It said, in part:

> . . .There can be little doubt that the wind will become the prime motive power of the future, not only for all kinds of work to be done in rural districts, but also in the cities for such work as requires but a moderate expenditure of power.
>
> Work which does not require any definite time for its accomplishment, such as wood-sawing, pumping water, grinding grain and cutting

feed, is now accomplished by the wind wheel, and it only needs the invention of some convenient means of storing up the energy of the wind, so that the power derived from it may be available at any time, to make it a universal labor-saver.

It is most probable that the conserving of wind power will take place through the use of storage batteries, and its transmission will occur electrically.

. . .There is no reason to doubt that in the course of time there will be erected great machines which shall collect the wind power in such quantities as will allow its transmission from central power houses, as at present accomplished by other sources of energy.

In the same vein, an editorial item in the *Fargo Forum and Daily Republican* of North Dakota said on May 24, 1912:

Electric light, heat and power can be brought within the reach of the farmers of North Dakota and the residents of the smaller cities and villages by harnessing the winds and putting them to work, according to Prof. A. H. Taylor of the state university, who has studied the problem from many angles and has put the result of his study and investigation into a bulletin entitled: The Development, Storage and Utilization of Wind Power.

"Christian at Work" raised some energy questions in the *San Marcos Free Press* of Texas, on November 17, 1887, including:

. . . The great problem evermore is, at which shop can we get our sunshine most cheaply. Direct solar power can only be had very occasionally, and the cost of bottling is high. Water power can only be had at certain places, and hence often leads to expenses which prevent it being economical.

Similar is it with wind power. Horse power is dear; the growth of the food of the animal, his stable and attendants run into money. At present coal power is the cheapest. Electric machinery is not a source; it is only a medium; not a bottle, but a glass, from which energy is consumed. It needs power to produce an electric current. Its value in the conveyance of energy is very great; so that in time it may prove a cheap way of getting sunshine to work.

Charles Greeley Abbot, astrophysicist and secretary of the Smithsonian, poses between 1913 and 1917 with his silver-disc pyrheliometer, which measures direct beam solar irradiance, converting heat to an electrical signal that can be recorded. (Courtesy of Library of Congress)

Solar power was also the subject of a piece in the *Gem State Rural* of Caldwell, Idaho, on March 9, 1905, that said, in part:

> Boston, New York and London capitalists have undertaken the manufacture and installation of solar motors for pumping and irrigation purposes in the arid sections of Nevada, Arizona and California, but the probabilities are that the solar motor is still very much in the air.
>
> That the day will come, however, when a method of securing energy direct from the sun will be devised is probable, and the fact that men of

affairs have been interested in the subject to the extent of investing dollars in experiments is a good sign of not distant solution of the problem.

Frederic J. Haskin wrote an informational column that regularly appeared in more than 100 newspapers around the country. His column that ran in the *Muscatine Journal* of Iowa on May 15, 1916, included the following paragraph:

> This study of the sun's energy also opens another fascinating possibility — that of putting the sun to work. The construction of a practicable motor which would use the heat of the sun would solve the power question forever. The price of gasoline would worry us no longer. Power would be free and inexhaustible.

On January 6, 1887, the *Wahpeton Times* of Dakota (now North Dakota) published an account of Captain John Ericsson, who spent twenty years working on an engine propelled by heat from the sun. The write-up included this description:

> The leading feature of the device is that of concentrating the radiant heat of the sun by means of a rectangular trough, having a curved bottom lined on the inside with polished plates so arranged that they reflect the sun's rays toward a cylindrical boiler placed longitudinally above the trough.
>
> This boiler contains the acting medium, steam or air, employed to transfer the solar energy to the motor, the pistons and valves resembling those of motive engines of the ordinary type.

The *Indianapolis Times* of October 31, 1924, had an article from its Washington bureau that said, in part:

> . . . Future generations of mankind will either live in greater luxury than we know today, or they will be galley slaves and serfs, all depending on the progress made in coming years in discovering how plants transform the sun's rays into energy.
>
> We face a time when all sources of stored energy will be depleted, says Prof. H. A. Spoehr, Carnegie Institute of Washington, Carmel Coastal Laboratory, in the annual report of the Smithsonian Institute.

"To save civilization, botanists, chemists and physicists must unite now and work together to find a new mode of obtaining energy," Spoehr declares.

". . . Coal is really nothing but fossil solar energy, rays of sunlight stored beneath the earth for centuries. This stored energy has made possible the civilization of today.

"Throughout nature, the young are protected and nurtured until they can care for themselves. So man has had his great patrimony of fuel to help him as he struggled feebly to overcome his environment. But the supply will he gone some day and civilization will have to depend on the daily quota of energy from the sun."

James Means had a prescient letter, headlined "Substitutes for Coal" in the *Boston Evening Transcript* of Massachusetts on March 19, 1898, that outlined the three chief renewable energy sources. The long letter by Means, an inventor and entrepreneur, said, in part:

To the Editor of the Transcript:

The article which appears in your issue of the 2d instant, giving an account of experiments with a solar engine at Longwood, is interesting and suggestive. It gives new proof that man will persist in his efforts to unlock those reservoirs of nature's energy which so far have remained closed to him.

It may be interesting to consider briefly three sources of energy which have attracted the attention of investigators. Mentioned in the order of the degrees of difficulty which they present, they are as follows: First, the solar rays; second, the wind; third, the tides.

. . . The utilization of the sun's rays is the least promising of the three methods mentioned, and this is so clearly because of the great expense of reflecting or refracting instruments. Experimenters who, facing this difficulty, work on undaunted, can only command admiration.

When we consider the possibilities of the extension of the use of wind energy, we find a much easier problem, yet it is difficult enough. In your issue of the 29th of last December, under the heading, 'Wind Power as a Substitute for Coal,' I gave a brief account of the work that has been done in this direction in recent years.

Charles F. Brush of Cleveland, the inventor of the modern form of storage battery, for ten years or more has been lighting his house and grounds with electricity generated by power from his windmill and stored in a large battery so that the current is available at all times.

. . . We are led to inquire why it is that the power of the wind has not been more extensively used in large units on land?

There are two reasons: First, because it is only in recent years that the storage battery has become a decided commercial success, and, second, because the steam engine has had so much more done for it than the windmill ever has.

. . . Coming now to the third source of energy, tidal movement, we find that there are fewer difficulties to overcome than are met with in applying wind energy to the uses of man.

. . . The coast of New England from Cape Cod to Eastport, with its numerous estuaries and abundant ebb and flow of tide, offers excellent facilities for the development of tidal power; while if we go farther east, we find in the Bay of Fundy a Niagara of undeveloped power surrounded by what is lacking at Niagara Falls, cheap land. That it will eventually be possible to utilize these waters will, I think, be conceded by electricians who are familiar with the performances of the enormous storage batteries now used as equalizers by very many of the great electric corporations.

A story in the *Opelousas Courier* of Louisiana, on September 7, 1901, addressed the water picture in the Southwest, advocating for solar power to improve it. Since then, drought and water usage in that region has become a bigger issue, garnering much recent attention in Washington and the American media.

In a May 2022 statement before a U.S. Senate subcommittee on natural resources, Bureau of Reclamation Commissioner Camille Calimlim Touton stated that the "unprecedented drought" in the West, highlighted "the need for immediate actions as well as for thoughtful planning and on-the-ground work to make both our infrastructure and operational decisions more resilient to withstand future water resource scarcity and variability." (As an aside: the *Detroit Free Press* reported in April 2017 that Jay Famiglietti, the chief water scientist at NASA's Jet Propulsion Laboratory, had said in an interview that eventually water from the Great Lakes might have to be piped to Western cities such as Phoenix and Las Vegas, calling it "part of our future.")

The earlier story in 1901 said, in part:

> . . . Government officials have estimated that fully one-third of the area
> of the United States is embraced in arid America — that immense tract
> where water can be had only by sinking wells of varying depths, and where
> even then there is no means of distributing the life-giving fluid to the
> famished land. To this region the solar motor is likely to prove a godsend.
>
> Here the sun shines almost continuously during the daylight hours,
> and when a model engine, such as has been erected at Los Angeles, is
> capable of lifting sufficient water to irrigate several hundred acres, it may
> readily be imagined what will be accomplished when the deserts of the
> Southwest are dotted with solar motors as the plains of Nebraska are
> now with windmills.

And speaking of Nebraska, besides wind power, the state was serious about
water as an energy source, as a long piece, compiled and published by the *Nebraska Press Association*, and that appeared in the *Alliance Herald* of Nebraska,
on December 11, 1913, noted. It said, in part:

> . . . The possibilities for the development of water power in the state for
> mechanical, industrial, and domestic uses excites the envy of everyone,
> who knows the facts. There is water power enough going to waste to fur-
> nish all the light and all the heat and all the mechanical energy required
> by the state.
>
> As yet very little attempt has been made to turn to practical uses this
> immense amount of waste energy.
>
> . . . The immense waste of the water power of the state awaits only
> development to make it available for agricultural, commercial and in-
> dustrial uses.

In a lecture before the National Electric Light Association that was published
in the *Electrical Review* and that ran in the *Washington Standard* of Olympia,
Washington, on September 10, 1897, L.B. Stillwell, a well-known electrical
engineer, said, in part:

> There is an important difference between using the energy of coal and
> utilizing the energy of water powers for power purposes. Coal once

The interior of the generating plant of the American Falls Water, Power & Light Co., on the Snake River in Idaho, c. 1925. (Courtesy of the Library of Congress)

burned cannot be used again. Water powers, on the other hand, are solar engines perenially (sic) renewed. We may utilize the energy of Niagara to-day without subtracting a single horse-power from that which nature intended, not only for our age but for future ages.

The thought, therefore, immediately suggests itself that we should, so far as possible, utilize our water powers in the mechanic arts, burning coal only for our protection from cold, for the preparation of food, for necessary metallurgical purposes, etc.

The *Daily Gate City* of Keokuk, Iowa, reprinted an article on April 17, 1909, that first appeared in the *Register and Leader* of Des Moines, and that said, in part:

It is estimated that the horse power of Iowa rivers is annually equal to 10,000,000 tons of Iowa coal. This is worth $20,000,000 at lowest average cost at the furnace door. This amount of power generated by coal by the present methods of generating in Iowa would cost $60,000,000.

A letter from H.D. Dibble in the *Black Hills Union* of Rapid City, South Dakota, on January 29, 1892, emphasized the immense power of the sun, saying, in part:

> During the past year I have been greatly interested in the discussion regarding the artificial production of rain.
>
> . . . It is calculated that, the sun is pouring on this earth on an average of one horse power to every ten feet square of surface. Basing a calculation on this we find that on an area of ten miles square the sun is constantly pouring its energy to the extent of more than 26,880,000 horse power, which in one year amounts to more than 228 trillion foottuns of energy. In other words the great center of the solar system is showering down on us more than twice the energy of the Niagara falls for every 10 square miles of surface on this earth.
>
> The vast output of energy is constantly being used up and stored by every growing plant or creeping animal. The wind that moves our wind engines and the streams of water that turns the wheels and spindles that add so much to the wealth of the world, all received their inspiration from this source. The steam engine of to day (sic) that converts the heat contained in coal into useful work, is but resurrecting energy that was stored in the growing plants myriads of ages ago.
>
> I do not believe the figures I have given, as vast as they seem, are near as large as they should be, in other words I believe that the sun is pouring much more than 425 horse power of energy on every acre of surface this earth contains.

The *St. Louis Republic* printed a little piece that was picked up by the *Sioux County Journal* of Harrison, Nebraska, on March 25, 1897, and was headlined "Solar Heat on House Roofs." It said, in part:

> The calculating genius figures on everything. He can tell you exactly how far you could hear the whine of a mosquito if the little insect should develop into a creature as large as an elephant, or how far a flea could jump if his weight were equal to that of the average man.
>
> . . . His latest calculation is on the amount of solar heat received by the roofs of our large cities. He finds that In Philadelphia enough of

sun heat is wasted each day to keep 5,000 20-horse power engines in motion.

Theophilus Sargent of Hallowell, Maine, had a brief letter in that state's *Daily Kennebec Journal* of Augusta on December 20, 1882, that simply said:

> Editors Kennebec Journal:
>
> I saw in the daily, patent No. 268,942, 'Apparatus for Converting Motion' reported to some one else. I have that patent and live in Hallowell. It is a machine for propelling a boat, hand car, etc., or an extension of horse, steam, water or any other power needed.

A letter from W.B. Crumpton in the *Montgomery Advertiser* of Alabama, on September 25, 1921, had random thoughts on "a morning's ride" on a few topics, including the work of Dr. Little, "a distinguished chemist." Little had said the supply of natural gas is "dwindling fast." Crumpton's letter said, in part:

> Editor The Advertiser:
>
> . . . Briefly here are some of the sources of supply to which Dr. Little 'looks with varying degree of confidence' in respect of the future supply:
>
> Solar energy derived from the sun's rays. The Sahara desert, Dr. Little calculates, with its 6,000,000 square kilometers of area, receives daily solar energy equivalent to that of 6,000,000 tons of coal. The world, he adds, awaits the genius who will convert that radiant energy into electric current.

On January 1, 1903, a wire story that ran in a number of newspapers, including *The Sun* of Baltimore, Maryland, asked experts what was ahead for the new year. The story included a paragraph that said:

> Prof. W. J. McGee, chief of the United States Bureau of Ethnology — Some of the signs of the time that attract attention are connected with the prospective exhaustion of the anthracite fields, with the consequent necessity of utilizing new sources of energy. Among these the most promising is solar energy, long neglected, but amply sent to drive all the mills, factories and dynamos of the world as soon as the requisite solar engines

are devised. Whether such engines will attain perfection during the new year is questionable; but they will undoubtedly be perfected during the century so newly begun.

On May 13, 1908, a three-day conference convened at the White House on conserving natural resources. Conference attendees included President Theodore Roosevelt, the governors of 44 states, cabinet members, judges, members of Congress, and science experts.

The *Daily Oregon Statesman* of Salem, Oregon, ran a wire story on May 14 that included the following:

> The most promising check on coal consumption is the substitution of other power. Naturalists tell us that coal is a reservoir of solar energy stored up in ages past, and that the same is partly true also of other chemically complex substances, including ores. The sun-motor still runs; its rays render the globe habitable, and may yet be made to produce power through solar engines, or may be concentrated in furnaces — as in the Portuguese priest's heliophore at the St. Louis exposition with its temperature of 6,000 degrees F., in which a cube of iron evaporated like a snowball in a Bessemer converter.

The *New York Sun* of September 7, 1879, ran a story on Captain John Ericsson's solar engine that said, in part:

> . . . Ericcson claims to have at last perfected his long-sought-for solar engine. If erected near the seaboard, where water is to be had, the solar engine will, he claims, generate steam, and that where water is not procurable atmospheric air may be made the medium for transmitting the solar energy to the motor.
>
> . . . Capt. Ericcson, during a recent interview, stated that he is ready to build solar engines of any power. A beautifully finished model occupies a table in the front parlor of his house in Beach street. He intends to offer the principle of the solar engine as a free gift to the world, and he will apply for a patent only for the purpose of protecting the public.

Along similar lines, the *Boston Sunday Post* of Massachusetts, on December 11, 1910, published a story on the work of professor R.A. Fessenden of

Columbia University, whom it described as "one of the foremost savants in this country." It said, in part:

> With the curious patented arrangement embodying his latest idea regarding the production of power without the aid of coal, Professor Fessenden last week appeared before a body of scientists and outlined just how practical are his plans to produce power by corralling the heat of the sun.
>
> He also produced another invention which is intended to make use of the wind as a coal substitute when the sun does not shine.
>
> . . . What he considers his most important invention is the 'solar engine' — a device which he feels embodies all the advantages discovered in years of experimentation, and which he thinks will become the great power agency of the world.

A brief item, headlined "New Windmill Idea" in the *Thomas County Clipper* of Seneca, Nebraska, said, on May 19, 1921:

> A new French windmill, on the principle of the water turbine, is encased with a vertical cylinder bladed like a Venetian blind. The cylinder is stationary, but the blades or slats guide the wind from any direction to the turbine wheel. After acting on the wheel, the wind escapes from the bottom of the cylinder. The vertical shaft transmits the power through a succession of gears adapted to light or strong wind, and a centrifugal regulator controls the speed. The apparatus is designed especially for driving an electric generator.

On April 28, 1924, the *Akron Beacon Journal* of Ohio ran an editorial referencing Dr. Charles E. St. John, a physicist at the Mt. Wilson Observatory in Pasadena, California. St. John pointed to a future that would include not only solar power but seemingly atomic energy as well. The commentary said, in part:

> The study of the sun is really aiming toward the discovery and mystery of great sources of energy stored up in the sun and stars for man's use. We are using up our sources of energy in the world and must learn to store up the sun's energy or learn how to get energy out of matter. He

shows that the world is going to be up against it some day unless we can find out how to do some of the things going on in the sun, that great unexplained engine of energy.

Chapter 11

The Plight of Immigrants Back Then

A common, fundamental belief fixed in the minds of most Americans is that the United States is made up of immigrants coexisting in a metaphorical melting pot.

From the first settlers to reach the land inhabited by Native Americans until today, immigrants have come from all corners of the globe. Just between 1880 and 1910, some 17.7 million immigrants ventured to the United States for various reasons; some were simply seeking work, others were escaping oppression, and still others were chasing the desire for a better life in a democratic republic. In 1907, the largest number of immigrants arrived—1.2 million. The period is commonly known as the Age of Mass Migration.

For virtually all new immigrants, the transition to the United States wasn't easy. Historian and professor Erika Lee notes that Americans through the centuries have been wary of or downright hostile to foreign immigrants: the Germans in the eighteenth century; Irish and Chinese in the nineteenth century; Italians, Jews, Japanese, and Mexicans in the twentieth century; and Muslims today. Central Americans also have been targeted in recent times.

Despite the positive spin placed on the "melting pot" categorization, immigrants to American shores over the years, Lee wrote, have been labeled as poor, of a different faith, and "nonwhite."

Immigrants fill the deck of a transatlantic ship, c. 1906. (Courtesy of Library of Congress)

The public believed that there were too many immigrants, that they carried disease and promoted crime, that they weren't interested in becoming Americans, that they harbored dangerous political views, and that they were stealing jobs, according to Lee, in her book *America for Americans: A History of Xenophobia in the United States*.

Historian Roxanne Dunbar-Ortiz even argues that the U.S. has never been "a nation of immigrants," but has always been "a settler state with a core of descendants from the original colonial settlers, that is, primarily Anglo-Saxons, Scots Irish, and Germans."

In her book *Not a Nation of Immigrants: Settler Colonialism, White Supremacy, and a History of Erasure and Exclusion*, Dunbar-Ortiz also makes the case that the characterization of "a nation of immigrants" is a "benevolent version" of U.S. nationalism and that the "ugly, predominant underside is the panic of enemy invasion."

Many letters to the editor of newspapers in the nineteenth and early twentieth centuries, as well as the publications' often-snarky or prejudiced editorial comments, bear that out.

Even today as the presidential election of 2024 approached, the issue of immigration remained prominent. A Gallup poll in February 2024 ranked immigration as the No. 1 issue for American voters, driven by widespread Republican anger.

Democratic President Biden was repeatedly attacked for his administration's policy at the Southern border. Congressional Republicans, when presented with a bipartisan bill to address the border issue, took a pass at the urging of presidential candidate Donald Trump, who has referred to undocumented immigrants as "poisoning the blood of our country."

In 2018, Trump tabbed immigrants from Africa and places such as Haiti and El Salvador as from "shithole countries," and called for more immigrants from Norway. It was a refrain similar to what many letter writers said more than a century earlier.

In June 2024, Biden announced an executive order on immigration that included provisions to bar migrants who unlawfully crossed the Southern border from gaining asylum, to expand efforts to dismantile human smuggling and to speed up the resolution of immigration cases.

Going back to those earlier days, even before stepping foot on American soil, many poor immigrants from Europe first endured travails on the ships bringing them over, as addressed in a letter from "E. T.Y" that ran in the *New-York Daily Tribune* on October 25, 1850. It said, in part:

> To the Editor of The Tribune:
>
> Your noticing my communication relative to the mistreatment of some of the passengers of the ship 'Delphin,' in the kind manner you have done in the Morning Tribune, entitles you to the gratitude of Immigrants particularly, and of the community at large — and may, I hope, be the means of preventing, in future, a course of conduct and treatment so unworthy the officers and consignees of all emigrant vessels . . .
>
> . . . It is to be hoped, also, that the Commissioners of Emigration and those other particular Societies formed and organized for the ostensible purpose of 'protecting' Immigrants, will use some efficient means, or endeavor to, for their protection from the gross frauds and impositions practiced on them. I trust these gentlemen will avail themselves of your excellent suggestion of paying attention to the proper debarcation (sic) of passengers.

It may be proper for me to state that I have not witnessed the harsh treatment complained of in my letter, but had my information from some of the aggrieved parties, particularly the girl referred to, whose position called forth the commisseration (sic) of some of the passers-by. The statement may, however, have possibly been exaggerated.

More than two decades later, on August 1, 1872, the *New National Era* of Washington D.C., reprinted President Ulysses S. Grant's address to Congress on immigration. He said that he had forwarded legislation to the lawmakers that would protect immigrants while aboard ships bound for America and "upon their arrival at our seaports from the knaves who are ever ready to despoil them of the little all which they are able to bring with them."

The same edition of the *New National Era* detailed some of the hardships immigrants faced upon their arrival. It also indicated that in those days, children from poor families often were separated from parents, an immigration policy that generated much controversy during the Trump administration. The account said, in part:

> . . . Up to 1847 neither the Federal Government nor the several States took any cognizance of the immigrant. He was permitted to land, it is true, but no one was authorized to supervise or direct his movements. In New York, where the largest number of immigrants landed, the greatest abuses prevailed, and but few immigrants escaped from that city without the loss of nearly all their ready money.
>
> . . . No provision is made anywhere for supporting the pauper immigrant, since he has gained no residence in the United States.
>
> . . . Large and commodious buildings are constructed on Ward's Island, and paupers are sent there, but practically, this duty is shirked, and the poor, who are compelled to seek this refuge, and who have no friends who will probably pay their board bills, are treated in a manner that will soon drive them from their asylum.
>
> If a woman goes there with children, the testimony shows that every child two years of age is separated from the mother, and placed in charge of the commissioners of charity. The mortality among infants in the public institutions of New York is so great, that the separation amounts, in nine cases out of ten, to a sentence of death.

An illustration in *Harper's Weekly* in 1893 shows immigrants detained at Ellis Island in New York. (Courtesy of Library of Congress)

Many letter writers, such as John Brown of New York, believed new immigrants were incapable of assimilating. Brown's letter, in *The New York Times* on September 15, 1911, includes the German word "Hexenkessel," which means "cauldron." It said:

> To the Editor of The New York Times:
>
> The letter in your issue to-day speaking of immigrants and stating that a large number of them have Negroid intermixture, is interesting, but your correspondent failed to state that another large number coming from southeastern Europe have Mongoloid intermixture. So here is another inconsistency: In the west the Mongols are excluded; in the east they are admitted.
>
> Of course, this nation is in the making, there may be perfect assimilation, but it is difficult to believe. Ancient Rome went down because its population was like New York's, a perfect 'Hexenkessel.' Shall this kind of immigration be curtailed?

The notion that the foreigners coming to America were different in ways other than simply their physical appearance and language infused letters through the many decades. In their fear of what the immigrants might bring to America, the letters surely have overtones to today. One such letter, during World War I, was that of George O. Ford in the *Arizona Republican* of Phoenix, on October 13, 1918. It said, in part:

> Editor, Republican:
> . . . After this cruel, barbarous war has ended in the downfall of autocracy and monarchy all peoples will be to a far greater extent than now, their own master. What will follow? It will not be the boom inrush that poured into California when gold discovery became known, but it will be the landing on our shores as fast as money can be earned, of first, the father, who soon hoards enough to load these ocean plying ships with steerage droves, that, scorning suffocation or distress, bring bands of offspring to fill our jails, asylums and charity homes to overflowing, and to our depletion of revenue for their support.

The *Emmons County Record* of Williamsport, North Dakota, ran a letter from Maj. J.S. Murphy of Minot, North Dakota on July 12, 1895, that, while harsh, at least showed a willingness to accept *some* immigrants. It said, in part:

> To the Editor of the Record.
> . . . The immigrants who come frankly determined to accept Americanism with all it implies — who take up their duty to their adopted country, who look upon every one sheltered by our flag as a countryman — these, even if the assimilation is slower than we would wish, add to the material wealth and the moral power of the country. Their coming is in no sense a danger.
> But the immigrants who carry with them the insolent design of establishing here, instead of our 'national spirit,' some foreign nationality, who want to take a share in American affairs without ceasing to be foreigners, who strive to multiply languages, who distrust the native born citizen and despise every foreigner who is not of their own kin, who make political capital out of their own clannishness, and who endeavor to render even school and creed the means of preserving differences and preventing national unification — these men are enemies of our form of government at every point, and, so far as their influence extends, their coming is a source of danger and should be discouraged.

Still, through the years, a fair number of letters defended immigrants, even if they offered a convenient rhetorical foil. For example, William Stonebridge of New York had a letter in the *New York Tribune* on April 5, 1909, that said, in part:

> To the Editor of The Tribune:
>
> 'Aliens are to be admitted too hastily,' 'we admit to our shores men and women who become kidnappers, blackmailers,' etc., say our criminal authorities. Yet the Sicilian, Italian, Russian or Chinese immigrants are not the cowardly murderers who run the red and green high-powered street locomotives at sixty miles an hour through 'special privilege' parkways and speedways, leaving a trail of dying and maimed women, children and babies in their wake, and who kill and maim more people in one year in the public thoroughfares of this city than have been credited to anarchism and the Black Hand in the whole United States in a century.
>
> . . . The arriving steerage passengers are not the ones who wreck banks, railroads, trust and insurance companies, and who sell 'paper traction systems,' rob the public, buy and sell public officials, defy the Legislature of a state, the courts and the people with a high priced legal staff instructing them how to do it.

A letter decades earlier from "D.," offering a defense of immigrants, was published in the *Bossier Banner* of Bellevue, Louisiana, on August 16, 1873. It had run previously in the *Picayune,* of New Orleans, and said, in part:

> To the Editor of the Picayune:
>
> Immigration may add from five to ten fold to the staple crops of the State yearly shipped to New Orleans.
>
> Immigration may give us a good, an economical and substantial State government.
>
> . . . Immigration would establish schools, churches, order and law all over the State, and the next generation would rise up and call us blessed for the blessing thus secured for them.
>
> Immigration would give us good roads and good bridges, and more steamboat and railroad accommodations.
>
> Immigration would give value to our lands, make the State rich, and the people contented, friendly and happy.

TAKING ON IMMIGRANT GROUPS, ONE BY ONE

Years before the American Revolution, Benjamin Franklin, in 1755, espoused the view that immigrants were ignorant and a political risk, according to author Lee. He was especially wary of newly arrived Germans.

Later, in 1837, fifteen thousand Bostonians took part in a Protestant-organized riot against Irish Catholics. By 1840, Irish Catholic immigrants made up one-third of the immigrant population, rising to one-half with refugees fleeing the potato famine in their homeland after 1845, Dunbar-Ortiz wrote.

On August 6, 1855, members of the American Party, also known as the Know-Nothings, violently attacked Irish- and German-born voters in Louisville, Kentucky. (The party was anti-immigrant and anti-Catholic, fearing the immigrants' increasing political power and the Catholic Church's presence.) The violence that day came to be known as Bloody Monday.

The Know-Nothing Party created a new definition of *nativism*, naming white Anglo-Saxon Protestant (WASP) settlers as America's "natives," Lee wrote.

The *Weekly Dollar Democrat* of Louisville, on September 22, 1855, carried depositions from readers who had witnessed the attacks on Irish Catholic and German voters on August 6. One such deposition, from Edward Fuller, said:

> I went to the Seventh Ward polls before six o'clock Monday morning, August 6th. While there I saw Mr. Gardiner, who was attempting to go into the voting place, struck on the head with something that caused blood to flow very freely. Mr. G. intended to vote the Democratic ticket. About eleven o'clock I saw a crowd of about twenty-five or thirty persons on Eighth street, between Main and Market, pursuing two Irishmen, and firing at them with pistols.

J.C. Metcalf's deposition said:

> I went to the Second Ward polls a little before 6 o'clock. I am certain, from what I saw, that the polls were in the possession of the Know-Nothing party, and that no one could vote unless the Know-Nothings permitted him. I myself was not able to vote. While at the polls I saw a German struck by an American.

A torn American flag was a popular nativist symbol, as shown here on the cover of sheet music written to glorify the nativist cause shortly after bloody anti-Catholic riots in May 1844 in Philadelphia. (Courtesy of Library of Congress)

The *Weekly Indiana State Sentinel* of Indianapolis published a letter from George J. Langsdale of Vienna, Indiana, on August 16, 1855, expressing his horror about Louisville in strong wording that resounds today. The letter from Langsdale, who years later would serve as president of Indiana's State Soldiers and Sailors Monument Commission, said, in part:

EDS. SENTINEL: —
    . . . Who would have believed that the people of this country, (I can no longer call it a free country,) would have become so degenerate, so tyrannical, so sectarianized, so lost to all sense of justice, as to trample into the dust those inestimable privileges for which our forefathers fought and died. But such is the lamentable fact.
    A party of men, (fanatics I should say,) have usurped the privileges of the ballot box, punishing those who wish to vote in opposition to their doctrines, with death. A man who merely wishes to exercise the privilege which the constitution guaranties (sic) to him a privilege 'formidable to

tyrants only,' runs the risk of being shot down like a beast. In vain, after these things, may we indulge the fond hope of preserving our liberties, without a decided movement.

. . . If we wish to continue free; if we mean to preserve inviolate those privileges for which our forefathers shed their life blood, if we mean not basely to abandon the government of our country, to the tender mercies of a fanatical clique, we must bestir ourselves. Then if all milder measures fail, I repeat it, we must fight.

Later immigrants, mostly in the early twentieth century, that spawned distrust or incurred the wrath of natives were from Eastern and Southern Europe, particularly Italians, Jews, Slovaks, and Poles.

The *Herald and News* of Newberry, South Carolina, on October 1, 1907, ran a blatantly xenophobic speech by that state's U.S. Senator Asbury Churchwell Latimer, who addressed immigration at the invitation of the Farmers' Union. The speech, at the Court House in Greenville, promoted white supremacy, saying, in part:

. . . No one realizes more fully than I do the importance of white supremacy in the south, but I deny that the class of immigrants that I protest against being brought to South Carolina, viz, Russian Jews, Turks, Greeks, Roumanians, Southern Italians and Asiatic peoples, that will come over the Triest Line will aid us in maintaining white supremacy in the south.

Sewell Ford had a venomous letter in the *Five Mile Beach Journal* of Wildwood, New Jersey, on November 4, 1898, that ripped immigrants from southern Italy. It said, in part:

Perhaps you know that sometimes— frequently, in fact—when the tide comes in at Coney Island and other seashore resorts near New York it strews the beach with the repulsive refuse of the city which has been dumped on the waters. In the same manner the tide of immigration is now casting on our shores the human flotsam of southern Europe.

. . .. The northern races — Germans, Scandinavians, Scotch, Irish and Danes — we know as capable of appreciating the advantages of republican government and personal freedom. We are confident that they will

Early importers and distributors of bananas were mostly Italian immigrants, c. 1900. (Courtesy of Library of Congress)

soon become Americanized and take their places in the body politic, at the same time filling the ranks of our industrial and productive army.

But the immigrant from southern Italy has a far different reputation. He brings with him traits of character which do not fit in well with the condition of things here. He is generally ignorant, vicious and clannish.

Immigrants' perceived impact on the job market was a recurrent theme of critics. The *Globe* of St. Paul, Minnesota ran a letter on May 9, 1886, by J. Kearney of St. Paul, placing the blame for labor unrest squarely on the wave of new immigrants. It said, in part:

To the editor of the Globe.

In your editorial Wednesday you assert that trade unions are to blame for the riots in Chicago and Milwaukee. Now isn't this a rather intemperate assertion.

. . . Now all those men prominently connected with the rioters are Russians, Germans, Polanders and Bohemians, who were socialists in their own countries. Now, would it not be more sensible to throw the blame on our immigration laws, by which such men are admitted to the

STILL TRENDING

country. Surely this country should not become the dumping ground for
the refuse of the world.

Honest labor has an aversion for them, as they are a constant menace to it, owing to their natural discontent and their continual idleness,
which makes an apparent surplus in the labor market and which makes
their condition so impoverished that, in case of labor troubles, they are
too ready to accept money from the general fund.

The California Gold Rush, which began in 1848, was one factor that
led Chinese immigrants to arrive in the U.S. These immigrants in the mid-
nineteenth century were mostly male manual laborers who settled on the West
Coast not only for mining, but also for railroad construction, agricultural, and
other low-skilled jobs, wrote Jie Zong and Jeanne Batalova for the Migration
Policy Institute.

American workers felt they were at a disadvantage against the Chinese workers, who labored under extreme conditions for meager pay in the mines and
especially on the expanding railroad lines. During this period, the derogatory
term "Yellow Peril" was popularized.

As the number of Chinese immigrants increased so did pressure on the federal government to limit or reverse the tide. On May 6, 1882, President Chester
A. Arthur signed the Chinese Exclusion Act, banning the immigration of Chinese laborers for 10 years; a month earlier he had vetoed a version that called
for a 20-year prohibition.

Still earlier, President Rutherford B. Hayes in 1879 vetoed a version of an
Exclusion Act. In a snide—and racist—editorial comment, the *Ukiah City Press*
of California, on April 18, 1879, wrote: "Probably, if the bill had passed over
the president's veto, and the Chinese should be expelled, every tramp in this
broad land would start a laundry the next day."

The *Atlanta Constitution* of Georgia ran a one-sentence letter from "A.B." on
Jan. 19, 1889, asking a question about Chinese immigration. The letter and the
newspaper's terse response follow:

> Editors Constitution: Do the Chinese continue to come to this country
> since the passage of the act against Chinese immigration?
>
> Constitution: Yes, they come over the Mexican and Canadian bor-
> ders, disguised sometimes as Indians. It is impossible to keep them out
> of the country without resorting to rigorous and expensive measures.

A Harper's Weekly illustration in 1896 shows Chinese immigrants on Mott Street in New York City.

Elizabeth M. Bachman had a letter in the Akron Beacon Journal of Ohio, on July 2, 1918, during World War I, arguing in favor of maintaining restrictions on Chinese immigration, even invoking the "Yellow Peril" epithet. Her letter said, in part:

> Editor Beacon Journal:
>
> The manufacturers of the country are preparing to petition congress to repeal the law restricting the importation of Chinese labor into the United States, to replace the men who are in the army, and camouflaging their desire for cheap labor by saying they do not wish our women and girls to work in the factories and fields.
>
> . . . Many of the girls and women who have taken the places of our men in the war, have done so as a patriotic duty, and many more will volunteer if necessary to hold the places for the men, rather than allowing Chinese labor to supplant them.
>
> . . . We shall gladly do any work to hold the places of our men rather than have this 'Yellow Peril' lower our living to Chinese standards.

John B. Alexander had a letter in the Santa Ana Register of California, on June 4, 1913, defending Asian immigrants. His letter said, in part:

> The good people of the United States have for a long time been trying to solve the question: How shall we assimilate the immigrants that are coming to our shores; or shall they Europeanize us by changing our laws and customs?
>
> This question is a national one.
>
> . . . Now let us compare the merits of the different immigrants. I think all will agree that, comparatively speaking, the Chinese and Japanese are law-abiding and industrious. They do not spend their money in the saloons. They do not keep the police busy, and their trials in court and their hospital treatment after some of their fights do not keep up expenses to be paid by the taxpayers. In these respects I think the decision will be in favor of the Japanese and Chinese, compared with other foreigners.

Through the years, various revisions to immigration policy were passed or rejected by the powers-that-be in Washington. In addition to the Chinese Exclusion Act of 1882, the Alien Contract Labor laws of 1885 and 1887 kept certain foreign laborers out of the country.

The general Immigration Act of 1882 placed a head tax of fifty cents on each immigrant and excluded the entry of "idiots, lunatics, convicts, and persons likely to become a public charge," according to the *U.S. Citizenship and Immigration Services* website.

W.W. Husband, U.S. commissioner general of immigration, wrote a piece published by the *Gazette-Times* of Heppner, Oregon, on Aug. 24, 1922, that included a short recap of past American immigration policy. It said, in part:

> . . . Practically all of the Colonies enacted restrictive immigration laws, some of which clearly reflect the fears and also the intolerance of the founders, but the new republic took an opposite course and for a century following the Revolutionary war maintained an open door policy with respect to all classes and conditions of mankind from every land and clime.
>
> There was, of course, continued and, at times, violent opposition to this policy, but throughout the century the ideal of America as a refuge

for the world's oppressed prevailed, although it must be admitted that on occasions the refugees were treated with no little harshness.

Foreign nations banished their criminals to America and communities sent us their paupers. We complained and complained bitterly but continued to receive them until the year 1882 . . .

The question of whether a literacy test or some other means should be employed to filter out "undesirables" endured over the years. Once again, various restrictive legislative measures were approved.

The *Boston Daily Globe*, of Massachusetts on March 26, 1892, had this brief, pro-immigrant editorial comment:

> Hereafter, it seems, the immigrant who lands in New York and expects to stay here, must have at least ten dollars in his inside pocket. Had this rule prevailed in years past, America would have lost not a few adopted citizens who have risen to eminence and honor.

On the flip side, the *Progressive Farmer* of Raleigh, North Carolina, on December 23, 1902, ran an editorial headlined "One Serious Menace to American Supremacy," that said, in part:

> We are glad to see that the Senate has passed a bill prescribing a slight educational test for immigrants from foreign countries. It is not so strict as we should have liked, but the important fact is that Congress has at last come to realize the striking change for the worse in the character of our immigration during the last few years.

On March 10, 1917, the *Colorado Statesman* of Denver published an open letter from Amadeo P. Giannini, president of the Bank of Italy in San Francisco, that reacted to recent federal immigration legislation in which a large congressional majority overrode President Woodrow Wilson's veto of a bill that included a mandatory literacy test. Giannini's letter said, in part:

> It has been proved, I think, that a very large percentage of the immigrants who have come to this country illiterate have made the best sort of citizens. They have raised large families, and their children, who are American citizens, are among the very best people here.

> It has been often said, and I am convinced of the truth of the assertion, that the most dangerous immigrants are those who are educated.

Along similar lines, Dr. H.A. Elkourie, of Birmingham, Alabama, had a letter in the *Birmingham Age-Herald* of January 3, 1923, calling for morality to replace literacy as the accepted test for immigration. While it might be unclear what his motive was, Elkourie said, in part:

> To the Editor of The Age-Herald:
> . . . The writer has for many years advocated, both in public and in private, and before the committee on immigration of these United States, the test of morality rather than literacy.
> The literacy test admits the most dangerous, the most cunning and shrewd plotters. These types all read and write. On the other hand it eliminates the hard-working, honest, plain but morally clean illiterate.
> If American industry needs any immigrants at all it needs the type with muscle and brawn with a moral character instead of the kid-gloved, scheming artist, who comes as a propagator of bolshevism and anarchism.

SOUTHERN NEEDS

After passage of the Thirteenth Amendment to the Constitution in 1865—which abolished slavery and involuntary servitude, except as punishment for a crime—the South railed about the need for labor on its plantations and farms. The conundrum, however, was that while Southerners complained that waves of immigrants were congregating in Northern cities or on the West Coast, they didn't want certain immigrants. That opposition showed up in a large number of letters and editorials.

The *Florida Agriculturist* of Jacksonville, on August 28, 1907, reprinted an editorial commentary from the *Live Oak Daily Democrat* of Florida that acknowledged the severe labor shortage on the state's farms. It said, in part:

> None of us want the low classes from Europe, the 'scum' as they are called, with but little of mind or morals either, and we should keep them out as we would lepers, but we certainly need more people from somewhere unless we have been the victims of a false alarm for the past few years and our fields and factories are not really suffering from a shortage of labor.

. . . The simple question is do we need more people in the South to till our fields and work in our factories, and if so, where are we to get them from?

The *Abbeville Press and Banner* of South Carolina, on April 2, 1873, published a letter from "Long Cane" that discussed the plight of the South and blamed the North for the immigration imbalance. The rhetoric sounds similar to that heard nowadays when some on the right claim that liberals are trying to replace them with immigrants who would vote Democratic. Long Cane's letter said, in part:

> Editors Abbeville Press and Banner:
>
> Go to Europe and you will find the same discouragement — misrepresentations of the South, circulated through any railroad train, public inn, thoroughfare, or place of amusement — going to shew that the condition of the poor European immigrant is ten degrees lower than that of the veriest slave. The North is at the bottom of all this — knowing that if immigration sets in here we too will become great and powerful.
>
> What the North fears most now is manufacturing at the South, and she knows that without immigration, the South must go on producing cotton, to be manufactured elsewhere.
>
> . . . If South Carolina had two hundred thousand stout immigrants in her borders to-day, a tide of prosperity would set in which none can now anticipate. Railroads, cities, towns and villages would spring up, and soon the South would be named, as she really is, the garden spot of the United States.

The *Bossier Banner* of Bellevue, Louisiana, ran a letter from "M.G." on June 11, 1914, that expressed a desire for "certain" immigrants and an aversion to the "melting pot" concept. The letter said, in part:

> We need a class of people who will assimilate with our people, make this country their home and work for its welfare.
>
> Because of the extensive acres of cultivated and uncultivated fertile soil in the South, which is being deserted by our farmers for city life and which demonstrates to us the need of an influx of people to develop our resorces, (sic) we seek immigrants from the North and West who have spent years of hard work trying to produce profitable crops on soil that

is not suited to farming and who have studied the occupation more
thoroughly than the Southerner, who in his mild climate, as it appears
to the immigrant, merely puts his seed into the ground, and they grow.

. . . The brave and hardy English, German, Swede, Irish, and most
of the other Northern European inhabitants make desirable citizens in
our country. In the first place our ancestors, the founders of our present
Constitution and Government, were immigrants from these countries
and came here to be free in every manner, especially in their religious
rights.

. . . But, we do not seek all the immigrants from Europe, nor do we
wish those from Asia and Africa. Such immigrants as the Italians, Sicil-
ians, Greeks and Jews are very undesirable. They are not home builders
or land tillers, they do not make satisfactory workmen for our lum-
ber mills, which are numerous in Louisiana, Mississippi and the other
Southern States, and these are the places where the people from Southern
Europe and Asia land, for they are accustomed to a mild climate.

. . . The idea is held by some that America should be the 'Melting
Pot' and asylum for the oppressed; but Americans are the foremost and
leading class of people to-day and do not wish to become blended with
such classes of people.

Eliot Norton, president of the Society for Italian Immigrants in New York,
had a letter in the *Atlanta Constitution* of Georgia, on July 18, 1905, that suggested what might assist in steering Italian immigrants to the South. The letter
said, in part:

Editor Constitution: The need of the southern states for laborers, mill
workers and settlers is leading to many inquiries why, out of the large
number of immigrants coming from Europe, more cannot be diverted
southward than at present go.

. . . Accordingly the Society for Italian Immigrants will be glad to
receive printed matter relating to the advantages of settlement in the
south, and will distribute such printed matter, both in this country and
in Europe, where it will do most good in inducing immigrants to this
country to settle in the southern states.

Interestingly, Rabbi George Fox, editor of the *Jewish Monitor* of Fort Worth-Dallas, Texas, wrote a piece in the January 7, 1921, edition, saying Jewish immigrants should consider taking up farming. He said, in part:

> We are becoming urbanized at an alarming rate. One of the most serious of the objections to immigration, is that our people will drift to and settle in large cities and industrial centres. Let us admit that this objection is well-founded.
>
> Only the fewest of the Jewish immigrants go to the farms, and yet farming or rather land and agriculture are the very basis of all healthy economic life.
>
> . . . If the national organizations interested in Jewish immigration could divert the stream of those who come to these shores, from the cities and industrial centres, to the farms, the most serious objection to the incoming of foreigners would be removed . . .

As of 2021, Mexicans comprised the largest immigrant group in the United States, accounting for about 24 percent of the country's 45.3 million foreign-born residents, according to the Migration Policy Institute. Over the many years, seasonal Mexican laborers would work American farms and vineyards. The presence of the Mexican immigrants and laborers has been a subject of letters and editorials for more than a century.

The *Commercial Tribune* of Cincinnati, Ohio, on February 13, 1920, carried this wire service brief from Washington, D.C., regarding Mexican farmworkers:

> Mexican farm laborers can not be kept out of this country without an adequate border patrol of upward of 400 men, F.W. Berkshire, head of the Immigration Service at El Paso, testified today before the House Immigration Committee.
>
> Except at El Paso, Laredo and a few other points, the border, extending over a distance of 2,000 miles, is 'wide open,' he said in describing some of the difficulties encountered in trying to keep Mexican immigrants on their side of the border.

The *Daily Silver Belt* of Miami, Arizona, had a rather vicious editorial on September 21, 1923, regarding migrant workers from Mexico. Headlined "The Invading Horde," it said, in part:

Twenty-five hundred Mexican laborers crossed the border at Nogales within the past month, headed for the cotton fields and mines of Arizona. Probably at least an equal number came in during that period through other border ports as far east as middle Texas, destined for this state.

The immigration laws are ignored. Inspection of Mexican immigrants for contagious diseases is a farce; the educational test is not even perfunctorily enforced. Scouts for border employment agencies are scouring Mexico with feverish activity for labor recruits. The alien contract labor law is violated on a wholesale scale. The foreign horde is pouring into Arizona like a plague of seven-year locusts. Never before have they come in such a swelling tide.

. . . Taxpayers groan under the mounting costs of providing more and more school rooms for children who, even in the remote event that they grow up in this country to manhood and womanhood, seldom become real Americans, rarely assume the responsibilities of American citizenship, whose allegiance, with rare exceptions, remains always with the land of manana.

The *Brownsville Herald* of Texas reprinted a less-caustic editorial from the *Houston Post,* on June 11, 1918, in reference to Mexican farm labor. It said, in part:

In order to induce Mexican laborers to come into the Texas farming sections the Federal immigration authorities have modified considerably the rules governing importation of alien labor, and they can be brought in now under certain restrictions which contemplate the employer keeping check on each Mexican, holding back part of his pay to see that he does not become derelict and that he is returned to his native country in six months. While the rules are still rather severe, they do provide for securing Mexican labor to save the crops.

The Immigration Act of 1924 established nationality quotas for immigrants to the U.S. Those from Great Britain, Ireland, and Germany accounted for 70 percent of visas, while immigration was limited from Southern, Eastern, and Central Europe. The act also excluded Asians, except those from the American colony of the Philippines. But, many letters to the editor discussed the best way to "Americanize" those immigrants who did make it into the country in the early part of the twentieth century.

For example, the *Oak Leaves* of Oak Park, Illinois, on May 25, 1907, published a letter by O.C. Blackmer, who had a suggestion after a trip to Ellis Island in New York. The letter said, in part:

> Editor Oak Leaves:
>
> . . . It was a most interesting and even pathetic sight to see such crowds coming in day after day, eager and hopeful, but ignorant of our country, its laws, its manners and customs, and its language.
>
> It is especially necessary that these immigrants should learn to speak, read and write our English language at the earliest possible moment . . .
>
> . . . It is not difficult to prepare suitable elementary books in English for the use of immigrants to be placed in their hands on their arrival at Ellis Island and to take with them when they leave it for their various places in the country.

"Alliance" had a letter in the *New York Times* on September 18, 1906, on services being provided to immigrants, mostly Russian Jews. It said, in part:

> To the Editor of The New York Times:
>
> At the Educational Alliance, East Broadway and Jefferson Street, hundreds of newly arrived immigrants are being enrolled. This institution, one of the most helpful factors in the uplifting of our alien population, stands in the heart of the lower east side. It is a non-sectarian institution, but the Russian Jews, who people this neighborhood almost exclusively, constitute over 90 per cent, of those reached by the Alliance.
>
> The immigrant, a stranger to the customs and language of his adopted country, settles in the Ghetto, where alone he can make himself understood. It is the main purpose of the institution to Americanize him. To accomplish this object most effectively classes are formed in American history, civics, and kindred subjects. These are taught both in English and Yiddish, but as soon as some fluency is attained with the former the use of Yiddish is discouraged.

F. Francis had a letter in the *Brooklyn Daily Eagle* of New York, on February 1, 1917, with a strategy for Americanizing immigrants. Of course, a number of foreign-language newspapers already were being published in the United States. Francis' letter said, in part:

> Editor Brooklyn Daily Eagle:
> . . . The immigrants need to be instructed in American customs. Reading to the immigrants the Declaration of Independence in the English language would do little or no good.
> . . . The newspapers published in this country in the different languages spoken by the immigrants only keep them aliens in feeling.
> . . . What is needed to remedy this evil is the publishing of a daily newspaper, printed in the dialects spoken by immigrants. The editors and writers for this polyglot paper should be native Americans, whose ancestry should go back three generations in America. It takes three generations for the 'hyphen' to disappear from the family tree.
> . . . The bulk of the immigrants read and write their mother tongue. All they need is some newspaper to show them what pure Americanism is.

The *Courier Democrat* of Langdon, North Dakota, on February 26, 1903, ran a letter from reader Peter P. Kopriva of Langdon that had first appeared in the *St. Paul Daily News* of Minnesota, and which argued against singling out people by nationality. It said, in part:

> . . . This country owes much of its greatness to immigrants with un-American names. An immigrant from England or Ireland comes to this country and when here the short time necessary to become naturalized considers himself a full-fledged American, and because his German and Bohemian neighbors can speak one language more than he, they are to him foreigners, although their ancestors came here perhaps three generations ago.
> If Sam Jones is sent to the workhouse the papers do not tell that Jones is a Yankee, but if Fritz Schmidt and John Zeleny commit a misdemeanor some papers do not consider the item complete unless they state that Schmidt is German, or at least that Zeleny is Bohemian. Those little things do not go unnoticed by the 'foreigners' and many act accordingly.

Regarding the Americanization process, a letter from "Civil Engineer" in the *New York Tribune* on February 8, 1920, was directed at all parties concerned, saying, in part:

> To the Editor of The Tribune.
>
> Sir: I respectfully submit the following platform on Americanization: For the foreigner — Become a citizen as soon as possible; do not join any organization that advocates the overthrow of this country; learn the English language; honor and obey the laws of this country; do not abuse this country by speech or act.
>
> For the American — Do not exploit the foreigner; teach him the Americanism of Roosevelt; aid the foreigner in every way.
>
> For both — Practice the Golden Rule; make every effort to become a true American.

Chapter 12

Scandals Aside, Rise of the Big Screen and Pop Culture

When Emile Reynaud cranked small, hand-painted glass plates onto a screen for French audiences in 1892 or even when a year later a team assigned by Thomas Edison unveiled a Kinetoscope, a precursor to the modern projector, few could have envisioned what was to come: a film industry that would help create and largely dominate popular culture to this day.

Like any startup, the industry sought to establish its footing in the early 1900s. The initial makeshift film studios were in the New York metropolitan area, with one in Philadelphia and two in Chicago, according to author Greg Merritt in his book, *Room {1219}: The Life of Fatty Arbuckle, the Mysterious Death of Virginia Rappe, and the Scandal that Changed Hollywood*.

But the film industry began in earnest when the first permanent studio was established in 1910 by the Selig Polyscope Company in Los Angeles, and the first Hollywood studio was established on Sunset Boulevard in 1911. While D.W. Griffith's 1915 landmark film *The Birth of a Nation* created the first major stir in the feature film world, it wasn't until the 1920s that Hollywood really helped spawn pop culture in the United States.

The public began to glorify glamorous stars of the Silver Screen, encouraged by expanding newspaper coverage. By 1921, a number of papers were dedicating a full page to movie coverage—for example, the *Evening Public Ledger* of Philadelphia, Pennsylvania, had the *Daily Movie Magazine*.

But in September 1921, Hollywood and the world were jolted by the arrest at the St. Francis Hotel in San Francisco of popular actor Roscoe "Fatty" Arbuckle in the death of a twenty-five-year-old model/actress.

"The ensuing scandal created a firestorm of controversy not just around Arbuckle but the entire motion picture industry," wrote Aaron T. Whitehead in his 2015 paper, *The 'Fatty' Arbuckle Scandal, Will Hays, and Negotiated Morality in 1920s America.*

Arbuckle, who hailed from Kansas and was one of nine children, first appeared on stage when he was 8. He eventually sang and danced and clowned around in that venue. He first appeared on film with the Selig company in 1909 and occasionally played a role in other pictures for four years. In 1914, Paramount Pictures gave Arbuckle a lucrative contract to make movies with Mabel Normand.

Over the 1921 Labor Day weekend, model/actress Virginia Rappe had attended a big party in Arbuckle's honor. At the party, Rappe died, and Arbuckle was accused of killing the woman after sexually assaulting her. He was arrested and jailed for three weeks.

He claimed that after a few drinks, Rappe screamed that she couldn't breathe and started ripping off her clothes. He also said she vomited in the bathroom; he and some guests put her in a room of her own, but she ended up succumbing to a ruptured bladder.

A grand jury handed down an indictment against Arbuckle on a manslaughter charge. Arbuckle's arrest and his subsequent legal ordeal, involving three trials, were major fodder for the nation's newspapers, especially those owned by William Randolph Hearst. The sensationalist Hearst press, fueled by a simple desire to boost circulation, covered the Arbuckle case in a "criminally irresponsible" manner, wrote David A. Yallop in his book, *The Day the Laughter Stopped.*

The public's growing fascination with early silent-movie stars and the details of their lives morphed into the powerful role of pop culture today. A large chunk of the public nowadays clings to the actions, thoughts and other doings of film, music, TV, and sports stars in particular, even shaping the people's thoughts on societal affairs, including current politics. A star such as Taylor Swift can boast a huge following—and attract either adulation or scorn, depending on one's perspective.

In the 1920s, those concerned about what they perceived to be a moral decline in American life took aim at some forms of popular culture, such as jazz, which was often referred to as the "devil's music" largely because it was

Roscoe "Fatty" Arbuckle, c. between 1920 and 1925. (Courtesy of Library of Congress)

dominated by Black people, was viewed as the music of brothels, and it departed from structure into improvisation, according to PBS. By the end of the decade, more than sixty locales in America banned the playing of jazz in public dance halls.

Despite any societal misgivings, the century-old Arbuckle case proved that scandal titillated the public imagination back then and continues to do so. Early Hollywood also saw other scandals involving mysterious deaths and drugs and, of course, the incidents didn't end then.

In the contemporary film world, the counter defamation lawsuits of Amber Heard and Johnny Depp garnered much national attention in early 2022. A staggering total of 83.9 million hours were spent watching the trial, with the verdict announcement drawing 3.5 million peak viewers, according to Bohdan Zaveruha, writing on the *StreamsCharts* website.

And, actor Kevin Spacey faced legal travails in the United States and Great Britain. On July 26, 2023, he was found not guilty in Britain on nine charges,

A Black American military jazz band plays in the courtyard of a Paris hospital for wounded patients in 1918. In the 1920s, jazz was viewed by many as a threat to the American way of life. (Courtesy of Library of Congress)

including multiple counts of sexual and indecent assault. He also was exonerated in 2022 in federal court in New York in a civil case brought by actor Anthony Rapp in which the latter alleged sexual abuse.

In addition, cinematographer Halyna Hutchins was killed when a gun held by actor and co-producer Alec Baldwin fired on the set of the film "Rust," on October 21, 2021. In April 2024, the film's armorer, Hannah Gutierrez, was found guilty of involuntary manslaughter and was sentenced to eighteen months in prison. Previously, first assistant director David Halls, who was responsible for a safety check on the gun, received six months' probation. Baldwin was to go on trial in July 2024 on an involuntary manslaughter charge to which he pleaded not guilty.

In the sports world, quarterback Deshaun Watson was accused by more than two dozen women who worked at massage parlors of coercive and lewd sexual behavior—even sexual assault in two cases. He is now on the Cleveland Browns team.

In the music world, R&B singer R. Kelly was sentenced in June 2022 to thirty years in prison on federal racketeering and sex-trafficking charges. And in March 2024, federal agents raided two homes of music mogul Sean "Diddy" Combs, who is facing multiple civil lawsuits accusing him of sexual abuse, rape and sex trafficking.

The public got a taste of pop culture scandal even before the Arbuckle ordeal when eight Chicago White Sox baseball players, including star "Shoeless" Joe Jackson, were accused of throwing the 1919 World Series. Although the players were found not guilty in court, league Commissioner Kenesaw Mountain Landis issued a lifetime ban against them.

Recently, controversy surrounded quarterback Colin Kaepernick for taking a knee prior to his National Football League games as a statement against oppression of Black people and other people of color. His stance basically cost him his career as a player.

The above scandals all captured the public's attention through traditional and social media. Still, it was the Arbuckle case, which coincided with the soon-to-be spectacular rise of Hollywood in the American psyche, that really triggered the almost obsessive coverage of and thirst for popular culture. Perhaps it was the fact that the case involved an individual rather than a group or team of people, or perhaps it was because the "big screen" presented the characters as larger than life.

As columnist Deliha Suraha wrote in the *Mirror* of Stillwater, Minnesota, on August 30, 1923:

> Nearly thirty million American people read the newspapers every day in the week and on Sunday one half as many additional readers join the throng and they are morbidly curious as to how the scandal runs on the morals of Hollywood; who get a divorce and why; what and where the current source of moonshine is; what prominent personalities eat for breakfast, luncheon, dinner and supper and what they drink, how they drink it and why.

After Arbuckle was indicted, at least some movie theaters stopped showing his films. But that action wasn't supported by everyone. The *Daily Ardmoreite* of Ardmore, Oklahoma, ran an editorial on September 13, 1921, that said, in part:

> If 'Fatty' Arbuckle is guilty of a capital offense it is up to the courts to do their duty, and one who has been in the west can vouch for the fact that justice is meted out in all cases. If his guilt is proven, he alone should be made to suffer; his masterpieces that have brought laughs to millions should not be burned; the public should be allowed to continue to laugh at his antics, his humor and smile at his beaming countenance from the billboards.
>
> Turning thumbs down on the comedian, means thumbs down on popular comedy, both on the screen and stage.

The *New York Herald* of New York City, on September 18, 1921, ran a brief wire story with a dateline of Thermopolis, Wyoming, that showed how Arbuckle's case fomented passion. The article began:

> A mob of 150 men and boys, many of them cowboys, entered the Maverick Theatre here last night where a 'Fatty' Arbuckle film was being shown and shot up the screen and seized the film, taking it into the streets and burning part of it.

A key witness against Arbuckle was Rappe's friend Bambina Maude Delmont, who had been at the fateful party but also had a questionable past that included criminal activities. A newspaper wire account in the *Arizona Republican* on the day of the indictment, September 14, 1921, said, in part:

> Arbuckle's mood throughout the day was one of indifference to everything but the weaving out of the story over the tragedy in the inquest. He paid no attention to newspaper photographers snapping him from all sides, disdained the many questions that were asked him by newspaper and other interviewers and seemed to show a disposition to let things take their course without direction from him.

Arbuckle was tried three times for manslaughter. The first two trials ended in hung juries. In the third trial, the jury, on April 12, 1922, deliberated five minutes before acquitting him. Ultimately, Delmont changed her story so many times prior to the trial that the prosecution didn't call her to the witness stand.

In announcing the not-guilty determination, the jury foreman read a statement:

> Acquittal is not enough for Roscoe Arbuckle. We feel that a great injustice has been done him. We feel also that it was only our plain duty to give him this exoneration, under the evidence, for there was not the slightest proof adduced to connect him in any way with the commission of a crime.

Despite the seeming conclusion to the Arbuckle case, it continued to generate much reaction among newspaper readers. W.W. Wall had a letter in *The Birmingham News* of Alabama on January 3, 1923, that said:

> To the Editor The Birmingham News:
>
> I have been reading with some interest the letters appearing in The News exchanging views on the Arbuckle case. Personally, I am not particularly interested in seeing Mr. Arbuckle's pictures, because I do not care for that type of comedy. However, I think it a very serious undertaking for every individual to pass judgment or express opinions that might be detrimental to the success and prayers of any man.
>
> In my opinion this actor was vindicated by the courts that tried him and under the circumstances I feel that the opinions of our courts should be final. If we are not to uphold the decision of American courts, why have courts?

In the same edition of the *News*, J.G. Sedberry of Birmingham also had a letter defending Arbuckle—with biblical references and criticism of the city's movie censor, Myrtelle Snell. It said, in part:

> To the Editor The Birmingham News:
>
> When the Master was on earth, He preached a gospel of love and forgiveness, and yet the churches, preachers and so-called reformers are making a concerted effort to deprive Roscoe ('Fatty') Arbuckle of the means of earning a livelihood, forgetting, it seems, that it was the Master

Himself who said, 'Let him that is without guilt cast the first stone'; and if we use that idea as a basis for our Christianity, how many of us would be in a position to criticise (sic) the other fellow for his misdeeds?

That Arbuckle made a big mistake every one knows, and 'Fatty' himself admits, but that he deliberately committed murder is an absurd and ridiculous idea to which no reasonable person will subscribe . . .

. . . Mrs. Snell should let the patrons of the various motion picture theaters decide for themselves whether or not they want the Arbuckle films, bearing in mind that while she is the city's official movie censor, she is not the guardian of our morals.

The *Cordova Daily Times* of the Alaska Territory, on January 2, 1923, had a letter from Frank H. Foster, who had a very different take on the matter. His letter said, in part:

. . . Arbuckle was never anything more than a clever clown whose gross shape coupled with much agility, made his antics popular among the young people.

. . . He got himself into a mess and in spite of the fact that a jury acquitted him, the great mass of the people consider him in a large measure responsible for the death of Virginia Rapp. (sic)

The disgusting details of the offense charged have been dissected by every yellow journal in the country and every kid who once shouted with merriment at Fatty's amusing or has read the sorry tale.

To drag these films out of the dust into which the public has condemned them for the purpose of saving the bacon of some film promoter can help no one other than the promoter and will make a hero of a disreputable and indecent character. Personally I wouldn't let one of my youngsters go near a show house whose proprietor thought so little of his public as to exhibit Fatty Arbuckle films.

On January 18, 1923, the *Belt Valley Times* of Belt, Montana, published a letter from "A Father of Three Growing Boys" that initially was in the *Great Falls Leader* and that had praise for Ohio officials regarding Arbuckle. The letter said, in part:

Editor Leader:

Hats off to the board of censors of Ohio who most emphatically state that they do not propose to allow persons of the Fatty Arbuckle type to be paraded before the youth of their fair state in the guise of a reformed hero.

Coming nearer home, again hats off to the editor of our own Belt Valley Times, whose editor, after spending his best years in training of the youth of his locality, condemns the maudlin sentimentality which seeks to throw a halo about the head of the discredited comedian, in the following terse commentary:

'We imagine that Fatty Arbuckle could repent just as sincerely by slinging hash in a restaurant as he can making a quarter of a million in the movies. At least we are willing that he should try it. . . .'

. . . If Fatty is really sincere in his desire to reform, let him get out of the parasite class and join the ranks of the producers. Let him get back to nature and establish his 'location' upon some sunny slope near to nature and there by some real honest, callus-building (sic) toil assist in producing a portion of the things upon which we live.

"I.M.H." had a letter in the *Seattle Star* of Washington on January 6, 1923, defending Arbuckle and curiously placing the blame for a societal lack of morality elsewhere. It said, in part:

> . . . I do not care for straight comedies, but have seen them in connection with some other plays I wished to see, and will say I do not think 'Fatty' will corrupt the morals of any of our twentieth century boys and girls. It will be the mothers, in most cases, who are to blame.
>
> If they did not attend so many clubs, dances, political meetings, etc., leaving the children to servants, there would be little danger from outside influences if the homes were right, and if Christ's teaching is followed, viz., 'Let him that is without sin amongst you cast the first stone,' and not even 'Fatty' would need to dodge, large as he is.

The *Omaha Morning Bee* of Nebraska printed a letter from T.P. Ward, of Howells, Nebraska, on New Year's Day 1923 that criticized Arbuckle's detractors, saying, in part:

> To the Editor of The Omaha Bee: The discussions of country editors regarding Fatty Arbuckle are disgusting in the extreme.
>
> . . . Arbuckle is no worse than thousands of others that are defaming him, and I hope the day may come when I can take his hand and tell him I believe in him, also that l may meet some of these knockers face to face and tell them to go jump in the lake.

However, the same newspaper had a series of letters on Christmas Day 1922 that had a different view of Arbuckle and Hollywood generally. One letter, from George Grimes, said:

> The return of Fatty Arbuckle to the films can do no good to the movies. The public would like to believe that the majority of screen stars lead more wholesome lives than his was revealed to be by the trial of the Rappe case.
>
> To set him up now as a hero, winning the applause of millions is unwise. The producers may find his films unprofitable. This, at least, will offer the public a chance to demonstrate whether it is sincere in demanding that Hollywood folks live clean lives.

In a letter to the *Seattle Star* of Washington, on January 11, 1923, "A Mother's Appeal" compared the Arbuckle case to that of her son, who apparently took his own life. It said:

> Editor The Star:
>
> May I say a few words in regard to the Arbuckle strife? My reason for so doing is this: I am a mother whose son had committed a sin very similar to Arbuckle's. And this misfortune was visited upon him in exactly the same manner. And, l am sorry to say, it was womankind that was strongest against my boy's forgiveness.
>
> My boy's atonement was sincere, which, I believe, is also the case with Arbuckle. However, my boy did not get his chance to come back, and so, with a broken heart, he committed self-destruction and appeared at a higher tribunal, to face a Judge who says, 'Tho your sins be as crimson, I will wash them white as snow." And as this unfortunate trouble with Arbuckle is so very similar to my poor, broken-hearted son's, I wish to

appeal, just as a mother would do, in behalf of 'Fatty' Arbuckle's forgiveness. Please give him a chance to make good.

On February 12, 1922, the *Arizona Republican* of Phoenix published an editorial that, in citing the Arbuckle case, criticized Hollywood while grudgingly conceding that the quality of its product was improving. It said, in part:

> . . . The industry has come to stay. It was accepted at first only because of its novelty. The acting in the beginning was at first absurd. It would not have been tolerated at a cross roads school house by speaking actors. It was the motion of the pictures that instantly attracted and held long enough for the character of the pictures to improve. Then it was permanently fastened and the industry has fairly well advanced as the popular taste demanded advancement.

A.G. Pickett of the Rialto theater in Phoenix had a letter in the same newspaper on February 18, 1922, in response to the editorial. Pickett's letter in defense of Hollywood included the following on the Arbuckle case:

> To the Editor:
> . . . The first paragraph of the editorial, referring to the Arbuckle matter, dwells on 'the eagerness with which the movie colonists and a pastor of the church rushed to the defense of this outrageous character.'
> Was that eagerness any greater than the eagerness with which the newspapers and newspaper writers rushed to the condemnation of the motion picture industry as a whole, and is that eagerness on the part of the newspapers and newspaper writers any less restrained even today, in the light of the recent developments?

Still, there were many public calls for Hollywood to clean up its act.

Even before the Arbuckle case, on July 24, 1921, the *Kansas City Star* published a poem in letter form from "A.S.A." While the tone was tongue-in-cheek, the moral for the film industry was clear. It said:

> Dear Editor: I'd like to air a protest if you will, a prayer, from one of that abused clan, the humble motion picture fan. Our sturdy frames are

A Hollywood set for the movie *In the Palace of the King*, produced by the Goldwyn Studio in 1923. (Courtesy of Library of Congress)

all but wrecks, from endless plays of muck and sex. Films flaunting sin, we've long endured; we liked 'em once but now we're cured. We're fed up quite on bathing girls, whose chief assets are legs and curls. On heroes tall with brawny arms, truants from long neglected farms. They say the outlook's mighty slim, the box receipts are growing slim. Oh, 'movie kings,' the fault's with you, if all this hard times talk is true. Give us, pray harken to our plea, we supplicate on bended knee, a change. Films that the famil-ee, the kiddies, ma and sis can see. Something that's wholesome, virile clean; our shekels then again you'll glean.

Others more formally took aim at Hollywood and its perceived lack of morality. Church, women's, and youth groups demonstrated throughout the nation, calling for Hollywood movies to be censored. By 1922, the federal government and 36 states were weighing laws against the industry, which in defensive response formed the Motion Picture Producers and Directors Association (MPPDA).

Will H. Hays, a Republican who had been President Warren G. Harding's postmaster general, was named head of the new organization on January 14, 1922. He created a strict movie production code—with a long list of informal rules for everyone from producers and directors to writers to follow—to stave off the censors.

Following Hays' appointment, the *South Bend News-Times* of Indiana, on February 8, 1922, had an editorial comment that included the following:

> . . . The exhibitors, owners of many millions of dollars in theater build-ings, made a brave start when, under pressure of the Arbuckle scandal, they demanded a moral clean-up of the industry.
>
> The exhibitors who show pictures have no control over those who make them except through concerted action and they tried their best. It seems that their best was futile and that the millionaires who control film production have the same old disregard for decency and moral con-ditions which they showed before the Arbuckle disclosures.
>
> The same men who hired Will Hays away from the cabinet employ these favorites whose popular diversion is the holding of 'dope parties.'
>
> Will they boss Hays or can Hays boss them?

If the intention of the film moguls was to control Hays and relegate him to figurehead status, their plan failed miserably, according to author Andy Ed-monds. "They had created a power-hungry monster to whom the studios now had to answer," he wrote in his book *FRAME-UP!: The Untold Story of Roscoe 'Fatty' Arbuckle.*

In fact, "The Cavalier," in a letter to the *Washington Herald* of the District of Columbia, on April 23, 1922, questioned Hays' power grab. The letter said, in part:

> To the Editor, The Washington Herald:
>
> "Will Hays, late chief postman and now guardian angel of the mov-ies, has ruled that no more pictures may be shown in this country of Roscoe (Fatty) Arbuckle. The comedian of the screens has just been acquitted of a charge of manslaughter after spending a fortune for his defense.
>
> . . . By what divine act of God has Will Hays possessed himself with the papal power of depriving Mr. Arbuckle of the freedom of the screen? Who is Will Hays to take such a holier-than-thou attitude? Is he so base as to inflict punishment on a man who has suffered enough just to estab-lish a certain amount of prestige in his new office of King of the Movies?

However, "A Constant Reader of the Post" had a letter in the *Boston Sunday Post* on December 31, 1922, praising Hays. It said, in part:

> To the Editor of the Post:
> Sir — Will Hays is doing a splendid thing to the public and to Hollywood. He did a splendid thing to Mary Miles Minter and to Wanda Hawley and also to Arbuckle, but as long as Fatty Arbuckle was arraigned and found not guilty, I think Mr. Hays has done right when he issued a Christmas pardon. Arbuckle should continue his pictures.
> . . . Let me also continue, that Mr. Hays is worthy of his job.
> . . . He is a great help to Hollywood, and to the public, and the public thanks him.

And, Hays' actions had the support of more conservative citizens. The Brookings, South Dakota, chapter of the Woman's Christian Temperance Union adopted a resolution in mid-January 1923 against "moral depravity" in Hollywood, even referencing the Volstead Act, which Congress passed to enforce the national prohibition on the sale of alcohol.

The resolution said:

> Although not proven guilty of murder Mr. Arbuckle stands before the court of public opinion as guilty of violation of the Volstead act and is therefore an unconvicted criminal in the eyes of all law-abiding citizens. The W. C. T. U. disapproves any action, however charitably intended, that may cloak such moral depravity as that which marked such an association of actors as those from Hollywood who met in San Francisco by Mr. Arbuckle's invitation.

On a lighter note, the *Paragould Soliphone* of Arkansas, on October 30, 1922, commented: "The ten-year-old geography student who pronounced 'Los Angeles' as 'loose angels' must have heard some of those Hollywood scandals."

A number of newspapers continued ganging up on the movie industry. The *Free Trader-Journal and Ottawa Fair Dealer* of Illinois, on February 4, 1922, had such an editorial, which said, in part:

> . . . Hollywood, as a representative colony of the craft, has been pictured by many who have visited that vicinity as a hotbed of immorality and a place of open defiance to the laws of sobriety and decency.

. . . Take Arbuckle, for instance, a man taken from behind the bar, where his clownishness made business for his employers, and elevated to stardom with an income equalling or exceeding that of a cabinet officer. Could it be expected that he would indulge in anything but extravagant and questionable pleasures, with all the ostentation possible?

Kitchel Pixley had a letter in the *Seattle Star* of Washington, on October 24, 1922, that made fun of British Lord Louis Mountbatten's plans to visit the American film capital. It said, in part:

Editor The Star:

Lord Louis Mountbatten, cousin of King George IV., is visiting Hollywood 'to see how things are done there,' and he says that American newspapers are wonderful, and he's 'just wild over American slang.'

. . . But His Cousinship Mountbatten is an ace we've drawn to our hand of four kings. He makes the boilings of our pot safe.

. . . He's the cheese, in short, and every newspaper man should get wise to it.

Nor are there any horseflies on Louis when he selects Hollywood as the emporium where 'things get done.' At Hollywood they pull off every sort of act known, from promiscuous swappin' of wives to swattin' of the conks of make-believe kings with custard pies.

At Hollywood he'll see art, clad in the clothes that mother gave her, out hangin' up moral dictates on the wash line. At Hollywood he'll find joy-stuff that's far above one-half of one per cent. Atta boy, Louie! You're the purple necktie! Take the city's key and glimpse all the key holes!

Colonel Billie Mayfield, who wrote a weekly column for newspapers in Temple and Houston, Texas, was even more vituperative in a piece that *The Call of the North*, a Ku Klux Klan propaganda publication based in St. Paul, Minnesota, reprinted on February 15, 1924. Some of his rhetoric sounds familiar today, as Hollywood often remains the target of many on the right. Mayfield's column said, in part:

. . . Today the American people are beginning to learn the source of the present day degeneracy. The school of the movie is solely and absolutely responsible for the evil that saturated the social life of the day.

. . . Old Satan himself, were he the reigning czar of Hollywood, instead of an assistant, couldn't design more soul destroying propaganda than is daily coming out of that great cancer on American life, with approval of every censor board in America save those of Ohio and Pennsylvania.

No man can forever revel in the salacious and debauching propaganda of the screen without absorbing some of its evil influences.

An editorial in *The Evening Star* of Washington, D.C., on February 25, 1922, pushed back on such screeds about Hollywood's perceived immorality, dismissing generalizations about an entire industry. It said, in part:

. . . It is manifestly unfair to think of the people of one trade, or profession, or art, as being scandalous because a small fraction of 1 per cent of them get into trouble. To denounce Hollywood as an improper place to live because they have had a murder there is to speak unfairly, foolishly. People of good brains and good instincts do not thus make charges against a whole class.

John W. Sibley of Birmingham, Alabama, had a letter in that city's *Birmingham Age-Herald* on October 28, 1922, that defended Hollywood based on a personal visit. It said:

To the Editor of The Age-Herald:

. . . On my recent trip to the west I spent 10 days in Hollywood, and can testify to the good order and quietness that prevailed, and the splendid behavior of the citizens of that interesting city.

It is certainly a splendid church-going town, as was evidenced by the fact that on the two Sundays I was in Hollywood the church was crowded that I attended, and I heard as fine an orthodox sermon as I have ever listened to anywhere.

It was my good fortune to be honored with a pass through the Lasky studio, where I witnessed the production of scenes in a number of forthcoming pictures. The behavior inside the studios was as fine as I have ever seen anywhere, and I was amazed at the immense amount of work and capital necessary in producing pictures.

I feel sure that if the good citizens of America would patronize the best type of pictures that it would soon revolutionize the industry and eliminate things that are objectionable.

In fact, Hollywood was expanding by massive strides. As an unsigned column in *The Sunday Star* of Washington, D.C., on April 8, 1923, noted:

There were 4,000 people in Hollywood a dozen years ago.

It has a population of nearly 100,000 now. At that time the board of trade made an announcement which some people thought was too optimistic. They heralded their faith in the future of the little town at the edge of the mountains by predicting for Hollywood a population of 8,000 in ten years.

And, the *Bismarck Tribune* of North Dakota, on February 16, 1922, while castigating Hollywood's perceived debauchery and lamenting the moral state of society, acknowledged that the motion picture industry was here to stay. The editorial comment said, in part:

Do you remember the first movie houses in the old home town? People shook their heads when shoe-string plungers threw caution to the winds and opened 'nickelodeons' in small store-rooms.

. . . Well, the future is here and we've found out. The nickelodeon has become a palace. The stars make more than President Harding. They roll in luxury, which breeds decay.

After all, though, the Hollywood intrigues and debauches are merely boils that have broken out from the foul jazz blood that races through present-day life.

In his movies column that ran in the *Seattle Star* of Washington, John D. Howard, on April 5, 1924, hyperbolically summed up the majesty of Hollywood—for better or worse:

HOLLYWOOD, accused enigma of the world, has ushered in more empires and kingdoms, more villages and townships than all history has recorded.

In the bed of its own realm, centuries come and go. Peacefully, Hollywood sits by and sees empires totter and fall.

It views love in its lustrous bloom; sees hate; knows duty; nurses sickness; sits beside death.

An unsigned column on the movies page of the *New York Tribune*, on June 12, 1921, included this paragraph:

Twenty years ago there was no motion picture industry. To-day only three industries in America — railroads, meat packing and clothing manufacturing — have more money invested in them than motion pictures. To-day the fourth industry in America, and not yet of age. That is certainly coming up from nowhere.

And, the *Arizona Republican* of Phoenix, on February 12, 1922, spoke in an editorial of the public's growing love affair with the new industry:

. . . The pictures are what the American people want and will always want with improvements, to the demands for which the industry is quickly responsive.

And the movie industry is yet young and increasing in virility. When audiences are not approving they are tolerant. They seldom or never describe a picture as 'rotten,' a term which is of frequent application to shows on the speaking stage.

Afterword

Most books and research projects begin at the library. This one was no exception. The Central branch of the Enoch Pratt Free Library system offered an inviting starting point, and the wonderful librarians there provided the service and support that I needed. Likewise, staff in The Library of Congress' Prints & Photographs Reading Room and its Copyright Office were extremely helpful. I wish to thank them all.

I also want to thank my editors at Sentient Publications, Deborah Weisser and Marissa Cassayre, for their much-appreciated diligence, patience, and expertise. On my end, a sincere thanks to Jill Yesko for all her hard publicity work.

I would be remiss without recognizing Chris Corbett, Matt Mulcahy, and Ramsey Flynn, accomplished authors, for their sage advice on the publishing industry.

Other journalists who have offered support and inspiration over the years include my hiking buddies, Mike Ahlers and Pete Pichaske, as well as John Scheinman, Beth Hughes, Mary Robbins Phelan, and Steve Kelly.

I also would like to recognize and express my love for my siblings, Laurie, Mark, Debbie, and Rich and their assorted spouses. In addition, I really value the input and goodwill of friends Eileen O., Jay S., Barbara D., Rick G., Dan B., Vanessa I., Deb M., Howard M., Paul S., and Terri F., as well as Baltimore neighbors the Simmons and Kelly/Reilly families.

Bibliography

BOOKS

Adams, David Wallace. *Education for Extinction: American Indians and the Boarding School Experience, 1875-1928.* Lawrence: University Press of Kansas, 1995.

Allen, John. *Thinking Critically: Renewable Energy.* San Diego: Reference Point Press, 2014.

Barclay, Donald A. *Disinformation: The Nature of Facts and Lies in the Post-Truth Era.* Lanham, MD: Rowman & Littlefield, 2022.

Barclay, Donald A. *Fake News, Propaganda, the Plain Old Lies: How to Find Trustworthy Information in the Digital Age.* Lanham, MD: Rowman & Littlefield, 2018.

Bartlett, Bruce. *The Truth Matters: A Citizen's Guide to Separating Facts from Lies and Stopping Fake News in its Tracks.* New York: Ten Speed, 2017.

Bianculli, Anthony J. *Trains and Technology: The American Railroad in the Nineteenth Century; Volume 1, Locomotives.* Newark, DE: University of Delaware Press, 2001.

Bok, Derek C. and John T. Dunlop. *Labor and the American Community.* New York: Simon and Schuster, 1970.

Boyne, Walter J. *The Smithsonian Book of Flight.* Washington, D.C.: Smithsonian Books, 1987.

Brody, David. *Workers in Industrial America: Essays on the Twentieth Century Struggle.* New York: Oxford University Press, 1980.

Cooper, Michael L. *Indian School: Teaching the White Man's Way.* New York: Clarion Books, 1999.

Cousins, Mark. *The Story of Film.* Glasgow, UK: Pavilion Books, 2011.

Daly, Christopher B. *Covering America: A Narrative History of a Nation's Journalism.* Amherst, MA: University of Massachusetts Press, 2012.

Dick, Ron and Dan Patterson. *Aviation Century: The Early Years.* Erin, Ontario: Boston Mill Press, 2003.

DuBois, Ellen Carol. *Suffrage: Women's Long Battle for the Vote.* New York: Simon and Schuster, 2020.

Dudden, Faye E. *Fighting Chance: The Struggle Over Woman Suffrage and Black Suffrage in Reconstruction America.* New York: Oxford University Press, 2011.

Dunbar-Ortiz, Roxanne. *Not a Nation of Immigrants: Settler Colonialism, White Supremacy, and a History of Erasure and Exclusion.* Boston: Beacon Press, 2021.

Edmonds, Andy. *FRAME-UP!: The Untold Story of Roscoe "Fatty" Arbuckle.* New York: William Morrow, 1991.

Fenton, Tom. *The Failure of the Media in the 21ˢᵗ Century.* Golden, CO: Fulcrum, 2009.

Frank, Andrew. *The Birth of Black America: The Age of Discovery and the Slave Trade.* New York: Chelsea House, 1996.

Naff, Clay Farris, ed. *Fueling the Future: Solar Power.* Farmington Hills, MI: Greenhaven, 2007.

Gant, Scott. *We're All Journalists: The Transformation of the Press and Reshaping of the Law in the Internet Age.* New York: Free Press, 2007.

Gladstone, Brooke. The Influencing Machine: Brooke Gladstone on the Media. New York: W.W. Norton, 2011.

Grant, H. Roger. *Railroads and the American People.* Indianapolis: Indiana University Press, 2012.

Hacker, Jacob S. and Paul Pierson. *Let Them Eat Tweets: How the Right Rules in an Age of Extreme Inequality.* New York: Liveright, 2020.

Hamilton, Alexander, John Jay, and James Madison. *The Federalist.* New York: Modern Library, original date 1787; intro written in 1937.

Harcup, Tony, *Oxford Dictionary of Journalism.* New York: Oxford University Press, 2014.

Henderson, D.A., M.D. *Smallpox: The Death of a Disease.* Amherst, NY: Prometheus, 2009.

Hills, Richard L. *Power from Wind: A history of windmill technology.* New York: Cambridge University Press, 1994.

Holt, Michael F. *By One Vote: The Disputed Presidential Election of 1876.* Lawrence, KS: University Press of Kansas, 2008.

Hull, N.E.H., Williamjames Hoffer, and Peter Charles Hoffer, eds. *The Abortion Rights Controversy in America.* Chapel Hill: University of North Carolina Press, 2004.

Johnson, David Alan. *The Last Weeks of Abraham Lincoln: A Day-by-Day Account of His Personal, Political, and Military Challenges.* Amherst, NY: Prometheus, 2018.

Knowles, Michael. *Speechless: Controlling Words, Controlling Minds.* Washington, D.C.: Regnery, 2021.

Langguth, A.J. *Union 1812: The Americans Who Fought the Second War of Independence.* New York: Simon and Schuster, 2006.

Lee, Erika. *America for Americans: A History of Xenophobia in the United States.* New York: Basic Books, 2019.

Lynching in America: Confronting the Legacy of Racial Terror. Montgomery, AL: Equal Justice Initiative, 3rd edition, 2017.

McCann, Carole R. *Birth Control Politics in the United States 1916-1945.* Ithaca, NY: Cornell University Press, 1994.

McCorquodale, Sara. *Influence: How social media influencers are shaping our digital future.* London: Bloomsbury Business, 2020.

McLuhan, Marshall. *Understanding Media: The Extensions of Man.* New York: McGraw-Hill, 1964.

Manning, Chandra. *What this Cruel War Was Over: Soldiers, Slavery, and the Civil War.* New York: Vintage Civil War Library, 2007.

Maurantonio, Nicole. *Confederate Exceptionalism: Civil War Myth and Memory in the Twenty-First Century.* Lawrence: University Press of Kansas, 2019.

Mchangama, Jacob. *Free Speech: A History from Socrates to Social Media.* New York: Basic Books, 2022.

Merritt, Greg. *Room {1219}: The Life of Fatty Arbuckle, the Mysterious Death of Virginia Rappe, and the Scandal that Changed Hollywood.* Chicago: Chicago Review Press, 2013.

Miller, Joe, Dr. Özlem Türeci, and Dr. Ugur Sahin. *The Vaccine: Inside the Race to Conquer the Covid-19 Pandemic.* New York: St. Martin's Press, 2022.

Morris Jr., Roy. *Fraud of the Century: Rutherford B. Hayes, Samuel Tilden and the Stolen Election of 1876.* New York: Simon and Schuster, 2003.

O'Neal, Michael J. *Decades of American History: America in the 1920s.* New York: Stonesong, 2006.

Wagner, Viqi, ed. *Opposing Viewpoints Series: Labor Unions.* Farmington Hills, MI: Greenhaven, 2008.

Philbin, Tom. *The 100 Greatest Inventions of All Time: A Ranking Past to Present.* New York: Citadel, 2003.

Rawley, James A. with Stephen D. Behrendt. *The Transatlantic Slave Trade: A History, revised edition.* Lincoln, NE: University of Nebraska Press, 2005.

Rudy, Kathy. *Beyond Pro-Life and Pro-Choice: Moral Diversity in the Abortion Debate.* Boston: Beacon Press, 1996.

Simi, Pete and Robert Futrell. *American Swastika: Inside the White Power Movement's Hidden Spaces of Hate.* Lanham, MD: Rowman and Littlefield, 2010.

Simon, Rita J. *Abortion: Statutes, Policies, and Public Attitudes the World Over.* Westport, CT: Praeger, 1998.

Smith, Anthony. *The Newspaper: An International History.* London: Thames and Hudson, 1979.

Smith, C. Fraser. *The Daily Miracle: A Memoir of Newspapering.* Baltimore: Otter Bay, 2019.

Stagg, J.C.A. *The War of 1812: Conflict for a Continent.* New York: Cambridge University Press, 2012.

Stegman, Erik. "Native People Continue to Resist 1950s Policies," Aspen Institute, November 22, 2019. https://www.aspeninstitute.org/blog-posts/native-people -continue-to-resist-1950s-policies/

Turner Main, Jackson. *The Anti-federalists: Critics of the Constitution 1781-1788.* New York: W.W. Norton, 1961.

Van Dulken, Stephen. *Inventing the 19th Century: 100 Inventions that Shaped the Victorian World.* New York: New York University Press, 2001.

Wichowski, Alexis. *The Information Trade: How Big Tech Conquers Countries, Challenges Our Rights, and Transforms Our World.* New York: Harper One, 2020.

Yallop, David A. *The Day the Laughter Stopped.* New York: St. Martin's Press, 1976.

Yetman, Norman R., ed. *When I was a Slave: Memoirs from the Slave Narrative Collection.* Mineola, NY: Dover Publications, 2002.

Zeskind, Leonard. *Blood and Politics: The History of the White Nationalist Movement from the Margins to the Mainstream.* New York, Farrar Straus Giroux, 2009.

ARTICLES

Aizenman, Nurith. "Trump Wishes We Had More Immigrants From Norway. Turns Out We Once Did," Goats and Soda: Stories of Life in a Changing World, *npr*, January 12, 2018. https://www.npr.org/sections/goatsandsoda/2018/01 /12/577673191/trump-wishes-we-had-more-immigrants-from-norway-turns -out-we-once-did.

Andrews, Evan. "Why Was It Called the 'Spanish Flu?': The 1918 influenza pandemic did not, as many people believed, originate in Spain." *history.com,* updated July 12, 2023. https://www.history.com/news/why-was-it-called-the-spanish-flu.

Baker, Carrie N. and Kirsten Thompson. "A Brief History of Birth Control in the U.S.," *Our Bodies Ourselves Today,* accessed June 20, 2023. https://www .ourbodiesourselves.org/health-info/a-brief-history-of-birth-control/.

Blackford, Sheila. "Disputed Election of 1876: The death knell of the Republican dream," Miller Center, University of Virginia, accessed July 6, 2023. https:// millercenter.org/the-presidency/educational-resources/disputed-election-1876.

Britannica ProCon.org. "History of Abortion," updated April 24, 2023. https:// abortion.procon.org/history-of-abortion/.

Burns, Adam. "Early Passenger Trains: Rail Travel In The 19th Century," *American-Rails.com,* revised March 21, 2023. https://www.american-rails.com/early.html.

Cavallier, Andrea. "What are the allegations made against Sean 'Diddy' Combs?" *The Independent,* April 14, 2024. https://www.independent.co.uk/news/world/ americas/allegations-against-diddy-sean-combs-b2537439.html.

Centers for Disease Control and Prevention. "1918 Pandemic (H1N1 virus)," accessed June 20, 2022. https://www.cdc.gov/flu/pandemic-resources/1918 -pandemic-h1n1.html.

Dator, James. "Deshaun Watson's sexual assault allegations, explained," *SBNation,* June 16, 2022. https://www.sbnation.com/nfl/2022/6/16/22346818/deshaun -watsons-sexual-assault-allegations-explained.

Dawsey, Josh and Maxine Joselow, "Trump rails against wind energy in fundraising pitch to oil executives," *The Washington Post,* April 17, 2024. https://www .washingtonpost.com/climate-environment/2024/04/17/trump-wind-power-oil -executives/

Deliso, Meredith. "Alec Baldwin 'Rust' case: What the armorer's conviction could mean for the actor," *ABC News,* April 17, 2024. https://abcnews.go.com/US/ alec-baldwin-rust-movie-death-armorer-trial/story?id=109309497.

Dennis, Steven T. and Oma Seddiq, "Schumer's AI Plan Urges Billions in Spending to Challenge China," *Bloomberg,* May 15, 2024. https://www.msn.com/en-us/ money/other/schumer-s-ai-plan-urges-billions-in-spending-to-challenge-china/ ar-BB1mq4uF.

Ditmar, Kelly. "What You Need to Know About the Record Numbers of Women Candidates in 2020," Center for American Women and Politics, Eagleton Institute of Politics, Rutgers University, August 10, 2020. https://cawp.rutgers.edu /blog/what-you-need-know-about-record-numbers-women-candidates-2020.

Dwoskin, Elizabeth and Jeremy B. Merrill. "Trump's 'big lie' fueled a new generation of social media influencers," *The Washington Post,* September 20, 2022. https:// www.washingtonpost.com/technology/2022/09/20/social-media-influencers -election-fraud/.

English, Trevor. "Origins of the Morse Code and How It Works," *Interesting Engineering* website, March 17, 2020. https://interestingengineering.com/innovation /origins-of-the-morse-code-and-how-it-works.

Faircloth, Susan C. "The Education of American Indian Students," *aft.org,* Winter 2020-2021, https://www.aft.org/ae/winter2020-2021/faircloth_sb1.

Findijs, Alex. "Federal officials warn of impending water crisis in the American Southwest," *World Socialist Web Site,* June 23, 2022. https://www.wsws.org/en/ articles/2022/06/24/fkkg-j24.html.

Fuller, John. "Did da Vinci really sketch a primitive version of the car?" *HowStuffWorks,* accessed October 5, 2022. https://auto.howstuffworks.com/da-vinci-car1 .htm.

Gaynor, Gerren Keith. "What should be on Black voters' radar ahead of 2024 elections?" TheGrio, January 5, 2024. https://news.yahoo.com /news/black-voters-radar-ahead-2024-203605332.html?guccounter =1&guce_referrer=aHR0cHM6Ly9kdWNrZHVja2dvLmNvbS8=&guce _referrer_sig=AQAAAMNdyf9lOTQLM42TDiurPkqy0t-wefb9WcHZWFZj -JzA7mnL85Sk4Ba4tgxQl7h43hUj7KwC3nvPnEqXVHg7uL8aG IpnkSbOKQQbMp0BQAuhw6G9tQQCtkgotbv4hF36pqA -xu6003L86Q7xmc3wSLs454HRFcQaR6onTA9dp_N.

Grant, Nico and Tiffany Hsu, "Google Finds 'Inoculating' People Against Misinformation Helps Blunt Its Power," *The New York Times,* August 24, 2022. https:// www.nytimes.com/2022/08/24/technology/google-search-misinformation.html.

Grayer, Annie and Kristin Wilson, "House lawmakers lay out proposal for legislation to prevent another January 6," *CNN Politics,* updated September 19, 2022.

https://www.cnn.com/2022/09/19/politics/electoral-count-act-liz-cheney-zoe -lofgren/index.html.

Harlan, Chico and Amanda Coletta. "Pope apologizes for 'evil committed by so many Christians' in Canada's residential schools," *The Washington Post,* July 25, 2022. https://www.washingtonpost.com/world/2022/07/25/pope-francis -apology-canada-residential-homes/.

Hartmann, Thom. "America Doesn't Understand that Inequality Causes Crime," *Hartmann Report,* September 29, 2022. https://hartmannreport.com/p/america -doesnt-understand-that-inequality.

Herres, David. "Heinrich Hertz and Maxwell's theory of wave propagation." *Test & Measurement Tips* website, April 23, 2015. https://www.testandmeasurementtips .com/heinrich-hertz-and-maxwells-theory-of-wave-propagation/.

History.com Editors. "Treaty of Ghent," *History.com,* updated August 21, 2018. https://www.history.com/topics/19th-century/treaty-of-ghent.

Howard University School of Law. "A Brief History of Civil Rights in the United States: The Termination Era," January 6, 2023. https://library.law.howard.edu/ civilrightshistory/indigenous/termination.

Indian Affairs, U.S. Department of the Interior. "Federal Indian Boarding School Initiative," May 2022. https://www.bia.gov/service/federal-indian-boarding -school-initiative.

Horwitz, Sari, Dana Hedgpeth, Emmanuel Martinez, Scott Higham, and Salwan Georges. "'In the name of God,'" *The Washington Post,* May 29, 2024. https:// www.washingtonpost.com/investigations/interactive/2024/sexual-abuse-native -american-boarding-schools/?itid=hp-top-table-main_p001_f001.

Huston, Caitlin. "BuzzFeed Will Be Leaning Into AI and Creators After Shuttering News Division," *The Hollywood Reporter,* May 9, 2023. https://www .hollywoodreporter.com/business/business-news/buzzfeed-ai-creators-news-shut -down-1235483607/.

Jaumotte, Florence and Carolina Osorio Buitron. "Power from the People," Finance & Development, International Monetary Fund, Vol. 52, No. 1, March 2015. https://www.imf.org/external/pubs/ft/fandd/2015/03/jaumotte.htm .Kingsberry, Janay. "Gen Z is influencing the abortion debate — from TikTok," *The Washington Post,* June 28, 2022. https://www.washingtonpost.com/nation/ interactive/2022/gen-z-tiktok-abortion-debate/.

Layne, Nathan. "Trump repeats 'poisoning the blood' anti-immigrant remark," Reuters, December 16, 2023. https://www.reuters.com/world/us/trump-repeats -poisoning-blood-anti-immigrant-remark-2023-12-16/.

Levitt, Zach, Yuliya Parshina-Kottas, Simon Romero and Tim Wallace. "War Against the Children: The Native American boarding school system — a decades-long effort to assimilate Indigenous people before they ever reached adulthood — robbed children of their culture, family bonds and sometimes their lives," *The New York Times,* August 30, 2023. https://www.nytimes.com/interactive/2023 /08/30/us/native-american-boarding-schools.html.

Library of Congress. "History of the Cylinder Phonograph," accessed November 18, 2022. https://www.loc.gov/collections/edison-company-motion-pictures -and-sound-recordings/articles-and-essays/history-of-edison-sound-recordings/ history-of-the-cylinder-phonograph/.

Lindsey, Rebecca and Luann Dahlman. "Climate Change: Global Temperature," National Oceanic and Atmospheric Administration (NOAA), U.S. Department of Commerce, *climate.gov*, January 18, 2023. https://www.climate.gov/news -features/understanding-climate/climate-change-global-temperature.

Manchester, Julia and Julia Mueller, "Here's where women voters stand in the Biden-Trump rematch, *The Hill,* April 7, 2024. https://thehill.com/homenews /campaign/4577139-joe-biden-donald-trump-women-female-voters-gen-z -college-educated-black-women/.

Marr, Chuck, Samantha Jacoby and George Fenton. "The 2017 Trump Tax Law Was Skewed to the Rich, Expensive, and Failed to Deliver on Its Promises," *Center on Budget and Policy Priorities,* March 5, 2024.

https://www.cbpp.org/research/federal-tax/the-2017-trump-tax-law-was-skewed-to -the-rich-expensive-and-failed-to-deliver.

Marsh, Allison. "Morse Code's Vanquished Competitor: The Dial Telegraph," *IEEE Spectrum*, August 31, 2018. https://spectrum.ieee.org/morse-codes-vanquished -competitor-the-dial-telegraph.

Matheny, Keith. "Great Lakes water piped to Southwest 'our future,' says NASA scientist," Detroit Free Press, April 10, 2017. https://www.freep.com/story/news/ local/michigan/2017/04/10/great-lakes-water-piped-southwest-our-future-says -nasa-scientist/100301326/.

Mathews, Joe, syndicated columnist. "East Coast Americans warring over 1619, 1776 should see 1848 out West," *The Baltimore Sun,* October 3, 2021. https://www .baltimoresun.com/opinion/op-ed/bs-ed-op-1001-california-1848-20211001 -p4k5khr6xjgjhp4bwpzheq2q6q-story.html.

Matulka, Rebecca and Daniel Wood. "The History of the Light Bulb," U.S. Department of Energy, November 22, 2013. https://www.usailighting.com /stuff/contentmgr/files/1/92ffeb328de0f4878257999e7d46d6e4/misc/ historyofthelightbulb_doe.pdf.

Media Office, Federal Communications Commission. "History of Commercial Radio," updated April 12, 2021. https://www.fcc.gov/media/radio/history-of -commercial-radio.

Miller, Cassie. "Male Supremacy is at the Core of the Hard Right's Agenda," Southern Poverty Law Center, *Hate and Extremism in 2023,* 2023.

Moghe, Sonia and Dakin Andone. "R. Kelly sentenced to 30 years in prison for federal racketeering and sex trafficking charges," *CNN,* updated June 30, 2022. https://edition.cnn.com/2022/06/29/us/r-kelly-sentencing-racketeering-sex -trafficking/index.html.

Music and Dance, "Early Jazz, 1900-1930," *PBS.* https://www.pbs.org/wgbh/ cultureshock/flashpoints/music/jazz.html.

Myers, Steven Lee and Sheera Frenkel. "How Disinformation Splintered and Became More Intractable," *The New York Times,* October 20, 2022. https://www.nytimes.com/2022/10/20/technology/disinformation-spread.html.

Orlando Women's Center. "The History of Abortion," accessed November 10, 2022. https://www.womenscenter.com/history_abortion.html.

Patterson, Thomas E. "The Decline of Newspapers: The Local Story," *Nieman Foundation* website, accessed November 3, 2022. https://nieman.harvard.edu/articles/the-decline-of-newspapers-the-local-story/.

Pettersson, Henrik, Byron Manley and Sergio Hernandez. "Tracking Covid-19's global spread: The disease has spread to every continent and case numbers continue to rise," *CNN,* January 22, 2023.

Pruitt, Sarah. "Broken Treaties With Native American Tribes: Timeline," *history.com,* July 12, 2023. https://www.history.com/news/native-american-broken-treaties.

The Red Road. "Education of the First People," theredroad.org, accessed May 6, 2024. https://theredroad.org/issues/native-american-education/

Reuters Staff. "False claim: the 1918 influenza pandemic was caused by vaccines," *Reuters,* April 1, 2020. https://www.reuters.com/article/uk-factcheck-vaccines-caused-1918-influe-idUSKBN21J6X2.

Ritman, Alex. "Kevin Spacey Found Not Guilty in U.K. Sexual Assault Trial," *The Hollywood Reporter,* July 26, 2023. https://www.hollywoodreporter.com/tv/tv-news/kevin-spacey-uk-trial-verdict-not-guilty-1235543727/#!.

Roose, Kevin. "Twitter, Once a Threat to Titans, Now Belongs to One," *The New York Times,* October 29, 2022. https://www.nytimes.com/2022/10/29/technology/musk-twitter-legacy.html.

Rosenbloom, Raquel and Jeanne Batalova. "Mexican Immigrants in the United States," Migration Policy Institute (MPI), October 13, 2022. https://www.migrationpolicy.org/article/mexican-immigrants-united-states.

Schaeffer, Katherine. "6 facts about economic inequality in the U.S.," Pew Research Center, February 7, 2020. https://www.pewresearch.org/short-reads/2020/02/07/6-facts-about-economic-inequality-in-the-u-s/.

Spinney, Laura. "Smallpox and other viruses plagued humans much earlier than suspected: Genetic research is rewriting the history of diseases," Nature Portfolio, July 23, 2020. https://www.nature.com/articles/d41586-020-02083-0.

SPLC (Southern Poverty Law Center) Report. "SPLC: Twitter was a major tool in Capitol insurrection," Fall 2021. https://www.energy.senate.gov/services/files/792F68B8-391C-49A7-AF5C-79327E872429.

The White House. "FACT SHEET: President Biden Announces New Actions to Secure the Border," June 4, 2024. https://www.whitehouse.gov/briefing-room/statements-releases/2024/06/04/fact-sheet-president-biden-announces-new-actions-to-secure-the-border/.

Tishma, Mariel. "The global journey of variolation," Hektoen International, A Journal of Medical Humanities, Summer 2020. https://hekint.org/2020/09/29/the-global-journey-of-variolation/.

Touton, Camille Calimlim. "Statement of Camille Calimlim Touton, Commissioner, Bureau of Reclamation, U.S. Department of the Interior, before the U.S. Senate Committee on Energy and National Resources, Subcommittee on Water and Power." Senate Committee on Energy and Natural Resources, 14 June 2022, www.energy.senate.gov/hearings/2022/6/full-committee-hearing-to-examine -short-and-long-term-solutions-to-extreme-drought-in-the-western-u-s.

trvst.world. "The History of Hydropower & Hydroelectric Energy," revised August 3, 2022. https://www.trvst.world/renewable-energy/the-history-of-hydroelectric -energy/.

ul Hassan, Nabeel. "Which platform do young Brits use most to get news?" News-writ.com, July 22, 2022. https://newswrit.com/2022/07/22/which-platform-do -young-brits-use-most-to-get-news/.

U.S. Citizenship and Immigration Services, U.S. Department of Homeland Security. "Early American Immigration Policies," updated July 30, 2022. https:// www.uscis.gov/about-us/our-history/overview-of-ins-history/early-american -immigration-policies.

U.S. Commission on Civil Rights, "Voting Irregularities in Florida During the 2000 Presidential Election," Executive Summary. https://www.usccr.gov/files/pubs/ vote2000/report/exesum.htm

Watts, Jonathan. "'Case closed': 99.9% of scientists agree climate emergency caused by humans," *The Guardian,* October 19, 2021. https://www.theguardian .com/environment/2021/oct/19/case-closed-999-of-scientists-agree-climate -emergency-caused-by-humans.

Weber, Lauren. "Conservative attacks on birth control could threaten access," The Washington Post, June 5, 2024.

https://www.washingtonpost.com/health/2024/06/05/birth-control-access-abortion -ban/

John McCarthy's Original Website. "What is AI? / Basic Questions," Stanford University, accessed December 2, 2022. http://jmc.stanford.edu/artificial-intelligence /what-is-ai/index.html.

Whitehead, Aaron T. "The "Fatty" Arbuckle Scandal, Will Hays, and Negotiated Morality in 1920s America," Masters Theses & Specialist Projects, Paper 1469, Western Kentucky University, 2015. https://digitalcommons.wku.edu/cgi/ viewcontent.cgi?httpsredir=1&article=2478&context=theses.

Wike, Richard, Laura Silver, Janell Fetterolf, Christine Huang, Sarah Austin, Laura Clancy, and Sneha Gubbala. "Social Media Seen as Good for Democracy Across Many Nations, But U.S. is a Major Outlier," Pew Research Center, December 6, 2022. https://www.pewresearch.org/global/2022/12/06/social-media-seen-as -mostly-good-for-democracy-across-many-nations-but-u-s-is-a-major-outlier /#:~:text=Additionally%2C%20a%20median%20of%2065,has%20made%20 people%20more%20civil).

Williamson, Timothy. "History of Computers: A brief timeline," *Live Science* website, December 1, 2021. https://www.livescience.com/20718-computer-history.html.

Woodall, Candy. "Congress revises Electoral Count Act that Trump used to pressure Pence on Jan. 6," *USA Today,* yahoo*!* news website, December 23, 2022. https://news.yahoo.com/congress-revises-electoral-count-act-192913471.html.

World Health Organization. "Commemorating Smallpox Eradication — a legacy of hope, for COVID-19 and other diseases," May 8, 2020. https://www.who.int/news/item/08-05-2020-commemorating-smallpox-eradication-a-legacy-of-hope-for-covid-19-and-other-diseases.

Zakrzewski, Cat, "Schumer's long-awaited AI 'road map' is coming this week. It will cost billions," *The Washington Post,* May 13, 2024.

https://www.washingtonpost.com/technology/2024/05/13/congress-ai-laws-research-regulation-schumer/

Zakrzewski, Cat, Cristiano Lima and Drew Harwell. "What the Jan. 6 probe found out about social media, but didn't report," *The Washington Post,* January 17, 2023. https://www.washingtonpost.com/technology/2023/01/17/jan6-committee-report-social-media/.

Zong, Jie and Jeanne Batalova. "Chinese Immigrants in the United States," Migration Policy Institute (MPI), September 29, 2017. https://www.migrationpolicy.org/article/chinese-immigrants-united-states-2016.

NEWSPAPER ARCHIVES:

Google News Archive Search, Google, news.google.com/newspapers.

"Historical Newspapers from the 1700's-2000s." Historical Newspapers from 1700s-2000s - Newspapers.Com, www.newspapers.com/.

Humanities, National Endowment for the. "Chronicling America: Library of Congress." News about Chronicling America RSS, chroniclingamerica.loc.gov/.

"NewspaperArchive 1700s - 2024." NewspaperArchive, newspaperarchive.com/.

About the Author

Most recently, Kenneth N. Weiss was a content editor for the Baltimore Sun Media Group. In his long career, he worked for a number of daily and weekly newspapers in Maryland and New Jersey, including the defunct Journal newspapers in suburban Washington, D.C., The Capital in Annapolis, Md., and the Daily Record in Morris County, N.J.

In the past, he oversaw the Opinion pages of three different publications, including The Washington Post Co.'s defunct Gazette of Politics and Business, for which he served as editor. While at the Montgomery Journal, he won a "Best in Show" award for editorial writing from the Maryland-Delaware-DC Press Association.

He later was a managing editor for Patuxent Publishing Co., supervising staff for nine community newspapers in the Baltimore area.

For the past few years, he also has been a seasonal copy editor for the non-profit Global Integrity's and then the African Institute for Development Policy's project scoring African countries on democracy indicators.

In the more distant past, he was a researcher and helped write the treatment for the film *The War at Home*, which was nominated for the Academy Award for best feature-length documentary in 1979. He also worked in the late 1970s for New York Public Library's film library.

In addition, for about a decade, he taught an introductory news writing course at Towson University and then the University of Maryland, Baltimore County.

Weiss has an undergraduate degree from the University of Wisconsin-Madison and master's degrees in library service from Columbia University and journalism from the University of Missouri.

Weiss, who lives in Baltimore, is retired and had been thinking about a book of this sort for a few years. The current political divisions in the country might make this a prime time to do the book.